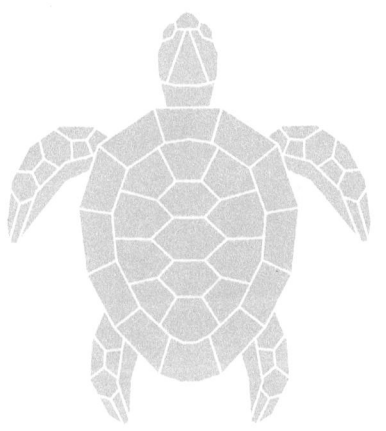

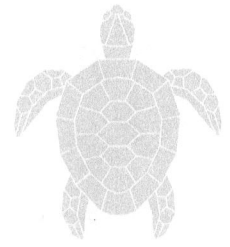

PERFORMING
TURTLE
ISLAND

INDIGENOUS THEATRE
ON THE WORLD STAGE

JESSE RAE ARCHIBALD-BARBER,
KATHLEEN IRWIN,
AND MOIRA J. DAY, EDS.

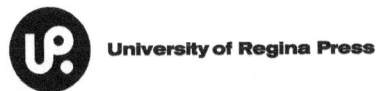

University of Regina Press

TURTLE ISLAND SONG: Jesse Rae Archibald-Barber
COVER ART: "Swimming sea turtle," Shutterstock
COVER AND TEXT DESIGN: Duncan Campbell, University of Regina Press
COPY EDITOR: Marionne Cronin
PROOFREADER: Kristine Douaud
INDEXER: Jason Begy Indexing

Library and Archives Canada Cataloguing in Publication

Title: Performing Turtle Island : Indigenous theatre on the world stage / Jesse Rae Archibald-Barber, Kathleen Irwin, and Moira J. Day, eds.

Names: Archibald-Barber, Jesse Rae, 1972- editor. | Irwin, Kathleen, editor. | Day, Moira Jean, 1953- editor.

Description: Includes bibliographical references and index.

Identifiers: Canadiana (print) 2019011388X | Canadiana (ebook) 20190115513 | ISBN 9780889776562 (softcover) | ISBN 9780889776760 (hardcover) | ISBN 9780889776579 (PDF) | ISBN 9780889776586 (HTML)

Subjects: LCSH: Indigenous peoples in literature. | CSH: Native theater—Canada. Canadian drama— Native authors—History and criticism. | Native peoples in literature.

Classification: LCC PN2301 .P47 2019 | DDC 792.089/97071—dc23

10 9 8 7 6 5 4 3 2 1

University of Regina Press, University of Regina
Regina, Saskatchewan, Canada, S4S 0A2
TEL: (306) 585-4758 FAX: (306) 585-4699
WEB: www.uofrpress.ca

U OF R PRESS

We acknowledge the support of the Canada Council for the Arts for our publishing program. We acknowledge the financial support of the Government of Canada. / Nous reconnaissons l'appui financier du gouvernement du Canada. This publication was made possible with support from Creative Saskatchewan's Book Publishing Production Grant Program.

This publication was made possible with the help of a grant from the Federation for the Humanities and Social Sciences, through the Awards to Scholarly Publications Program, using funds provided by the Social Sciences and Humanities Research Council of Canada.

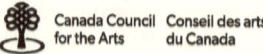
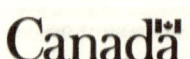
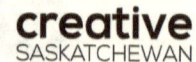

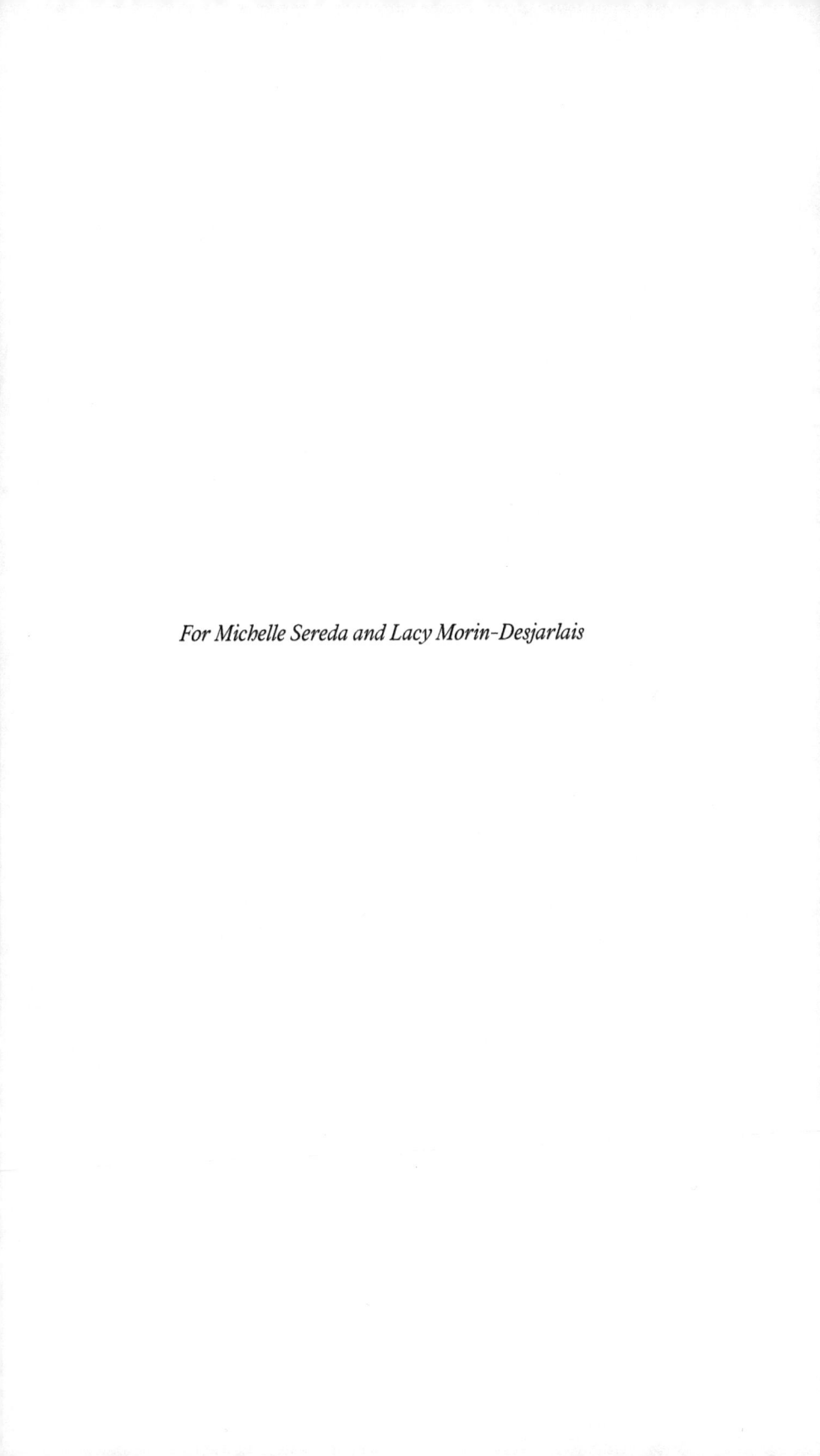

For Michelle Sereda and Lacy Morin-Desjarlais

Call to Action #83 of the Truth and Reconciliation Commission of Canada: We call upon . . . Indigenous and non-Indigenous artists to undertake collaborative projects and produce works that contribute to the reconciliation process.

CONTENTS

TURTLE ISLAND SONG

Turtle Island, land and water
We dance our journey home
Beneath the starry map
For those before, here, to come
The living earth our drum
We play on Turtle Island

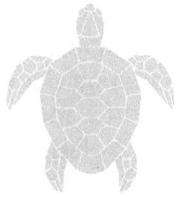

INTRODUCTION: PERSPECTIVES ON CURRENT PRACTICE

Jesse Rae Archibald-Barber, Kathleen Irwin, Moira J. Day

Our aim with this collection, *Performing Turtle Island*, is to open up discussion around Indigenous theatre and performance practices, considering current work by artists and scholars from a multidisciplinary perspective. Understanding Indigenous cultures as sovereign and living histories of knowledge, meaning, and identities, we see that the practices represented here are also profound opportunities for community engagement, education, and creative expression. Delving further, this anthology examines how Indigenous artists shape the aesthetic and theatre-related forms that we use to construct and represent land, community, and both Indigenous and Canadian identities. Now, more than ever, it is time to reflect on the images of Indigenous peoples in Canadian theatre and performance, and we hope this collection adds to previous scholarship on the subject.

To this point, in the introduction to the seminal work *Aboriginal Drama and Theatre*, Rob Appleford writes, "when looking at the variety and success of what we call 'Aboriginal drama' or 'Aboriginal theatre' in Canada, I am struck that this body of work's greatest strength lies in the delight of the unforeseen . . . the power of Aboriginal drama to combine emotional honesty with self-conscious critique in surprising ways."[1] Since its publication, this much-cited collection has stood as a landmark reflection on the wealth of Indigenous playwriting in Canada, with essays by Tomson Highway, Floyd P. Favel, Drew Hayden Taylor, Yvette Nolan, Geraldine Manossa, Daniel David Moses, and Armand Garnett Ruffo, as well as writing by a corresponding number of significant non-Indigenous academics, including Sheila Rabbillard, Alan Filewod, Reid Gilbert, Robert Nunn, Ric Knowles, and Appleford himself. The book illustrated in equal measure the vibrancy of the field and the volume's position as merely an opening volley, a discussion that marked "only the beginning of watching, studying and understanding the complexity and liberative possibilities of Aboriginal theatre and drama in Canada."[2] More recently, in the introduction to *Performing Indigeneity: New Essays on Canadian Theatre*, Yvette Nolan reflects on the collection as the first in which all the pieces were written by Indigenous scholars, artists, and academics. In this move she summons the notion of an Indigenous identity, an evasive term when applied to individuals who are rooted in diverse nations, such as Cree, Saulteaux, Mohawk, Creek, Ntlakapamux, Stó:lõ, Inuit, and many others. Accordingly, Nolan acknowledges that the anthology offers "a beginning, a way of inviting more voices into the conversation."[3]

In turn, the *Performing Turtle Island* anthology offers another kind of beginning, one that views performance as both a critical self-representation important to empowerment and self-determination and a way of placing Indigenous performance in dialogue with other nations, both on the shores of Turtle Island and on the world stage. Indeed, this notion of dialogue is what the editors use to order the articles in the anthology. As the editors, we step into these waters with eyes wide open in regards to the problematic categories of

1   Robert Appleford, "Introduction: Seeing the Full Frame," in *Aboriginal Drama and Theatre: Critical Perspectives on Canadian Theatre in English*, vol. 1, ed. Robert Appleford (Toronto: Playwrights Canada, 2005), viii.
2   *Ibid.*
3   Yvette Nolan, introduction to *Performing Indigeneity: New Essays of Canadian Theatre*, vol. 6, eds. Yvette Nolan and Ric Knowles (Toronto: Playwrights Canada Press, 2016), 5.

Canadian and Indigenous theatre within the relevant and colonizing national literatures. It is in this context that the editors and contributors, Indigenous and non-Indigenous, have expressed their cultural foundations, research interests, curiosity, and enthusiasm about Indigenous performance in Canada.

Speaking to both these national and international connections, this collection is in part the result of a gathering called Performing Turtle Island: Fluid Identities and Community Continuities, which took place at the University of Regina and the First Nations University of Canada from September 17–19, 2015.[4] The gathering brought together over one hundred established and emerging scholars and artists to focus on how Indigenous theatre and performance are connected to Indigenous ways of knowing and well-being, while also considering the role of Indigenous identity in shaping the country's. The gathering was simultaneously local and global: situated in Regina, it also served as the primary Canadian node of Performance Studies International's (PSi) Globally Dispersed Conference 2015, Fluid States: Performances of UnKnowing. This provided a way for the Regina gathering to interact live and online with multiple performance, symposium, conference, and festival programs across Europe, Africa, the Americas, Asia, Australasia, and the Pacific. In all, we aligned ourselves with fourteen other communities worldwide to examine "the fluxes, flows and currents that circulate around and in between fixed, stratified, and centralized cartographies of knowledge: conceptual spaces that are in-between and in-motion that problematize boundaries and remap the relations and limits of [un]knowing."[5] The threads we addressed locally echoed those proposed by the global PSi network. They included these questions: 1) How do we perform what we merely assume we know? 2) How do we respond responsibly to the particularities of our local, cultural, historical, ideological, social, and political conditions in relationship to others? 3) In what way does the performance of identity question and shift or confirm and standardize the elements, structures, and operational modes of the knowledge system that we take as given? 4) In what way is

....

4   See schedule, participants, videos, and images at www.performingturtleisland.org.

5   PSi #21 Fluid States, "Theme," *Fluid States: Performances of Unknowing*, http://www.fluidstates.org/page.php?par=16&id=18, accessed May 4, 2017.

the [un]known implied within the knowledge system? and 5) Does how we [un]know enable us to move, as interlaced local and global communities, towards a place of balance and healthfulness? With these questions at the forefront, Performing Turtle Island became a multiplatform event that was simultaneously actual and virtual, local and globally disseminated, interactive and docked on a website.

In the years since the gathering in 2015, when material in these articles was first presented, many things have happened on the Canadian landscape that have involved critical acts of knowing and unknowing: notably the completion of the *Final Report of the Truth and Reconciliation Commission of Canada*, a landmark document that outlines in its Calls to Action the many challenges of moving forward within the historic context of genocidal policies, while also articulating an imperative for a genuinely respectful understanding of Indigenous rights and sovereignties. Canada's sesquicentennial in 2017 is also notable as a year in which many Canadians (though not all) celebrated 150 years of Confederation, promoting the nation as a home to people from all over the world. At that moment, as the publication began to take shape, we also asked how Indigenous identities and communities are reflected and respected within the normative construction of the country's identity. In the same year, a strategic unsettling of Canada 150 was enacted through many grassroots movements that called for nation-to-nation recognition of collective Indigenous rights and titles, full implementation of the Truth and Reconciliation Commission's (TRC) Calls to Action, and implementation of the United Nations Declaration on the Rights of Indigenous Peoples. In 2018, the anger over the deaths of Indigenous youths and the subsequent acquittal of those charged and the intensity of reaction to the events all heightened the urgency of the conversation. The background to the *Performing Turtle Island* anthology also includes the National Inquiry into Missing and Murdered Indigenous Women and Girls (commencing in 2016), which has defined one of the most significant national crises of our times and underscores the necessity to, once and for all, address the violent legacies of colonialism. While the articles originated prior to these defining circumstances, each addresses issues in this country in ways that remain relevant and remind us that the way to reconciliation between Canadians and Indigenous people is neither straightforward nor easily settled. As Gabrielle L'Hirondelle Hill and Sophie McCall acknowledge, *reconciliation* is "a troubled and troubling term often used to impose a sense of closure on experiences of colonization that are very much alive and ongoing."[6] Yet, as artists and academics, Indigenous and non-Indigenous, we must engage with the concept of reconciliation in part or in full, "to shake it up, to wrestle with it, and to insist on other possible futures."[7] Indeed, the writers in this collection point beyond a simple notion of reconciliation as "the act of causing two people or groups to become friendly again after an argument or disagreement,"[8] to address the multilayered concept in both its constructive possibilities and shortcomings.

Specifically, this collection underscores the significant contributions artists make to the complex public discourse that surrounds performing identity both as critical self-representation important to empowerment and self-determination and as a way of placing Indigenous performance in dialogue with settler descendants and eventually with more recent newcomers as they become familiar with the country's foundational history. Through event and publication, *Performing Turtle Island* looks beyond the notion of performance as a way of educating or entertaining—although it is that as well. What we offer is, rather, a mustering of stories and performed knowledge by and for Indigenous storytellers, framed as an open and inclusive interchange. Granted, we recognize that the nature of this interchange will always call for an irreconcilable space of indigeneity where, as David Garneau describes, "individuals are not performing identity for others but simply are, where they express and celebrate their continuity . . . without the sense of feeling they are witnessed by people who are not equal performers."[9] At the same time, *Performing Turtle Island* is explicit in its conviction that public, live interaction produces a space of equanimity and empowerment through an embodied mutual call to action in which situations and relations are made palpable and transformative for all present. Indeed, as Lisa C. Ravensbergen attests, theatre makes

----

6   Gabrielle L'Hirondelle Hill and Sophie McCall, *The Land We Are* (Winnipeg: ARP Books, 2015), vii.

7   *Ibid.*

8   *Merriam Webster Dictionary*, s.v. "reconciliation," https://www.merriam-webster.com/dictionary/reconciliation, accessed June 9, 2018.

9   David Garneau, "Imaginary Spaces of Conciliation and Reconciliation," *West Coast Line* 74 (Summer 2012): 33.

one visible: "I have come to understand that it is a political act to be seen, to self-determine how I'm seen and what is done with that knowledge ... taking aesthetic action, like reconciliation and decolonization is a verb—it creates, reacts, chooses, it enacts change."[10] We might add that theatre is a space/act/process of seeing and being seen for both performer and spectator, while understanding that these categories are unstable, moving in and out of focus.

Since 2015, global fluctuations have continued to mobilize populations and change the way Canadians see themselves in relation to the rest of the world. In Saskatchewan alone, Statistics Canada shows that approximately 50,000 immigrants came to the province between 2011 and 2016, arriving from a wide variety of places, including Asia and the Pacific, Africa and the Middle East, Europe and the United Kingdom.[11] Certainly, this realization, as well as the relationship of the *Performing Turtle Island* conference with the thirteen other partner hubs that made up PSi's internationally dispersed event, prompted us to frame the local Saskatchewan demographic circumstances, in which fully 14 percent of the population is Indigenous, within the notion of a fluid globalism. Mindful of this, we identified a range of implicit considerations: 1) how Indigenous and non-Indigenous communities adapt to recent transformations, 2) how we include newcomers in our particular (de)colonial discourse, and 3) the aesthetic forms used to reflect changing ideas of land, community, and history within the ideational borders that designate Saskatchewan and Canada. This volume furthers the fluid blending of cultural expressions by looking at the ways contemporary Indigenous artists and scholars reconsider traditional ways of being as unfixed and flexible processes of human perception, making note of how they themselves respond to, adapt, or reinvent inherited models of theatre, in some cases by creating a distinct mode

10 Dylan Robinson, "Acts of Defiance in Indigenous Theatre: A Conversation with Lisa C. Ravensbergen," in *Arts of Engagement: Taking Aesthetic Action in and Beyond the Truth and Reconciliation Commission in Canada*, eds. Dylan Robinson and Keavy Martin (Waterloo: Wilfrid Laurier University Press, 2016), 190.

11 Ministry of the Economy, Government of Saskatchewan, *Saskatchewan Statistical Immigration Report 2012 to 2014* (Regina: Ministry of the Economy, Government of Saskatchewan, n.d.), http://publications.gov.sk.ca/documents/310/93353-2014%20Immigration%20Statistical%20Report%20-%20July%2020%202016.pdf,accessed June 15, 2018 .

that asserts, constructs, explores, and interrogates ways of being on Turtle Island that [un]know the narratives of colonialism.

Performative storytelling was a constituent part of Indigenous cultures and knowledge forms long before Europeans' arrival on Turtle Island, and while Indigenous traditions were disrupted and degraded by colonialism, residential schools, and assimilation policies, artists today have reclaimed many of these traditions, with an understanding of storytelling as essential to Indigenous ways of knowing. Encoded in stories is knowledge that encompasses all aspects of being, including performative and representational dimensions with their own direct lines of development. It is the ways in which Indigenous artists draw on those cultural practices to reclaim traditions as well as create new forms of knowledge and performance that make up the guiding threads of the works in this collection, with particular attention paid to the ways in which models indigenous to Turtle Island are in diverse, multidimensional, and fluid dialogue with models indigenous to other places, including Europe.

Addressing these overlapping legacies, a significant body of works by Indigenous playwrights has emerged over the last thirty years that responds to hackneyed representations of Indigeneity by creating robust and dynamic expressions of Indigenous peoples. Across Canada, established writers such as Tomson Highway, Daniel David Moses, Drew Hayden Taylor, Maria Campbell, Marie Clements, Penny Gummerson, Monique Mojica, Margo Kane, Michael Lawrenchuk, Floyd P. Favel, Alanis King, and Yvette Nolan, along with newer writers such as Darrell Dennis, Tara Beagan, Kevin Loring, Curtis Peeteetuce, and Kenneth T. Williams, have produced outstanding works that focus on a decolonizing effort, writing against the problematically fixed image of Indigenous peoples linked to the realities of historical oppression and inadequately supported education, housing, and health in their communities. Situating much of their work between Euro-Canadian and Indigenous traditions, the artists mentioned here, among many others, also raise the ethical problem of using Western theoretical approaches to interpret Indigenous literatures—in essence, another form of colonialism. In response, as the contributors to this collection work through the meaning of land, environment, and geography, we note much of their work is centred on body, landscape, mindscape, text, and performance as shifting sites of self-awareness, self-healing, and community well-being. Current performative practices in Canada have seen a provocative synthesis of Indigenous and settler cultures, and we hope this volume will advance the notion that all who live on Turtle Island need to continue deepening the processes of knowing and unknowing the world in performative, embodied, and grounded ways.

STRUCTURE

Because of the broad range of issues and diverse backgrounds of the writers, organizing this collection into thematic sections, while challenging, led to several insights about the importance of land and territory, language and language revival, centring of culture and experience in the body, survivance, and creative sovereignty, all of which are critical in understanding the role of performance in Indigenous cultures. This is certainly true when considering aesthetic practices, particularly in regards to the transmission of cultural knowledge as embodied and grounded in place(s) and inflected by a thorough engagement with interdisciplinary modes of creation, dramaturgies, and scenographies. Indeed, the writings in this collection highlight and reflect these fluid practices and approaches in order to foreground the richness of Indigenous self-representation and the complex forms of dialogue it requires. Out of this, the editors have identified two broad concerns and have accordingly structured the articles in two sections: Part I: "Critical Self-Representation in Production and Training," and Part II: "Performance in Dialogue with the Text."

The first section, "Critical Self-Representation in Production and Training," addresses the processes of performing Indigeneity and what this means to contemporary theatre and performance arts. More specifically, this section deals with writers, teachers, and performers, mostly in urban centres, who function largely within existing professional structures in the arts and education while still advancing efforts at decolonization and reconciliation as they understand them. These chapters involve exercises in decolonizing at the personal, professional, and community levels in conservatory and liberal arts training, in creative writing and composition, and in film, music, and theatre production. Each reflects the author's attempts to map out and critique performance through an Indigenous knowledge system that allows those engaged to replace or adapt old paradigms of settler colonialism with new models and methodologies.

In the opening chapter, "Stranger in a Strange Land: Views from an Indigenous Lens," Michael Greyeyes imagines a new playing field for Indigenous actors and performers by centring the perspective of the Indigenous performer and critiquing the standard representations of Indigenous people in film. He suggests that, with a few noteworthy exceptions, commercial attempts to create sympathetic Indigenous characters in historical dramas 'freed' of overt colonial bias ironically still tend to trap Indigenous actors in outmoded, fragmented, and formulaic versions of themselves—a problem further aggravated by conventional forms of actor training that emphasize building a role through immersion in text-based psychological analysis. Michael Greyeyes sees the physical aspect of theatre training as essential to Indigenous performance because of its ability to ground the actor in the 'knowingness' of a body that predates and transcends colonialism. He also promotes the equally critical introduction of Indigenous languages to theatre and film training. This is partially because of the ability of language to similarly ground the actor in the 'knowingness' of an oral tradition that again predates and transcends colonialism. However, the use of multiple Indigenous languages also evokes an earlier multilingual era on Turtle Island (still present in other places in the world), where it was seen as an important part of the social, economic, and political discourse for all parties to speak and know each other's languages. As recovered again, both within and outside of arts training in Canada, such Indigenous language learning could once again become a vital way in a decolonized world for people to reach out and authentically understand both themselves and each other.

As this chapter is based on Michael Greyeyes' keynote address at the *Performing Turtle Island* conference, it retains the oral performativity and spontaneity of his delivery, one that was enthusiastically received by his audience. Moreover, with its focus on Indigenous performance in the context of national and international film, history, actor training, embodiment, language, and education, this chapter opens up a wide range of issues and sets the stage for the chapters that follow, particularly in relation to embodied approaches to training following Indigenous cultural practices and methodologies.

Along these lines, in "Making a Movie: How to Carry an Elephant up a Mountain," Armand Garnet Ruffo draws on traditional story elements to describe the adventurous, and often humorous, process of adapting his play, *A Windigo Tale*, to the screen. Appropriately, Ruffo weaves the trickster figure of Nanaboozho through his own rich story of failure-to-success (or something close to it) within the context of the Canadian film industry, an industry where writers and performers invariably confront the difficulties of trying to produce even a simple feature film as an Indigenous artist, often with little support, training, funding, or distribution. In short, Ruffo's chapter is a cautionary tale, a warning and a lesson to Indigenous artists to be careful what they wish for when dreaming about producing a small-budget, independent film.

While raising similar problems about professional training and production, composers Spy Dénommé-Welch and Catherine Magowan focus more on the composition and performance of music (an often rather urban, white, and male-centred practice). Their article "Decolonizing Counterpoints: Indigenous Perspectives and Representations in Classical Music and Opera" explores the theoretical and practical applications of interdisciplinary and intercultural collaboration in the creation of new music dealing with Indigenous topics. They examine the implications of decolonizing music education, development, and performance within contemporary Canadian arts and cultural contexts. Through their own musical creation they investigate the deeper meanings and implications of intercultural collaboration and how these can be used to (re)envision and (re)tell Indigenous oral histories and contemporary stories on the stage. They call for a careful consideration of what work is being created and produced, and a redistribution of resources by funding bodies, to allow Indigenous organizations to do their work to, as Ravensbergen says, "govern the telling of [their] own stories, whether or not it is recognizable to existing power/knowledge structures."[12] Overall, Dénommé-Welch and Magowan suggest collaborative approaches connected to land as a means to start to move beyond traditional Western practices.

In "Making Our Own Bundle: Philosophical Reflections on Indigenous Theatre Education," Carol Greyeyes moves the discussion

----

12 Robinson, "Acts of Defiance," 189.

west, returning to the topic of actor training and exploring its decolonization with reference to some existing training paradigms. Like Michael Greyeyes, she moves Indigenous theatre away from Eurocentric conventions of dramatic literature and actor training towards methods that stress language recovery and embodiment. However, she also uses the medicine bundle as a metaphor for an expanding collection of organic, improvisational, and healing approaches to Indigenous life and drama education that are more grounded in everyday being, embodiment, and experience. As a performer and teacher for over three decades, Carol Greyeyes has been a participant and witness to the emergence of Indigenous theatre and the development of a culturally affirming praxis and education methodology in the lands currently called Alberta, Saskatchewan, and Ontario. In this chapter, she unpacks items from her metaphorical bundle not only to express the evolution of her own teaching philosophy and practice in creating a more Indigenous theatre bundle, but to show how those "key experiences with the development of teaching and performance training"[13] can also further the process of reconciliation. The drama classroom, she posits, as structured on the egalitarian principle of the circle, is a place where newcomer, settler, and Indigenous performers and audiences can meet and start again together.

The next chapter shifts format to include Annie Smith's "Conversation with Daniel David Moses, August 2016," in which Moses discusses his understanding of script development, his sources of inspiration, and the development of Indigenous theatre over the past decades. As the local correspondent for the broader PSi context of the Performing Turtle Island conference, Smith's interview prompts a rich reflection on the residue of colonialism in the structures of Canadian theatre, a world still dominated by patriarchal, commercial, and professional realities. In response, Moses raises the perennial questions about identity in Canada, which ironically resonate with both First Nations and immigrant artists: "Can we be Canadian? Do we have a place here, or are we still the Other, always from elsewhere?"[14] Similar questions are posed in Moses'

---

13 Carol Greyeyes, "Making Our Own Bundle: Philosophical Reflections on Indigenous Theatre Education," this volume, 51.

14 Daniel David Moses, in Annie Smith, "Interview with Daniel David Moses," this volume, 73.

work around gender. Openly gay, many of his works explore the complexities of two-spirit or queer identities. Asked whether his own two-spiritness might be construed as a gift, Moses counters by saying that, in this world, in this moment, anyone can, perhaps *must*, be willing not just to imagine but to connect with the Other. The essential challenge that Moses throws us, in his work, is to decolonize settler colonialism as surely as we must decolonize love. Resisting the simple answers, Moses provides an urbane overview of his experience of being a successful Indigenous playwright in Canada and the contradictions that go with that.

The second section, "Performance in Dialogue with the Text," shifts the focus back to the problematic area of the dramatic text, conventionally understood in the Western tradition as a durable literary document intended to be realized in the non-durable medium of live performance before a live audience. All the chapters in this section are intensely focused on how traditional concepts of 'text' and 'performance' have been complicated, subverted, exploded, and radically transformed by processes of decolonization that also 'dialogue' in complex, edgy, and provocative ways with the ends of reconciliation. Some chapters aim at reclaiming texts, now grown canonical through production, publication, and scholarship within colonial institutions, while revitalizing them through radically new Indigenous interpretations in production and scholarship. Other chapters consciously situate the dialogue on the liminal ground existing on the margins of, in opposition to, or simply beyond settler-colonial paradigms and institutions. These chapters deal more with the impact of transnationalism, as intertwined with more radical reworkings of aesthetics, identity, and land, to significantly reframe the terms of the dialogues between text and performance— and the peoples that produce them—on Turtle Island.

Picking up on the work of one of the outstanding playwrights that Carol Greyeyes and Moses mention in their chapters, in "Performing the Bingo Game in Tomson Highway's *The Rez Sisters*," Jesse Rae Archibald-Barber examines the play's Indigenous performance in dialogue with Western literary theory. Historically, the play was groundbreaking, featuring the Trickster figure, who, while a primordial hero to Cree and Ojibwa cultures, was little known to Canadian audiences at the time of the play's debut in 1986. However, while the play was immediately celebrated as ushering in a new era of Indigenous theatre, most contemporary scholarship invariably interpreted its themes and aesthetic structures through a Western critical paradigm. Archibald-Barber critiques this textual approach and recentres an Indigenous spiritual perspective as essential to advancing the ends of decolonization for its performers and audiences.

Along similar lines, but in reference to a story about an Indigenous woman written by a non-Indigenous author, in "A Prayer for Rita Joe," Yvette Nolan recounts her experience restaging George Ryga's *The Ecstasy of Rita Joe* at the National Arts Centre in 2009. While Ryga's play was groundbreaking when it was first commissioned for the centennial of Confederation in 1967, by taking a stark rather than a celebratory look at the country's colonial legacies, the play has also received intense criticism for presenting a non-Indigenous view of Indigenous experience. In her restaging, Nolan set out to redeem the play's historical and aesthetic significance by showing how the play also lends itself to an Indigenous perspective. The play, as originally written, was unruly by conventional standards and open to diverse interpretations; Nolan's striking 2009 reinterpretation of the play is supported by the research of James Hoffman and Christopher Innes, who both suggest that some of what Nolan identifies as being implicitly open to Indigenous interpretation in the text was actually there in earlier drafts but was winnowed out to make the play more stageworthy for Canadian audiences of 1967. For example, Ryga's original 'Rita' was depicted as less of a victim than she became in the final published version. Nolan's chapter shows how her interpretation of the play addresses the interaction between Indigenous and Eurocentric perspectives and helps to decolonize the text.

In "Cradling Space: Towards an Indigenous Dramaturgy on Turtle Island," Dione Joseph proposes the notion of cradling space, a conceptual and pragmatic understanding of land-based practices and land-based dramaturgy from an Indigenous practitioner perspective. Working through the nuances of land-based dramaturgy, she describes how different environments, specifically Indigenous lands, have the potential to contribute to an understanding of how the materialities of Indigenous performance shape multilayered creative works. She views an Indigenous dramaturgy as having two functions: to nurture the narratives of its people and to provide a framing of theatrical convention that is relevant, necessary, and important to the broader dialogue on dramaturgy. Drawing upon conversations with Indigenous playwrights from Saskatchewan, Joseph explores how the concept of dramaturgy as cradling space reflects the unique theatrical and performative landscape of the province and how such a practice is intrinsic to the development of a distinctive Indigenous voice in Canada, particularly in Saskatchewan, where land and the way it shapes and defines people is, arguably, more important than in large-city-based traditions. Admittedly, Joseph still reaches back to dramaturgy as defined by Europe, as well as current practices in contemporary Canada, but she also ties it to transformative models drawn from Indigenous practices in Canada and New Zealand, bringing a more transnational perspective into view.

Kahente Horn-Miller's chapter, "Standing With Sky Woman: A Conversation on Cultural Fluency," picks up on several themes raised by Joseph, and to some extent, Carol Greyeyes and Nolan, by referencing the importance of embodiment and storytelling in the move away from colonial and male narratives. Specifically, Horn-Miller discusses how her performance of the Sky Woman narrative, *We Are In Her and She Is In Us*, demonstrates the transformation of the story from an aspect of her doctoral work, to a performance piece, and to embodied knowledge through which she inscribes and communicates the history of her Haudenosaunee people on and through her body. The writing provides an example of cultural fluency and rematriation of foundational stories in which the cultural metaphors in the language and cultural principles of Rotinohnsionni-Haudenosaunee philosophy are reinvigorated. In revisiting the creation story, Horn-Miller begins to transcend disciplinary boundaries, moving from researcher to storyteller, to woman, to mother, and finally, to performer. Importantly, she centres the concept of matrilineality and the transfer of knowledge through female bodies as key to her reading, emphasizing the point that our futurity lies in our children.

Following this multidisciplinary framework, in "Resurgence, Recognition, and Remaining Settled Through *Changes* at UpFront '91," Megan Davies looks specifically at the Tunooniq Theatre Company in Pond Inlet, Nunavut, and its goal of engaging community youth, using theatre to develop skills in problem-solving and self-expression. Davies follows the company's production history of *Changes*, from 1986 to 1991, examining how the play subverted the colonizer's gaze by staging the colonizer's role from an Inuit perspective and by using

Inuktitut almost exclusively. With this, Davies considers more generally the role of language translation and (mis)communication in Indigenous performance, publication, and subsequent reviews and scholarship. Davies further suggests that Canadian audiences may have moved beyond the primitivism of Robert J. Flaherty's *Nanook of the North*, now coming to festivals that include Indigenous works out of a desire to have their gaze and ears deliberately subverted.[15] Nonetheless, the persistence of older paradigms of the Canadian north, promoted by Canadian writers like Farley Mowat, still leaves many tone-deaf to deeper and possibly more subversive and unsettling messages of social and political autonomy.

The collection concludes with Floyd P. Favel's "Red People, Red Magic," a poetic alternative to the formal essay. Favel draws on his personal experiences, from which emerges a dream of the epic hero who travels and returns with new visions and insights about the nature of Indigenous theatre and performance, which have implications for First Nations cultures. Favel navigates a diverse range of voices and a delicate balance between remembering and forgetting, to draw insights from both European and Indigenous performance conventions. Although the poem concludes with the provocative notion of "an impossible theatre," it along with this entire collection of essays speaks emphatically to its viability.[16]

AUDIENCE

To return to the gathering that launched this publication, Performing Turtle Island took up the (PSi) global themes of knowing and unknowing to call on Canadian Indigenous performers, playwrights, scholars, and artists to show and discuss notions of transidentity—what it means to signify across a range of practices and

---

15 "*Nanook of the North* is a 1922 American silent documentary film by Robert J. Flaherty, with elements of docudrama, at a time when the concept of separating films into documentary and drama did not yet exist." The film depicts the lives of the indigenous Inuit people of Canada's northern Quebec region. Although the production contains some fictional elements, it vividly shows how its resourceful subjects survive in such a harsh climate. "Nanook of the North," *Wikipedia* , https://en.wikipedia.org/wiki/Nanook_of_the_North, accessed June 21, 2018.

16 Floyd P. Favel, "Red People, Red Magic," this volume, 203.

global perspectives. The gathering also drew inspiration from *In the Balance: Indigeneity, Performance, Globalization*, a conference staged in London, UK, in 2013 that focused on "the growing visibility of artistic networks and ideological coalitions among indigenous peoples on a transnational scale urg[ing] a fresh look at the cultural entanglements that have accompanied colonization and globalization."[17] The *Performing Turtle Island* collection extends those networks and coalitions by addressing the topics of identity, land, language, and culture, and the process of /un/knowing colonialism, on and beyond Turtle Island.

With this in mind, the intended audience for the publication encompasses a range of readers, both Indigenous and Canadian, including undergraduate and graduate students in Indigenous arts, theatre, performance studies, and Canadian studies programs. This collection will likewise be of interest to established Indigenous and settler artists and scholars in theatre, performance, and cultural studies, along with international readers interested in Indigenous, Canadian, and intercultural performance. More critically, this collection is aimed at those who desire to come together in a post-TRC environment—a coming together, as Dylan Robinson and Keavy Martin describe, "of Indigenous communities to support one another alongside the coming together of members of the Indigenous and non-Indigenous public."[18] Whether this new era results in radical transformation and necessary change to Canadian society is a question left for later. In the meantime, it is important to consider where and how we come together. Robinson and Martin suggest that aesthetic spaces (stages, galleries, found space, and so forth) that support ritualized relationships of performance interaction may offer new opportunities for societal interaction.[19] In the context of the TRC and its Calls to Action, rather than the formal platforms of courtroom and review panel where justice may or may not be served, we may look to performing bodies and performative spaces

---

17 In the Balance: Indigeneity, Performance, Globalization, call for papers (2013), http://www.indigeneity.net/events/Cfp-In%20the%20Balance%20conference-final.pdf, accessed February 12, 2018.

18 Dylan Robinson and Keavy Martin, eds., *Arts of Engagement: Taking Aesthetic Action in and Beyond the Truth and Reconciliation Commission in Canada* (Waterloo: Wilfrid Laurier University Press, 2016), 11.

19 *Ibid.*

to find a way forward through witnessing and healing, actions and effects held in the body at the moment of their occurrence. For, to exist and to be seen, as Ravensbergen attests, are embodied political acts of defiance that transcend formal artistic form. They are "living, breathing act[s] of transformation."[20]

Where does this leave the Canadian and more recent newcomer, whether as reader of this publication or audience member witnessing performances by Indigenous artists? In addition to the PSi objectives laid out above, the aim of *Performing Turtle Island* is to approach performance as a critical self-representation important to empowerment and self-determination, as well as to place Indigenous performance in dialogue with Western perspectives. We also want to show how Indigenous artists and scholars consider traditional concepts in relation to Eurocentric theatre models and to manifest how this might enact positive change towards, if not reconciliation, a better understanding of our shared histories. The collection, we hope, serves to show the vibrant and abundant cultural gestures to which Canadians must attend in addressing their inherited colonial legacies.

To truly attend to these legacies will require a thorough decolonizing of settler ways of looking and being. Can this happen through performing and witnessing stories? Leanne Simpson writes that "storytelling is at its core decolonizing because it is a process of remembering, visioning and creating a just reality." She suggests that it is "a lens" through which Indigenous people "can envision a way out of cognitive imperialism" and "create models and mirrors where none existed," and wherein can be found the "spaces of freedom and justice." In this sense, for Simpson, storytelling becomes a space where Indigenous people may "escape the gaze and cage of empire."[21] Above all, *Performing Turtle Island*, the event and subsequent publication, envisions performance to be a space of creativity, knowledge practice, criticality, and unknowing—a space shared, if only partially, with Canadian and more recent newcomer audiences, so that they might acknowledge and understand it fully.

20 Robinson, "Acts of Defiance," 190.
21 Leanne Simpson, *Dancing on our Turtle's Back: Stories of Nishnaabeg Re-creation, Resurgence and a New Emergence* (Winnipeg: ARP Books, 2011), 33–4.

EDITORIAL NOTES

The editors would like to thank all the contributors whose hard work has made this rich and important collection possible. We'd also like to thank all the staff at the University of Regina Press for their commitment to bringing this publication to fruition. And we'd like to thank all the participants who presented at the original gathering, as well as all those who attended, as it is to our audience and readership, teachers and students, producers and performers that we acknowledge the purpose of and support for this book. In this process of writing and editing we are made acutely aware of how this work reaches out to a growing audience curious about Indigenous performance. We are reminded again and again that readers, spectators, artists, and performers alike are equally part of this shared creation.

Indeed, the process of editing this collection has been a profound learning experience for the editors, and each of us would like to take this opportunity to offer our reflections on the process, particularly on the politics, ethics, and principles that must be properly addressed with this kind of intercultural project.

KATHLEEN IRWIN: I am, first and foremost, a theatre artist, a scenographer whose practice focuses on performance space, specifically site-specific performance. My work is grounded in places. Inherent in my practice is an understanding of the meanings imbued in a site—social, historical, psychological, and metaphorical. These aspects lend meaning to performance situations, though these meanings are also in flux. When one meaning is set in motion, its opposite is also implicitly mobilized. For example, embedded in the notion of site and rootedness is its antithesis: mobility. Implied in stasis are notions of change; in homecoming one understands departure.

As an artist, I feel obliged to underscore the impossibility of a fixed state and to explore the tension between fixity and mobility, which is, as Anna Birch writes, "both creative and critical and one that reverberates with our experience of an increasingly globalized and mobile world."[22] Things change; art is ambiguous. We move; we move forward. Working with First Nations and Métis artists has allowed me to see how others relate deeply to place in immutable

22   Anna Birch, Editorial, *Contemporary Theatre Review* 22, no. 2 (1999): 199.

ways; how some places can be shared while others cannot. I try to think more deeply about this now—along with the issues of ownership and authorship.

My involvement with this project has been enriching and has problematized my own (Scots-Irish-Welsh ancestral) position within the process of transcultural art-making. I say problematized because, in a sense, this was simultaneously my work (in part, conceiving the initial idea, writing the grants to fund the process, and co-editing this publication) and not my work—something that could never be my work. The tension was particularly acute in the editing process, during which I often had to make suggestions to authors to use other words, reshape sentences and paragraphs, and sometimes restructure entire pieces of writing. I understand that this is the inherent challenge of the editorial process; however, when working across cultures, there are inevitably other pressures that come to bear in publishing work by and about Indigenous people.

It was not until the process was well underway that I discovered a small but significant book by Gregory Younging called *Elements of Indigenous Style,* and this changed, I hope in a good way, everything about my position as a settler-descendant editing several chapters by Indigenous authors. Younging writes, "The body of natural scientific knowledge encompassed in the Indigenous voice ... contains valuable paradigms, teachings, and information that can benefit all of the world's family of nations."[23] However, while over the past five decades Indigenous authors have expressed and developed a voice that establishes a higher level of authenticity, the writing down of it and its attendant editorial practices are still in a state of evolution and flux.[24] Still, the *Performing Turtle Island* collection is a concrete example of what we need now to move forward towards some kind of reconciliation, even (especially) in publishing.

I understand that while steps towards decolonizing and reconciling, such as the Performing Turtle Island gathering and the subsequent anthology, may be few, faltering, at best naive and at worst ignorant, they are among a range of actions that lead in a healing direction, towards a better understanding of what is Indigenous knowledge alone

....

23 Gregory Younging, *Elements of Indigenous Style: A Guide for Writing by and about Indigenous Peoples* (Edmonton: Brush Education Inc., 2018), 13.

24 *Ibid.,* xi.

and about which places and stories can be shared and which cannot. These realizations may play a small but important part in restoring balance, altering periodically but finding an equilibrium in time.

MOIRA DAY: As an editor and writer, I find that good editing tends to work from a place of humility and generosity. Engaging with the 'sacred ground' of another person's writing is an intensely dialogic process requiring close listening, careful thought, and perceptive questions on both sides. Nonetheless, even if the editor's completely praiseworthy intention is to help another writer to become his or her best possible self in a written medium, it is a process that even at the best of times has its flaws and limitations—both human and systemic. As Jessica Riley has suggested in her book *A Man of Letters: The Selected Dramaturgical Correspondence of Urjo Kareda*, even great dramaturges and editors, and the institutions they serve, can carry biases and assumptions into the process of shaping the works of others—and in ways they may not be aware of themselves. And if that is true of stars of Kareda's magnitude, all the more cause for lesser lights to be doubly cautious on that score, especially in dealing with writers and artists who write and work out of a different tradition of 'sacred ground.'

In this instance, I found it was essential to do more extra reading than usual before I felt I was anywhere near listening as intelligently as I needed to, or even knowing what questions I needed to ask. I think the article that probably stayed with me the most was Tuck and Yang's in its uncompromising interrogation of whether any attempt at reconciliation could be successful, let alone valid, without first completely deconstructing or decolonizing the system as it currently exists, and in going back to restart the history of the Americas anew.[25] With this in mind, I think the *Performing Turtle Island* book is a reflection of the hope and belief of its participating editors, writers, and artists that, while it is possible and in fact critical to start that process of reconciliation now, any dialogues or actions involved need to be done with a strong awareness of the multiple complexities and difficulties involved in both reconciliation and decolonization.

25 Eve Tuck and K.W. Yang, "Decolonization is not a Metaphor," in *Decolonization: Indigeneity, Education & Society* 1, no. 1 (2012), https://jps.library.utoronto. ca/index.php/des/article/view/18630/15554, accessed January 28, 2019.

In that regard, I think Tuck and Yang, among others, are correct in cautioning against the tendency of educators and scholars to gravitate too easily towards the comfortable stability of closed systems that assimilate all knowledge into symmetrical comparisons, contrasts, and dichotomies leading to tidy, satisfying conclusions.

As regards the question of constructing or reconstructing histories, in teaching my senior-level contemporary theatre history and aesthetics class, I often start by asking people to read the concluding chapter of R.G. Collingwood's *The Idea of History.* Among other things, Collingwood makes the point that histories are important, not just on a communal but on an individual level, because our "knowledge of the past," as shaped into narratives or stories, profoundly shapes our understanding of who we are now and just as critically "condition[s] our creation of the future."[26] He also suggests, to the extent that those histories are manifestations of a human consciousness that is perpetually in flux and motion, our understanding of the past shifts and changes every time our understanding of the present does. It is a perspective that validates the power of individuals to create narratives or histories that matter, while also charging them with the enormous responsibility of bringing the full integrity of who and what they are to that process. Ultimately, we need to reach a place of understanding past and present, and the systems and histories involved in both, in their full integrity, in a way that does not shortchange or underestimate the immensity of that challenge. Otherwise, in trying to create the future, "there will once more as so often in the past, be change but no progress."[27]

The reservations of Tuck and Yang and Collingwood came very much to mind during the long editorial process involved in producing this volume. Every article, including the introduction, is a personal narrative or history of that kind, some of them revised again and again in the process of trying to eliminate the easy comparison, the facile analogy, the sweeping generalization that seemed to tie the bow of the argument together neatly—only for the latter to start to unravel again under closer examination and questioning from a variety of cultural perspectives. Editors and writers were continually challenged to ask: What do I know and how do I know it? When

....

26 R.G. Collingwood, *The Idea of History* (Oxford: Clarendon Press, 1946), 334.
27 *Ibid.*

am I speaking authentically based on the integrity of who and what I am and what I know, both in the past and present tense? When am I making assumptions or speaking for others in ways that I should not? I believe that as human beings we are more than the sum of our gender, our race, and our class; but we cannot write authentically without an awareness of how those factors, among others, make us the individuals that we are and give us the particular voice in which we speak, create, and write. I also think that part of good listening involves knowing when our voices may need to harmonize, become quieter, or even fall silent to allow others to speak.

As a scholar, editor, and writer, I may speculate that the value of the *Performing Turtle Island* collection lies more in the questions it raises than in the answers it gives. However, as a parent and a teacher, I find that the insight that resonates the most with me is the suggestion in Kahente Horn-Miller's paper that the most profound embodied knowledge that many of us experience in our lives is our children: they are the people whom we ultimately create the stories with and for, in the hopes that their narratives will have deeper roots while reaching farther, beyond the limits of our own. I feel that the volume will have been worth creating if it plays even a small role in helping to free people from earlier, more restrictive definitions of art, of humanity, and of history in ways that will help prepare us for the reality of a world where, in Maria Campbell's words, all our children are of different colours now, sometimes even within the same family.

JESSE RAE ARCHIBALD-BARBER: The process of compiling and editing this collection has been a wonderful learning experience for me as a teacher, writer, and theatre producer—as well as for my students. I include my students here because, while co-editing this anthology, I had the opportunity in 2017 to offer an Indigenous performance course at the First Nations University of Canada, where we focused on laying the groundwork for a major project called *Making Treaty 4*. While I often consulted with colleagues and theatre professionals throughout the course and the subsequent production of the work, I was also fortunate to be able to draw from the chapters in this book important insights into the elements and considerations that go into developing and staging an Indigenous theatre piece. As I completed both the *Making Treaty 4* project and the *Performing Turtle*

Island collection, I realized that I had serendipitously been engaging in a kind of 'proof of concept' for the collection.

Far from an assemblage of theoretical musings, each chapter of this book provides direct knowledge and applicable advice on how to navigate the many challenges that may arise when creating and producing Indigenous performance. This kind of resource is critical for teachers and practitioners, especially considering how Indigenous performances often aim at confronting the violent legacies of our colonial past while opening new pathways to self-empowerment through the very process of performance. This imbued the entire editorial process for me with a deep sense of confidence in the materials and gratitude for the writers, along with the excitement of seeing the collection finally come to publication.

This whole experience also gave rise, for me, to reflections on the spiritual aspects of Indigenous performance. In particular, I carried with me several principles as outlined by Blair Stonechild in *The Knowledge Seeker*, where he emphasizes how spirituality is foundational to Indigenous knowledge, reminding us that we are "spirit beings embarked on a temporary physical journey."[28] This principle is clearly evident in performance arts, given both the ephemeral and embodied nature of theatre. Indigenous performance in particular speaks to this notion of the spirit engaged in human activity, at the threshold of *knowing* and *unknowing*—a space that includes the complex relations between Indigenous and non-Indigenous cultures, whether in tension or alliance. The *Performing Turtle Island* collection offers many paths of guidance across this threshold.

❖ ❖ ❖ ❖

In closing, the following chapters carry forward the main threads of the argument drawn throughout this introduction, all of which involve in their own way the process of reclaiming Indigenous cultural practices and spiritual traditions, in order to create new forms of knowledge and performance in a dialogue that engages a diverse range of historical and contemporary issues. These issues include

---

28 Blair Stonechild, *The Knowledge Seeker: Embracing Indigenous Spirituality* (Regina: University of Regina Press, 2016), 67.

self-representation and community engagement, education and creative expression, empowerment and self-determination, decolonization and reconciliation, language revival and storytelling, connections to land and images of body, meanings of the text and sites of performance, self-healing and community well-being. All these threads have shaped our relationships and contemporary lives, particularly in a time of heightened political, economic, and environmental crises. But it is also a time where the possibilities for self-transformation are evermore open to us, and the writers in this collection draw those new paths to imagine and persevere through them. From the shores of first contact on the east coast to the residential school legacy in northern Ontario, from classical music on the opera stage to the unpacking of a medicine bundle in the classroom, from a community centre in Nunavut to the theatre halls in Toronto, from the cradling space of land in Saskatchewan to the rematriation of foundational stories in Kahnawà:ke, from the audience member's gaze to the dream of an impossible theatre—all these and more are part of a thriving Indigenous performance culture in Canada, and the chapters in this book run the gamut, expressing how we engage our past traditions with ever new ways of knowing and performing Turtle Island.

REFERENCES

Appleford, Robert. "Introduction: Seeing the Full Frame." In *Aboriginal Drama and Theatre: Critical Perspectives on Canadian Theatre in English*, vol. 1, edited by Robert Appleford, vii–xiii. Toronto: Playwrights Canada, 2005.

Collingwood, R.G. *The Idea of History*. Oxford: Clarendon Press, 1946.

Garneau, David. "Imaginary Spaces of Conciliation and Reconciliation." *West Coast Line* 74 (Summer 2012): 28–38.

Hoffman, James. *The Ecstasy of Resistance: A Biography of George Ryga*. Toronto: ECW Press, 1995.

Innes, Christopher. *Politics and the Playwright: George Ryga*. Toronto: Simon and Pierre, 1985.

In the Balance: Indigeneity, Performance, Globalization. Call for papers. 2013. http://www.indigeneity.net/events/Cfp-In%20the%20Balance%20conference-final.pdf. Accessed February 12, 2018.

L'Hirondelle Hill, Gabrielle, and Sophie McCall. *The Land We Are*. Winnipeg: ARP Books, 2015.

Ministry of the Economy, Government of Saskatchewan. *Saskatchewan Statistical Immigration Report 2012 to 2014*. Regina: Ministry of the Economy, Government of Saskatchewan. http://publications. gov.sk.ca/documents/310/93353-2014%20Immigration%20 Statistical%20Report%20-%20July%2020%202016.pdf. Accessed June 15, 2018.

Nolan, Yvette. Introduction to *Performing Indigeneity: New Essays of Canadian Theatre*, vol. 6, edited by Yvette Nolan and Ric Knowles, 1–4. Toronto: Playwrights Canada Press, 2016.

PSi #21 Fluid States. "Theme." *Fluid States: Performances of Unknowing*. http://www.fluidstates.org/page.php?par=16&id=18. Accessed May 4, 2017.

Riley, Jessica, ed. *A Man of Letters: The Selected Dramaturgical Correspondence of Urjo Kareda*. Toronto: Playwrights Canada Press, 2017.

Robinson, Dylan. "Acts of Defiance in Indigenous Theatre: A Conversation with Lisa C. Ravensbergen." In *Arts of Engagement: Taking Aesthetic Action in and Beyond the Truth and Reconciliation Commission in Canada*, edited by Dylan Robinson and Keavy Martin, 181–92. Waterloo: Wilfrid Laurier University Press, 2016.

Robinson, Dylan, and Keavy Martin, eds. *Arts of Engagement: Taking Aesthetic Action in and Beyond the Truth and Reconciliation Commission in Canada*. Waterloo: Wilfrid Laurier University Press, 2016.

Simpson, Leanne. *Dancing on our Turtle's Back: Stories of Nishnaabeg Re-creation, Resurgence and a New Emergence*. Winnipeg: ARP Books, 2011.

Stonechild, Blair. *The Knowledge Seeker: Embracing Indigenous Spirituality*. Regina: University of Regina Press, 2016.

Truth and Reconciliation Commission of Canada. *Final Report*. http://www.trc.ca/websites/trcinstitution/index.php?p=890. Accessed June 9, 2018.

Tuck, Eve, and K.W. Yang. "Decolonization Is Not a Metaphor." *Decolonization: Indigeneity, Education & Society* 1, no. 1 (2012): 1–40. https://jps.library.utoronto.ca/index.php/des/article/view/18630/15554. Accessed January 28, 2019.

Younging, Gregory. *Elements of Indigenous Style: A Guide for Writing by and about Indigenous Peoples*. Edmonton: Brush Education Inc., 2018.

PART I

CRITICAL
SELF-REPRESENTATION
IN PRODUCTION
AND TRAINING

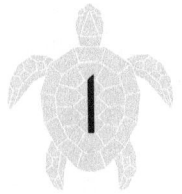

STRANGER IN A STRANGE LAND: VIEWS FROM AN INDIGENOUS LENS

Michael Greyeyes

*The following was presented as a keynote address during the
Performing Turtle Island conference at the University of Regina
and First Nations University of Canada, September 2015.*

have the great pleasure to call American director Anne Bogart one
of my teachers. In 2005, in upstate New York, I worked with her
and members of Saratoga International Theatre Institute (SITI),
a theatre company she founded with Japanese director, Tadashi
Suzuki. Working in the spacious studios of Skidmore College, a
liberal arts university where SITI hold their annual training program, it was a brutally hot summer, I recall.

I was then a tenure-track assistant professor at York University—
where I am now the graduate program director of the Master of Fine
Arts (MFA) program. The work we pursued in the sweltering July
heat was career changing. I was introduced to two major forms of
study that summer: the actor training of Suzuki, and Viewpoints, the

movement improvisation practice first developed by Mary Overlie and subsequently rearticulated by Bogart. Together Overlie, Bogart, and Wendell Beavers are now recognized as the co-developers of Viewpoints, a movement practice taught across the United States and, increasingly, in Canada.[1]

Both forms radically changed my approach to teaching. Viewpoints, which provides lenses through which to examine the various structures of theatrical activity, is also a system of analysis that allowed my professional and lived experiences as a dancer, choreographer, and then-nascent director to take root. As part of subsequent research as a theatre maker and educator, through Viewpoints I found a way to convey experiential knowledge to my students and collaborators in a tightly structured way. I have taught Viewpoints ever since—at York University, at the Banff Centre (for five years), at the Soulpepper Academy in Toronto (two seasons), and for a number of years as part of Volcano Theatre's summer Conservatory in Toronto.

Although I chose to study in Saratoga because of my interest in Viewpoints, it was Suzuki's highly physical actor work that caught my imagination. The Suzuki method involves, among many other things, rhythmic stomping. Because every culture in the world stomps, it seemed natural to incorporate this pedagogy into my own movement practice as its genesis spoke to me powerfully. Suzuki and his company developed the work as an outgrowth of their highly stylized performance work. An example of this is his adaptation of *The Trojan Women* (first premiered in 1974) that electrified the world. As he and his actors developed new forms of physical staging and subsequently needed to replace actors as they left the company, they instituted training to bring new company members up to speed on how various characters moved in his works. Suzuki's technique is

---

[1]   Viewpoints is a composition technique that provides a vocabulary for thinking about and acting upon movement and gesture. Originally developed in the 1970s as a method of movement improvisation, the Viewpoints theory was adapted for stage acting by directors Anne Bogart and Tina Landau. Overlie's Six Viewpoints (space, story, time, emotion, movement, and shape) are considered to be a logical way to examine, analyze, and create dances, while Bogart's Viewpoints are considered practical in creating staging with actors. *Wikipedia*, s.v. "Viewpoints," https://en.wikipedia.org/wiki/Viewpoints, accessed January 21, 2019.

rigorous. For example, in Saratoga I would typically sweat through (at minimum) three T-shirts in a single training session. During such exertion there are moments when you wonder how you will continue standing or moving through a given exercise. I've seen participants with tears rolling down their face as they performed an exercise, somehow grinding through a bad day on the deck. The technique blew my mind! In it, I found a movement practice that effectively replaced the emotional/physical/intellectual void left once I had retired from dance.

Today, both these forms are intrinsic to my work as an educator and theatre maker. They are demanding, highly structured, and invigorating. I returned home to Canada after that summer in 2005 energized in a way that was palpable both to me and, I believe, to my students. Recently, I introduced a new class of devised theatre students at York University to one of Bogart's simple consciousness-raising spatial relationship exercises. I could see eyes widening as we unpacked the exercise. Then I saw the fire in them as their imaginations and critical thinking were piqued.

Bogart taught us a great deal that summer. One story she shared was about her journey as a young director. She told us that she was obsessed with German theatre. Everything about the Germans caught her imagination. They were the cutting edge of theatre making and all she desired was to go to Berlin and immerse herself in their milieu. After years of trying, she finally scraped the money together to travel to West Germany, but as soon as she got there, she realized she'd made a mistake. She was an American director. Her ethos, her tastes, her mores and knowledge were based in the culture of her homeland, the United States, and its theatrical past: vaudeville, early American Expressionism, jazz. She told us that she had to travel to Germany to realize she was an American director. I was struck by that.

I've been away from home—my territory in Saskatchewan—for a long time, working across Canada, the United States, and abroad. For example, in the summer of 2015 I was working in Cape Town, South Africa, for over two months filming a miniseries in four parts called *Saints and Strangers*.[2] It was a long way from home, but it was necessary for me to go, just as travelling to Skidmore College in New

---

2   Paul A. Edwards, director, *Saints and Strangers*, written by Eric Overmeyer and Seth Fisher (Sony Pictures, 2015).

York State was necessary for me eleven years earlier. As I discovered, being so far from home refocuses your eyes so that you can see your home and your place in it differently.

South Africa is a stunningly beautiful country. There is a quality of light there that is difficult to describe; it has a tangible magic. The film industry has long realized this and many film projects and television series have been and continue to be shot there to take advantage of its beauty. There are also significant financial incentives offered by the South African government. These include low wages for the film crews, terms that readily convince Hollywood producers that the twenty-three-hour flight is worth the investment.

But my journey actually begins with a script description of the character I was cast to play in the project in Cape Town. It reads, "Canonicus, a Sachem of the Narragansett, stands. He is tall and muscular." Honestly? As I finished reading this I put the half-eaten doughnut I was holding in my hand down on the table. The previously delicious sugary dough rapidly losing its flavour now mixed with a distinctly acid taste in my mouth. Great. Just great.

The project in question, a four-hour miniseries for the National Geographic Channel, was called *Saints and Strangers*. Written by Eric Overmeyer and Seth Fisher, it is a provocative retelling of the voyage of the *Mayflower* and how the Atlantic coastal nations reacted to the settlement of Plymouth. It is a period piece, which meant the actors playing First Nations (in the American parlance: Native Americans) would be wearing period clothes and that, inevitably, there would be a sequence in which the men are shirtless. The project had just such a moment, and the character descriptor had given me all the warning I needed. I had to get back into pre-Columbian shape! Historically, our communities were active, healthy, and vibrant—and we looked it. But in mid June of 2015, when the script arrived, I was none of these. I was exhausted, overworked, and desk-bound. Plus I'd gone soft in the middle. I had become the thing I'd always feared: an out-of-shape movement professor.

A casting director who had previously cast me in a number of productions had suggested my name. Because of this, I did not have to audition for the part. Evidently she did not realize that I no longer looked like the pictures, so plentiful on the Internet, showing a buff, twenty-something actor recently retired from a professional dance career. Needless to say, I had my work cut out for me. Over

the course of about twelve weeks, beginning here at home, I began
to train physically and I changed my diet completely. To overcome a
few nagging injuries, I started slowly. Then I began to gain strength
and some momentum. The changes were subtle at first but became
palpable by the time I was about to film the first scenes in South
Africa. It was revelatory.

As an Indigenous performer I have an uneasy relationship with
period-film work. On the one hand, such work represents more than
half of my professional output as an actor. On the other hand, I
resent how we are depicted in period films, as it entrenches, for a
worldwide audience, the idea that our cultures and communities
exist primarily in the past—as a vestigial trace.

Because I do not work on many film or television projects, as my
work as professor and as artistic director of Signal Theatre precludes
it, I entered the process with a certain degree of wariness. Also,
as an established performer, I am judicious about where I lend my
name and put my efforts. However, *Saints and Strangers* represented
an interesting opportunity. First of all, the storyline appealed to me.
It looks at the passenger manifest of the infamous *Mayflower* vessel
through a new lens, asserting that half of the passengers were religious zealots fleeing persecution in England, while the other half
were con men fleeing justice. It proposed that the *Mayflower* and the
settlement of Plymouth provided the American nation with a DNA
blueprint which still resonates to this day. Secondly, Rene Haynes,
the film's casting director only involves herself in projects with artistic and political integrity. All these factors intrigued me, so I said yes.

Working on this miniseries was also significant because of the
writing. Non-Indigenous writers usually create Indigenous characters having little connection to our respective cultures. There are
exceptions to the rule—John Fusco is an obvious example.[3] However,
without cultural knowledge or experience, writers usually have
only one choice: since they can no longer safely depict us as savages, they represent us as some version of noble. Thus portrayed,
the depiction of our community is monolithic. We're all wonderful! However, there is no such family or community in existence.

----

3   John Fusco is an American screenwriter and film producer born in Prospect,
    Connecticut. His screenplays include *Crossroads, Young Guns, Young Guns II,
    Thunderheart, Hidalgo,* and the Oscar-nominated *Spirit: Stallion of the Cimarron.*

Where is the crazy uncle, the demented grandmother, the maniac cousin? Of course, these are all clichés too, but writers from outside the community steer away from them for fear of offending or painting us negatively. *Saints and Strangers* took another path. In it, the Indigenous characters vary widely and the characterizations are complex and sophisticated. It is the best writing for Indigenous characters coming out of Hollywood in a long time. The character of Canonicus is especially so. He is, in fact, paradoxical. On the one hand, he is insufferably arrogant and ambitious; on the other, he is fully cognizant of how the English will change the entire region, despite his position as a Sachem. The Narragansett, whom Canonicus led, were a superpower with 5,000 warriors that tithed neighbouring nations mercilessly. This depiction of him provided a fascinating frame of reference for Massassoit, Sachem of the Pokanaket people, who, due to plagues and other incursions, had a mere 500 survivors. Massassoit played a pivotal role in the survival of the Plymouth colony, but in the context of the Narragansett presence and Canonicus' predations, the Europeans were the lesser of two evils. This interpretation allowed Raoul Trujillo, the very experienced actor playing Massassoit, to play a wide range of tactics and responses. In *Saints and Strangers*, no one wanted the *Mayflower* settlers to remain—they were filthy, scurvy ridden, and divisive. Canonicus certainly wanted them wiped from the earth. Having to decide between these horrible new pilgrims and the lunatic Canonicus, Massassoit chose to ally himself with the settlers, thereby creating a tenuous and sophisticated relationship that shifted continuously. The script followed these changed closely.

By creating a foil in Canonicus, writers Overmeyer and Fisher took a risk by giving the Indigenous characters three-dimensionality. In the end, it is evident that Massassoit was neither villain nor fool, but his decision to help the settlers was based on immediate needs and born out of urgent political necessity. This is not usually the kind of latitude we are given to play in period films. Even Canonicus, a seeming blowhard, was allowed room to grow, change, and contradict himself. In a crucial two-page scene near the end of hour three, he confides to Massassoit that he is actually afraid of the English. He sees in them the "end of us all, our ways, and our future." For me, the level of discourse and the range of intentions and backstory provided to Indigenous characters were equal in complexity to the range of characterization and intention in the non-Indigenous cast.

Was the film historically accurate? Of course, we will never know if Canonicus was exactly as he was written or played. The point is that the writers abandoned any putative notion of authenticity in order to paint vivid and breathing portraits. In so doing, they provided me with a full understanding of how to play the character. This allowed me to consider as a prototype an arrogant, wealthy, power-mad contemporary character—Donald Trump, *sans* comb-over. In the end, the fact that it was challenging period work, coupled with the fear of looking like an out-of-shape professor preserved forever on film, motivated me to address my physical conditioning as an actor.

It was this double process that I found eye-opening. By preparing myself physically to play such a character, I was reminded that any approach to good acting must be physically grounded, connected, and rigorous. In every scene I prepared myself to take physical risk, whether or not I had anticipated the scene would be action based or not. Using this as a point of departure, my portrayal of Canonicus, aching to stretch his muscles and assume control of the whole region, bristled with fear and energy.

So I walked away from the project, filmed on the other side of the planet and set in a time period far from today, coming to a realization about performance in the Indigenous context. I now believe we must look at performance and, in particular, the training of our actors through a strictly physical lens. Firstly, this connects us to our pasts, wherein we relied on our physical knowledge and prowess to survive. At the same time, it charts a course through contemporary performance—one that does not follow the psychological approach championed by the American pedagogues of the Group Theatre, whose philosophy still has an iron grip on the academy and performance training.[4] In fact, Michael Chekov and others—even the guru Konstantin Stanislavski himself—claimed that the approach, which

....

4   "The Group Theatre was a New York City theatre collective formed in 1931 by Harold Clurman, Cheryl Crawford, and Lee Strasberg. It was intended as a base for the kind of theatre they and their colleagues believed in—a forceful, naturalistic, and highly disciplined artistry." *Wikipedia*, s.v. "Group Theatre (New York City)," https://en.wikipedia.org/wiki/Group_Theatre_(New_York_City), accessed January 21, 2019.

became known as The Method, was misconstrued. He insisted that his approach was primarily a physical one.

Within our traditional cultural practices we see a vibrant physical terrain. Why would our performance training not emerge from within this?—especially as intense physicality is already required for working in the professional realm. Considering the broad landscape of contemporary Indigenous performance in Canada, one sees a number of companies—some new, some more recently established—making exciting work. They include: Kaha:wi Dance Theatre, Article 11, Ravenspirit, Compagnie V'ni Dansi, Red Sky, Damelahamid, and my own company, Signal Theatre.[5] These companies are leading our community in terms of energy, risk, rigour, and public reach. Their work includes dance, physical theatre, movement—all relying on physically fluent and physically engaged performers. What is consistent through each company is that the somatic landscape of their theatre is heightened, requiring performers who are physically adept.

Recently, the Australian performance company Marrageku and performer Dalisa Pigram presented an astonishing theatre piece, *Gudirr, Gudirr*, at Harbourfront Centre Theatre in Toronto as part of the 2014–2015 DanceWorks season. As I watched it, I realized that this was a wake-up call to every Indigenous actor in Canada. Pigrim's work was intensely physical, emotional, and seething with energy. Although her body is ferociously strong and lithe, the physical demands of the piece were daunting. This represents the new playing field. Indeed, it already exists. The profession is demanding such performers to fill its stages. If we do not bring ourselves to play there, we remain shadows. As my friend and mentor Denis Lacroix has stated, we will be left "playing ghosts of ourselves." We need strength to portray members of our community and, without doubt, it is easier to portray this if we are actually strong.

....

5   Michael Greyeyes founded Canadian-based Signal Theatre in 2010. Emitting images, ideas, and stories, Signal Theatre is committed to the collaborative process, experimentation, and intercultural research. Signal explores both physical and text-based theatre that moves through the disciplines of dance, opera, music, design, and the spoken word. "About Signal Theatre," Canada Dance Festival, http://canadadance.ca/buy-tickets/signal-theatre/, accessed February 7, 2017.

This brings me back to my experience in South Africa. After twelve weeks of physical conditioning to prepare for my work there, I felt I might be ready to engage at this extreme level in my performances. I had become a different actor after the training. I had tremendous confidence in myself as I walked on to the set. Undeniably, confidence is a tenuous thing in the world of acting. It is the one thing an actor must be able to project without guile or falsity when auditioning for a role. Confident actors are the ones hired most often and work itself gives you this confidence. When one gets outside of the loop of employment, one struggles, but a physical practice, through which one attains mastery, can be maintained without the imprimatur of industry or casting decisions. Walking into a room full of physical confidence, bristling with energy and health, is not something easily dismissed.

While central, the training paradigms that I experienced in South Africa were not solely focused on the physical aspect. Language training was also important. The decision for our characters in *Saints and Strangers* to speak the western dialect of Abenaki was key to the success of the project. We who find ourselves working within the power structures and narratives of Hollywood have always battled, literally and figuratively, to find an acceptable level of subjectivity in the work offered us, as well as a way to rewrite and assume authorial power in our representation. The question before us is simply put: where do our original languages sit inside the paradigms of mainstream media representation? Positive examples of this are few and far between. For example, I was working in New York City when the landmark feature film *Dances With Wolves* (1990) was released. Seeing it in at the cinemas on Broadway, downstairs from where I was dancing with the choreographer Eliot Feld, made a significant impact on me. In fact, it was this film, along with *Last of the Mohicans* (1992), that convinced me to transition from a dance career to one in filmed media. In *Dances With Wolves* the Indigenous actors spoke Lakota. I had never seen a film in which our original languages were so dominant. The purpose of language in the film was obvious: the Lakota were alien to the character of Dunbar (Kevin Costner) and the settlers were equally alien to the Lakota people. Language was the separator. As a non-Lakota person, and English speaker, the Lakota language was also for me a signifier of otherness. Hearing it spoken in the context of a major studio release was extraordinary. It was one of the first times that watching a film depicting us made me feel pride in how we were portrayed. The Lakota language was, for the most part, subtitled, with the Indigenous characters learning rudimentary English in order to erode the distinctions and communications gap between Dunbar and the Lakota characters. As they learned English they became less Other. It is impossible to forget, for example, the endearing attempts of Graham Greene's character, Kicking Bird, to pronounce the word 'buffalo.' This was purposeful because the film's *raison d'etre* was to bring the viewer inside the Lakota community, to show the beauty, integrity, and complex relationships of its history. In order for the film to work, it was as important to empathize with the Lakota as it was to despise the settler soldiers and racketeers. The use of an original language both was a brilliant artistic choice and reiterated problems of identification with the cultural Other.

Gil Cardinal, an Indigenous writer, filmmaker, and producer, used another approach in addressing the notion of subjectivity through language. In 1998, filming in southern Saskatchewan on the Pasqua First Nation Reserve, I participated in an experiment that eroded the perception of us as Other. Cardinal had cast me in the CBC miniseries *Big Bear*, starring the esteemed late Gordon Tootoosis. Based on Rudy Wiebe's novel *The Temptations of Big Bear*, the screenplay, adapted for television by Cardinal, had a unique premise. All the Indigenous characters in the miniseries spoke English, while all the settler characters spoke in an invented language that each white actor had to learn and master. When they spoke 'English' (now Jabberwocky) to each other, the Indigenous characters in the film would scratch their heads and wonder what the settlers were saying. At the time, I felt sorry for the white actors, all wonderful Anglophone and Francophone performers who continually practiced their nonsense language and agonized over their double workload. While I enjoyed working on the project and playing one of our cultural heroes, Wandering Spirit, what was truly unique was the decision of the Indigenous director, who found in the structure of the work itself a means by which our stories were portrayed empathetically while positioning the settlers as the *new* Other.[6]

In *Saints and Strangers*, director Paul Edwards was equally obsessed with the question of language. He frequently cited, as an example of language use, the film *Tora! Tora! Tora!* The silky voiced narrator for the advertisements intoned:

> The Incredible Attack on Pearl Harbour: As Told from both the United States and Japanese Sides. Once two nations made war. Today they have collaborated to make a motion picture of unequalled magnitude and importance. Recreating the actual events leading up to . . . the day that changed the course of history, Twentieth Century Fox Presents . . . [then with the crackly sound of a period 1940s radio headset . . .] *TORA! TORA! TORA!*, an unprecedented film bringing you the answers to one of the most controversial mysteries of our age: How could the attack on Pearl Harbour have happened? Why was one nation unprepared, while another was geared for war?

In this seventies film, Edwards explained, the Japanese actors began all their dialogue in Japanese, but then a cut would

---

6 Big Bear (Mistahi-maskwa) (ca. 1825–1888), a powerful and popular Cree chief, played a pivotal role in Canadian history. He is most notable for his involvement in Treaty 6, acting as one of the few leaders who objected to the signing of the treaty with the Canadian government. He felt that signing would have devastating effects on Indigenous nations, causing them to lose their free, nomadic lifestyle. He also took part in one of the last major battles between the Cree and the Blackfoot nations, leading his people in the last largest battle on the Canadian plains. *Wikipedia*, s.v. "Big Bear," https://en.wikipedia.org/wiki/Big_Bear, accessed February 11, 2017.
    Wandering Spirit (Kapapamahchakwew, Papamahchakwayo, Esprit Errant) (1845–1885) was a Plains Cree war chief. Angered by treaties with the Canadian government that he and Big Bear perceived as unfair and by the dwindling bison population, Wandering Spirit led young Cree warriors in an attack on the small settlement of Frog Lake (February 4, 1885). The Cree uprising, in which nine people were killed and three were taken as captives, was known as the Frog Lake Massacre. For his involvement, Wandering Spirit was hanged on November 27, 1885, at Battleford, Saskatchewan. *Wikipedia*, s.v. "Wandering Spirit," https://en.wikipedia.org/wiki/Wandering_Spirit_(Cree_leader), accessed February 11, 2017.

introduce a new camera angle that would begin with a dolly shot of someone's back moving to the same group, now speaking English. The filmmaker used this technique to avoid the viewer's eye shifting from actors' faces down to the subtitles at the bottom of the screen, a movement he felt that would effectively alienate and 'other' the Japanese. The suggestion for *Saints and Strangers* was to have the native characters speak English, but the director wanted to use an original dialect—in this particular case, an endangered dialect. The research he had done on subtitling was also a revelation. Media analysts have long been testing the viewer's ability to absorb text appearing on screen. It appears we are becoming extremely fluent at it. What is revealed in eye tracking research is that contemporary audiences no longer track subtitles through up and down eye movements. Rather, through practice, we have become adept at reading text without the eye physically shifting to the bottom of the screen—a movement noted in our parents' generation. Because of this, Edwards realized that North American audiences could watch our performances and understand us, through both our performance work and through subtitles. After the first day of speaking Abenaki on set, he knew he had nailed it, or rather, the Indigenous actors had nailed it. We had been coached brilliantly by Jesse Bowman Bruchac, a language specialist and one of only twelve Western Abenaki speakers left in the world. As depicted in the show, this dialect was chosen as the language common to various tribal nations (Narragansett and Pokanet, among others) during the seventeenth century. The dialect was extremely difficult to master as it is an Algonquian language with unique word sounds and grammar that I had not encountered in over twenty years working in the film industry. To say the cast was challenged by the language is an understatement—we were flummoxed. We understood, however, the political and artistic importance of doing it correctly, and this drove us. As non-speakers, we relied on the precision of the teaching and our ability to mimic the sound combinations and rhythms we heard. Here are two examples from the script:

N'nodabnob Iglismonak wijokahalid jiligiliji Namaskik. Ni, Nalagonsek kadawi sôgenaozin ta gwezioholit.

Kizilla, ônda n'wawaldamowen, kanwa n'wawinawô Kinjames. W'wizwôgan. Ônda nidôbanna, ônda kindôba Teskwatem.

The 'i' is pronounced 'ee,' as it 'beet.' The circumflex above the 'o' turns that letter into a double sound 'o(n),' as in 'bone' with an unvoiced 'n,' as in the French nasal 'n' in 'un.' The accent, indicated by the underline, is on the final syllable, unless the word is a three- (or greater) syllable word. Then, the accent is on the third syllable. A 'w' followed by a consonant is pronounced 'oo,' as in 'cool'; when it is followed by a vowel this makes it a regular 'w' sound. These are just a few of the language rules! In addition, some of the words were very long. A medium-length one like this—'jiligiliji'—gave me fits of anxiety. To learn it properly we would start with the last syllable: liji; then giliji; and finally the whole word—jiligiliji. We had to do this with nearly every word we had. The language coaching was laser-like in its precision and our approach as actors was born-again religious. We were competing with each other to sound fluent. It took hour after hour, coaching session after coaching session, day upon day of individual practice walking on Cape Town's streets with the coach feeding us lines while we dodged pedestrians, traffic, and other hazards, so that when we arrived on set we were like ninjas. It usually took a mere two takes, but never more than three or four, for the actors to deliver their dialogue. If more takes were required, it was because of the camera or sound issues—never because of language inaccuracy.

The Pilgrim characters were played by English and Irish actors, who are famous for their professionalism and crisp technique. They stood at attention when we spoke—deadly accurate in our mastery of language, our words flowing with energy, conviction, and power. Remember—this was language that we didn't understand! We did double translations to achieve a parallel understanding of the text, paying attention to what we said and how it translated in our minds in relation to the English text. Since the Abenaki dialogue required us to learn another Indigenous thought process embedded in the structure and words themselves, this was not a simple one-to-one translation. By learning how Abenaki is structured, we glimpsed the heart of it—the meaning embedded in a language obscured by the English translation.

As a professional, I always know my lines when I go in front of a camera or step onto a stage. However, this was work at another level, a more rigorous and exacting level than any one of us, veterans of numerous high-level projects, had known. We were on the ground floor of a new paradigm. This is the new playing field. It also made abundant professional sense. It was like training an actor how to ride a horse, drive a car, or handle a firearm safely. Those three skills alone are used again and again in movies that feature our communities. If we teach our emerging actors this vocal approach, using Indigenous language as the foundation, we teach them a methodology for working, in any language, with precision and craftsmanship.

Just as I had found a new strength in performance through my physical approach and level of conditioning, working in dialect inside Indigenous language constructs I glimpsed a future for training Indigenous performers—and I did so by travelling halfway across the planet. I needed that distance, it seems, to see something else, something that I'm still unravelling.

While in Cape Town, I had to simultaneously get into shape and rehab some old injuries that precluded me from actually doing the exercises required to get me back into condition. I sought out a team of therapists, including a massage therapist and two physiotherapists, recommended by the production, a short distance from my hotel. I worked with them through the two months of filming in Cape Town, during which time we discussed the project, Canada, our families, the politics of South Africa, the still tangible and powerful legacy of apartheid, the black majority, the so-called coloured population, and the white minority, which still held the wealth of the country in its hands. Even as I was growing up, the notion of apartheid loomed powerfully in my consciousness and, in Cape Town, I could never shake the thought that I was walking on cobblestone streets and roads paved with black labour. I bought the anti-apartheid *Sun City* EP and watched the protests on TV. Big Bad Apartheid. Both my physiotherapists were white. In fact, they were both blonde. In our lengthy conversations, I discovered they were also multilingual, both speaking English and Afrikaans, one spoke Zulu, while the other Xhosa! Then a realization hit me like a train—blacks in

South Africa are the majority in a country that was colonized and ransacked by robber barons, just like North and South America had been before them. Black people remain the majority, with white Africans speaking their languages. We should be the majority here, as we once were. If that were the case, settlers would know Abenaki, Cree, Anishinaabe, Mohawk, Mi'kmaq, Coast Salish, in addition to their settler languages. But we are not the majority and the settlers do not speak our tongues. Ours was a different sort of experiment. In Canada, the ethnic cleansing was nearly total.

Since my return from South Africa, I walk on the streets with a new perspective. I am painfully aware that I speak only one language fluently. We were all multilingual once, because we had to be in order to trade and negotiate with the communities outside our own. As we were wiped from the face of the continent, we lost those opportunities and the obligation to communicate in each other's languages. Indian residential schools and other governmental policies furthered the experiment. Now we seek to recuperate what was lost in the fire or denied us. And I think about my journey, halfway across the world—a trip that allowed me to return and see with new eyes the terrain I call home.

REFERENCES

Canada Dance Festival. http://canadadance.ca/buy-tickets/signal-theatre/. Accessed February 7, 2017.

Costner, Kevin, director. *Dances With Wolves*. Tig Productions, 1990.

Edwards, Paul A., director. *Saints and Strangers*. Sony Pictures, 2015.

Fleisher, Richard, and Toshio Masuda Kinji Fukasaku, directors. *Tora! Tora! Tora!* 20th Century Fox, 1970.

Landau, Tina, and Anne Bogart. *Anne Bogart: The Viewpoints Book: A Practical Guide to Viewpoints and Composition*. New York: Theatre Communications Group, 2006.

Mann, Michael, director. *Last of the Mohicans*. 20th Century Fox, 1992.

MAKING A MOVIE: HOW TO CARRY AN ELEPHANT UP A MOUNTAIN

Armand Garnet Ruffo

he years fade away and I still shake my head at times and wonder how it is that a lowly poet fell into making a full-length feature film.[1] I think of this because it was quite unexpected and literally took years of heart-wrenching struggle. It is all the more poignant when I consider that, although the film circulated to a few national and international film festivals and garnered some acclaim when it was released, it now sits more or less dormant in an artist-run distribution office, like so many other small-budget independent films. What I am reflecting upon is the process I went through to make my feature film, *A Windigo Tale*, looking back over a period of fifteen years in which a small two-act play consisting of three characters transformed into a feature film of more than a dozen characters. I write this not to

....

1   An earlier reflection on writing the script appeared under the title of "A Windigo Tale: Contemporizing and Mythologizing the Residential School Experience," in *Aboriginal Drama and Theatre*, ed. Rob Appleford (Toronto: Playwrights Canada Press, 2005), 166–80.

thwart anybody's filmmaking ambitions, but on the contrary, to instil a sense of possibility despite whatever trials and tribulations one might have to go through to get it made. In this sense, I am writing about a path an Indigenous artist might take should the opportunity arise, while simultaneously offering a cautionary tale of paths to avoid.

THE CATALYST

In March of 2001, the CBC announced that my play, "A Windigo Tale," was one of three winners of their Performance Showcase Competition for that year. At the time, the competition existed to provide a so-called 'calling card' for dramatists wanting to move from stage to screen. The CBC would film a couple of scenes from the winning play and invite a studio audience, including people in the business, for a screening and reception. To say that I was surprised to be selected would be an understatement because the competition that year had over two hundred applicants, and the other two winning plays had both won Governor General's Awards for Drama. What I believe made the judges take notice of my little play was that it addressed the intergenerational impact of the residential school experience at a time when the issue was still not in the public eye, and it employed traditional Anishinaabek storytelling strategies based on the oral tradition.

As fate or Nanaboozho[2] would have it, that same year the newly established Aboriginal Healing Foundation (AHF) put out a call for projects. As their mandate included addressing the intergenerational impact of the residential schools, I decided to put together a project proposal to turn my play into a film. That it had won the CBC showcase award gave me confidence. It had occurred to me that nearly everyone back home in northern Ontario, specifically in the town of Chapleau and on the three reserves that surrounded the town, where I had family, had a satellite dish. The way I figured it was, if I could get my play on television then Indigenous people would have a better chance of seeing it. A couple of months later an official-looking letter arrived from the Aboriginal Healing Foundation. Like the

---

2   Nanaboozho or Nanabush is commonly referred to as the Anishinaabe Trickster.

CBC officials, those at the AHF had found value in the play script and offered financing, and so, unbeknownst to me at the time, I began a journey that would take me nearly ten years. To put it another way, I began to carry an elephant up a mountain.

THE FIRST TURNING POINT

What I immediately realized was that I knew nothing about film-making. Certainly I had an idea of what a movie is supposed to look like. My play script, however, was written for the stage. It consisted basically of people talking. The action was restricted to one room. When the CBC had filmed it, it looked exactly like a stage play that had been filmed. While there were some good things about it, mostly to do with the story elements, it did not work for the camera. My initial excitement accordingly soon turned to dismay, which inevitably turned to panic. Despite winning the CBC competition, I suppose I never really believed AHF would award me a grant. I had never done anything remotely like feature-film-making before. I was not trained. I was not prepared. I needed to figure it out, quickly. To begin, I would have to rewrite the script for an image-based medium. The first thing I did was to scamper off to the library, where I read everything I could about scriptwriting. At the time, Ottawa—the city where I was living—was host to The Summer Institute of Film and Television, which brought in some of the country's finest filmmakers; it was an amazing opportunity right on my doorstep, and I dived right into it, taking six of their workshops. If anything, I was determined.

I contacted a local film production company. Inexperienced as I was, I knew that if I did manage to cobble a film script together, I would need someone to produce it. Whatever that meant. At the end of any movie there is a long list of credits. I needed somebody to organize all those people. The thought of it made my head spin. When I told the company that I had a couple hundred thousand dollars, they were more than eager to jump on board. They promised me the sky, the stars, the moon, and the sun. They told me that the cost of the average small-budget film in Canada was between one and three million dollars. They would bring in the additional funds, using what I had raised for leverage. Being a poet whose art form is of no material consequence in the world of dollars, I readily agreed to their vision of the production. There was a contract. All I had to do was sign it. My great-great-great-grandfather had been a signatory to the Robinson Huron Treaty. Hadn't I learned anything? Obviously not; I naively signed.

I am not saying that this production company did not have the best of intentions. A well-known maxim is that the world of film and television is fickle. For example, the production company had a verbal agreement with an executive of the Aboriginal Peoples Theatre Network (APTN) for a broadcast licence. They would provide a substantial amount of money upfront and then broadcast the completed film. But, that same year, APTN went through a restructuring and that particular executive moved on, along with his roster of projects. To put it bluntly, my film got shelved. (APTN would come on board much later—for a fraction of their initial offer.) The producers tried other broadcasters like the CBC—the same organization that had selected my play for their 'showcase' award—and funding agencies like The National Film Board, but all to no avail. Nobody seemed interested. The NFB strung us along and then suddenly pulled out without an explanation. In the meantime, expenses accumulated—everything from salaries to phone calls—and the production money I had raised was virtually disappearing. It was then that I decided to part from the production company I had hired, and to their credit they let me break the contract. They were as frustrated as I was. So, there I was, out in the cold with nowhere to go, when Nanaboozho again tilted his hat in my direction.

THE MIDPOINT

One concrete thing the production company had done was to introduce me to the Toronto filmmaker and award-winning playwright Colleen Murphy. They knew from our initial meetings that I needed help turning the play script into a film script. Fortunately for me, Colleen realized that my story had potential, and, for a reasonable fee, she agreed to come on board as my script editor. I wrote a draft at home in Ottawa, traveled to Toronto for a meeting with her, and then returned home with revisions. We did that for about a year, and I have to say that I enjoyed the experience. I used my credit card to buy my train tickets and racked up more points in that year than ever before. She also helped me look for a director. We put out a call and did our initial interviews at her place in Toronto. Perhaps because it was a small independent production with a tiny budget, most of the people who showed up to the interview hadn't even bothered to read the script—even though we had sent it to them in advance—and they all wanted far too much money. After one particularly disastrous interview with a director dressed in mandatory black and totally unprepared, Colleen suggested that I direct the film myself.

"There's no way," I said. "I don't know the first thing about it."

"Nobody knows the script better than you." She reminded me that I really couldn't afford anyone with experience anyway. And if someone was going to wreck my movie, it might as well be me.

"Thanks," I said, and I soon found myself back in the library.

At this point I still needed a production company. Once again, Nanaboozho just happened to be in the neighbourhood. He reminded my partner that she had a friend, who had a friend, who had a husband who worked in film sound recording—but he wanted to get into producing. It sounded to me like the blind leading the blind, but what did I have to lose? I met Steve McNamee that winter, and his knowledge of the industry, enthusiasm, and confidence impressed me. We discussed doing it on a small scale, 'guerilla style,' with a hand-held camera, minimal equipment, and minimal expense. It sounded like the way to go. Then, because of my inexperience, he told me he had once worked with a cameraman, an older, experienced guy, whom he thought would be a good complement to the crew. He agreed to come on board, and we set up an office in Hamilton and planned to shoot the film on Six Nations Reserve, about a half-hour drive away. Since it was an Indigenous story, shooting on a reserve made a lot of sense, and it gave us the idea of setting up a mentoring project to get the youths on the reserve involved. As for casting, I already knew most of the actors I wanted personally, like Gary Farmer, Andrea Menard, Jani Lauzon, and Lee Maracle. The rest we auditioned in Toronto. We were finally ready to shoot the film.

THE CRISIS

We budgeted a twenty-day shoot and started principal photography on February 22, 2006. Fifteen days later we were twelve thousand dollars over budget and our canoe was sinking fast. With no alternative, I shut down the production. Blame it on inexperience. Blame it on the weather. Blame it on a ton of factors. Weetigo or Windigo reared its ugly head, and I was too involved in directing the actors to realize it. The cameraman became consumed. Our original concept for shooting the film 'guerilla-style' was thrown out the window. I found out later that the cameraman's experience came from TV, where they had major budgets to work with and lots of time. He turned out to be an equipment junkie, the bane of any small independent production. He rented a camera that alone cost the production over ten thousand dollars. When something went wrong he blamed it on his lack of equipment. With more equipment, the set-ups started taking forever, and we soon fell behind schedule. When my line producer cornered him, he growled and grew the size of the trees.

I won't even get into equipment failure or the just-plain-bad decisions. Suffice to say that my monitor crapped out on me the first week and I became dependent on the cameraman to tell me if a shot looked good. Sometimes they did, and sometimes they didn't. When I saw some of the shots later in the editing room, I wanted to scream. For some reason, he had decided to shoot 'day for night,' which essentially means using filters to give the illusion of night. It turned out to be a disaster—often the colour didn't match—and again I ended up with footage that I couldn't use. But you cannot point the finger at any one person. We were all in it together and were shooting up to five scenes a day. A big-budget film might do half of a scene in a day. Moving through the scenes so quickly prevented us from having the requisite time to think through the set-ups, let alone reshoot any of them. It was a luxury we just couldn't afford, and the pressure was intense.

There were other factors as well. As we know, March, Naabidin Giizis, Snowcrust Moon, can be fickle. One day we woke up to a blizzard and had to shut down the production, all while the money clock was ticking. You can see it in the scene where Dr. Shannon and David, who is intoxicated in this scene, drive from the bar to Doris' place. When David walks into the bar it looks like a spring day outside, but when he leaves there is literally a foot of snow on the ground. Because we couldn't afford to have a dedicated locations person, we found ourselves scrambling when weather conditions changed. We had lost the morning, but were determined not to lose the afternoon. At times like this we threw the shooting schedule out the window and looked for an indoor scene we could shoot. For example, there's a scene in the movie that takes place in a hockey arena. Again, because of the inclement weather, I was driven there and expected to set up the shots in about fifteen minutes—without ever having seen the arena before.

And, of course, we couldn't afford a dedicated continuity person either; continuity therefore became a nightmare. We would shoot a scene, only to realize afterwards that an actor had forgotten to take off a hat or put on some other garment, or we had forgotten to lower or raise a blind in a window. Watch the movie closely and you will see David's car drive into the yard at night without the headlights turned on. Shooting 'day for night' raised all kinds of continuity issues as well; the car actually drove into the yard during the day, and nobody thought about turning on its headlights. A simple error, but a glaringly loud mistake.

Then there were the half-hour trips back and forth between Hamilton and Six Nations. With the actors working on different schedules, they were constantly on the move. All this travel not only took time and wore people out, it cost money as well. We soon realized that we didn't have enough cars to shuttle everyone back and forth and had to rent more. Between the cost of car rental and gas for the actors and crew, transportation expenses skyrocketed.

And how can I forget the cost of food? There's an old adage in the business: a happy stomach makes for a happy cast and crew. We started out with a catering company from Hamilton driving in every day, but as the costs mounted exorbitantly, we finally dropped it in favour of a local business on Six Nations. That helped. They were inventive and didn't let an opportunity slip past. There's a scene in the movie where Doris, the mother, walks in with a rabbit. It was an actual rabbit that one of the locals on the reserve had snared for us. We ended up eating it. That's why I can't write that no animals were harmed in the making of the film—we actually had one for dinner! But, hey, I grew up snaring rabbits. One last thing about creature comforts. We rented what is called a 'honey wagon' in the business, essentially a fancy trailer where the actors change, rehearse their lines, and basically chill out between scenes. In hindsight, a regular trailer would have served the purpose, but the co-producers had arranged it, and frankly I didn't know any better and just went with the flow. Again, my inexperience. Again, the sound of the cash register.

Incidents to do with the actors also made for an interesting production. One of the things I learned was that actors will often become 'consumed' by their role or by the 'life of the set.' For example, one of the actors got into her role so intensely she had difficultly getting out of it. It brought a lot of tension to the set, but in hindsight it speaks to that particular actor's heartfelt dedication to the project. In contrast, another actor was so self-involved he made the women working in make-up and wardrobe cry. While yet another, who I shall call persnickety, did not want to take his boots off in the old house we had rented. In one scene where he's supposed to jump up from bed and hurry downstairs, he tried to convince me that some people sleep with their boots on. Needless to say, I put my director's (bare) foot down.

THE SHOWDOWN

By the second week of March, we had shot 82 scenes out of 132 and had spent all the money I had raised, and we were in debt. In the grand scheme of things, it was a micro budget, but it was all the money I had. The co-producers suggested I go to the bank and take out a loan. Instead I decided to stop production. This was one of the most difficult decisions I ever made, but there was no way around it. For whatever reason, the crew had not jelled as a team—something I knew was essential for any small-budget film to thrive. We were all exhausted, frustrated, disappointed, and yet, I think more than a little happy to part ways. We had shot more than half the film, but not all of it, and we were missing scenes. To say that I wanted to take the footage and jump out of the nearest building is not an understatement. And, yet, when I think about it now, I have to say that together we accomplished a lot given our inexperience. Eighty-two scenes in fifteen days means that we shot about five and a half scenes a day, which is really unheard of. Despite everything we had been moving like crazy. So, there I was, alone and broke, with eighty-two scenes on three hard drives.

What else could I do but start looking for additional financing? I went online, made phone calls, read over the granting criteria from the likes of the NFB and Telefilm Canada. The applications made my head spin. I was so desperate that I even went to Indian and Northern Affairs and applied for an economic development grant. I had meetings with bureaucrats who met me stone-faced or were initially enthusiastic and then said "no" without explanation.

I learned quickly that people in power do not have to give explanations. I applied to the Canada Council for the Arts and the Ontario Arts Council. They both had programs earmarked for Indigenous artists, and I figured their officers might recognize the value of the project. I basically told them what I had done and what I intended to do. I had been at it so long there was no way I could just give up. It was also a point of honour for me. I had made a commitment to the AHF for the initial funding, and I intended to fulfill my obligation.

As I waited for a response, Nanaboozho again came knocking. After the shoot had come to a halt that March, I had plunged into writing a creative piece for the National Gallery of Canada's *Norval Morrisseau: Shaman Artist* retrospective (which would lead me to write a biography about him that would become a finalist for a Governor General's Literary Award). That summer, a woman with a sunny voice telephoned me to ask if she could interview me for a small documentary she was making about Morrisseau to coincide with the retrospective. I said sure, and a few days later Jean Versteeg arrived at my door with her cameraman and editor, Terry Bosy. In the course of our conversation I told her about the movie I was determined to finish, and she told me that it was the kind of project she was interested in. She told me she had been a social worker up in northern Ontario and she liked causes, and I guess she saw my film, and maybe me, as a cause. Terry Bosy also offered his services. They both made it clear that they did not have any expertise in movie making, but they would help in whatever way they could. I had had enough of so-called experts anyway, and I agreed to bring them on board. What did I have to lose? As it turned out, they proved to be worth their weight in gold.

Trouble was, time was quickly flying by. When I opened my garage and saw all the costumes stacked in boxes, hanging on racks, looking at me like sullen ghosts, the whole endeavour seemed to be getting further and further away. A year went by, and I came to the realization that I would never be able to raise the kind of money I needed to finish off the shoot as originally planned. And even if I did get the money, the locations had probably changed. The house we had rented on Six Nations was now being lived in. And what about all the actors? They had now moved on to other projects. They had changed. Grown older or fatter or grayer or balder. How could I ever get the same look? I fathomed that it would be impossible.

Fortunately, the eighty-two scenes we had shot on Six Nations were all the major dramatic high points in the story. The unfinished scenes were basically connecting stuff. I reread the original script and decided to write another script that would segue into the eighty-two scenes and tie them all together. In other words, I would create a frame to hold the original story together. Because I was teaching a course on the oral tradition at Carleton University at the time, I thought it fitting to include the element of storytelling to connect the disparate scenes. In other words, my film would consist of a story that someone was telling within a larger story. Questions naturally arose. Who would tell the story? I immediately thought of Harold, the grandfather figure in the first shoot, played by Gary Farmer. If any actor could pull it off, Gary Farmer could. Who would he be telling the story to? This would be a new character, his grandson. Since the first shoot had focused on the impact of the residential school system, the grandson would naturally be someone who has experienced the intergenerational impact of it. I had my basic idea. The grandfather would be driving his grandson home to reconnect with his roots. And in the midst of their travels, he would tell him a story about his family and community—the material I had already shot. I got to work on the new script, and I finished it that winter.

To my delight, the two arts council grants came in and we had just enough money to do a modest production. In the spring of 2008, we began casting for the youth. And hit a brick wall. Dozens of auditions later, I was once again panicking. None of them seemed right for the role. And again, Nanaboozho appeared, this time in the guise of a DVD that was sent to us, appropriately, from Manitoulin Island. Jean Versteeg had the foresight to post the casting notice online with a couple of pages from the script. Lo and behold, Elliot Simon saw the call and sent us an audition he had done with his own grandfather standing in for the Gary Farmer character. Elliot was a natural. The camera either loves you or hates you, and it clearly loved him.

The plan was to shoot for a total of five days: four days around Renfrew and one day in Ottawa. Although the road trip was supposed to take place in northern Ontario, because of cost, we filmed those scenes in the Ottawa Valley in October. The warm reds of the maples provided excellent contrast to the cold blues of the Six Nations winter scenes. We also needed an art gallery, somewhere in Ottawa, for one additional day. That scene would introduce the concept of the Windigo and the troubled youth. The problem was, we didn't have a gallery.

We contacted a few galleries, but all to no avail. Nobody seemed keen to loan their gallery to strangers who had no budget line to pay them. Then, one day we were leaving one of the galleries on Cumberland Street, in the market area, when I spotted an empty building. Again, Nanaboozho smiled on me, because it just so happened Galerie St-Laurent + Hill had moved out a week earlier, and the space wasn't going to be occupied by the new owner until the end of the month. We told them that we would like to get in there before they handed it over. To our surprise, they said sure and even cleaned it up for us. I called my many visual artist friends in Ottawa, and without a second thought, they delivered their paintings. The people at Galerie St-Laurent + Hill came by to help us hang the paintings professionally, and a week later we had a fully functioning art gallery at no cost. To me this was a sign that the film was supposed to be made, and that the second shoot would go much smoother.

This is not to say that we didn't have our share of problems. Case in point is the antique Mercury we rented; it broke down after the second day of shooting, and we ended up having to tow it around. In all the shots you see—except for the few long shots that we fortunately took the first day—the car is being pulled or pushed. And, of course, there were the inevitable Windigo clashes that come when you put diverse, creative personalities together in close quarters under a stressful situation. We were still working with a very small budget. After four days, the shoot in Renfrew was over, and it was on to the gallery in Ottawa. The only thing I will say about that is, on October 20, 2008, the evening we were shooting the gallery scene, Ottawa had an unexpected snowstorm. And I mean a blizzard! Look closely at the windows in front of the gallery, and you will see it. I needed a shot of Elliot walking down the street and had to do it a week later with a 'stand-in' actor. For reasons of continuity, there was just too much snow to shoot the scene. In hindsight, I think Nanaboozho threw that into the mix just to keep me on my toes.

THE REALIZATION

Comparatively, the Renfrew production went smoother than the earlier one on Six Nations. For one thing, it was a much shorter shoot, and the weather was much better—the one time it snowed, we were scheduled to shoot indoors. In hindsight though, this is in large part due to the crew, which was small and cohesive, being made up mostly of Ottawa people who knew each other. This also goes for my Métis cameraman, Shane Belcourt, who lived in Toronto but had grown up in Ottawa. I also suspect it had something to do with youth and commitment. The crew was mostly young and nimble on their feet. They could roll with whatever Nanaboozho threw their way. Filmmaking was their passion. For a small-budget film, this is essential. You have to find people who believe in your project as though their lives depend on it. (Okay, that may be an exaggeration, but you get the idea.) Even us older folk took the job to heart. Jean Versteeg, my production manager, for example, dug her heels in and kept the production moving despite whatever was thrown at her. You cannot buy that kind of dedication. As for me, I had learned a ton from the previous shoot. There's nothing like getting thrown into a fire to know what it feels like to get burned. The second time around I had more confidence, and consequently I did my best to create a respectful atmosphere on set when Windigo threatened to rear its ugly head.

After the Ottawa shoot, I had five hard drives full of footage and no money to edit them. I contacted a couple of professional companies that do editing, but they wanted a minimum of one hundred dollars an hour. And that's when Terry Bosy, who I had first met with Jean Versteeg, offered to do a rough cut with me. He said he wanted to learn more about editing drama and this was the perfect opportunity. I knew the story. He knew the technology. And so from November until March we edited over thirty hours of footage down to two hours. I had my rough cut. And that's when Nanaboozho appeared again. She had always been more help than a hindrance. I just happened to mention my film to a neighbour who makes documentaries, and he suggested that I send it off to the Banff Centre for the Arts in Alberta. I had actually studied and later taught creative writing there and knew they had a media program, but it never occurred to me to contact them. I sent them the rough cut; they liked it and parachuted me in for nearly two months, where I worked with a professional editor on professional equipment. Come June, I left Banff with a finished movie that was ninety-one minutes and twenty-eight seconds long. After nearly ten years, my film was finished. I returned to Ottawa and tweaked the sound at a local studio and made copies. I printed a label: *A Windigo Tale, A chilling and redeeming drama inspired by Ojibway spiritualism and the history of residential schools.* A week later I screened it for the Aboriginal Healing Foundation. I had done it!

The movie finished, I sent it out to a number of film festivals, and for my first ever feature-length film, made with a minuscule budget under extreme conditions, I was surprised it did as well as it did. In 2010 it won Best Picture at the 35th American Indian Film Festival in San Francisco, Best Picture at the Dreamspeaker's Film Festival in Edmonton, and Best Aboriginal Film at the Brantford Film Festival; it received the Peoples' Choice Award at the Baystreet Film Festival in Thunder Bay and was selected to close the ImagineNative Film & Media Festival in Toronto. It then played in festivals in the United States, in Germany, and in Russia. And, even more importantly for me, it toured northern Ontario, thanks to the ImagineNative Film Festival, and played to full houses in Sault Ste. Marie and Sudbury. My neck of the woods.

The film was eventually screened on APTN and subsequently purchased by educational institutions across Canada and the United States. But despite the awards, the screenings, and the touring, it did not get picked up by a distributor that could have pushed the film to other venues, like Air Canada, and this is probably my biggest disappointment. Like any number of Indigenous films, it is being distributed by an artist-run media centre, and, while V-Tape in Toronto has done the best they can, they do not have the resources to promote their films to any great extent. And so, like the work of other Indigenous artists, *A Windigo Tale* has more or less come to a standstill because of the lack of industry support. While Indigenous peoples now have the creative talent—young Indigenous filmmakers are learning their craft from the ground up—we are still sorely lacking in the areas of production and distribution, and it seems to me that these are crucial areas that have to be addressed. As for my involvement, despite the rollercoaster ride, the work put into it, I have no regrets about plunging into the world of filmmaking for a time. When I now go back home to northern Ontario and walk the reserve road or the town streets on a clear winter night, and I look up to the satellite dishes on the roofs, see the faint blue flicker emanating from the living rooms, I think that just maybe someone is watching my film.

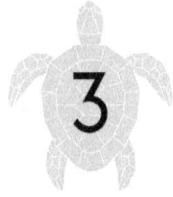

3

DECOLONIZING
COUNTERPOINTS:
INDIGENOUS PERSPECTIVES
AND REPRESENTATIONS
IN CLASSICAL MUSIC
AND OPERA

Spy Dénommé-Welch and Catherine Magowan

n this chapter we examine the theoretical and practical applications of interdisciplinary and intercultural collaboration in the
creation of new music dealing with Indigenous topics. Describing
our own collaborative and artistic processes, we look at the implications of decolonizing music development and performance
within the contemporary Canadian context. Using our own working relationship as an example, we discuss intercultural collaboration and how it can (re)envision and (re)tell Indigenous oral histories and stories on the stage and in classrooms. We also provide
some current and historical examples of the (mis)appropriation of
Indigenous music and culture, to illustrate how difficult, marginalized histories may be better represented and expressed through
a variety of musical forms.

Musical collaboration is never simple. Frequently, it is romanticized as a harmonious coupling in which two people make beautiful music together. Beyond such clichés, the reality is that collaboration is an intensive endeavour, particularly if the working relationship is to be productive. The fact is that the work will reflect both collaborators equally. Ideally, the collaboration will benefit from two people's experience and expertise; it will also reflect two sets of opinions, emotions, and personalities. Unless the collaborators are carbon copies of each other, these challenges need to be navigated and negotiated throughout development and production. Unique histories, cultural backgrounds, and personal tastes come into play and must be acknowledged, examined, and unpacked. Given that our identities are not static, we continuously reflect on our own constantly evolving artistic partnership. Our aim here is to share some of the complexities we have encountered in our own collaborations.

THE PERSONAL AND POLITICAL DIMENSIONS OF MUSIC CREATION

Cultural appropriation and (mis)representation are current and recurrent issues in twentieth-century Western music performance. Indeed, the representation of Indigenous ways of life in popular culture has often been distorted, histories have been disparaged and individuals humiliated. Examples of negative racial tropes are abundant in popular American entertainments such as Irving Berlin's *Annie Get Your Gun* and Walt Disney's *Peter Pan* and *Pocahontas*. These colonizing practices have emphatically reinforced stereotypes and propagated myths about Indigenous peoples that are perpetuated in subtle and harmful ways.

Theorizing the ways in which imperialism is embedded in disciplines of knowledge and tradition as regimes of truth, author Linda Tuhiwai Smith writes, "while being on the margins of the world has had dire consequences, being incorporated within the world's marketplace has different implications and in turn requires the mounting of new forms of resistance."[1] We ask, in the context

---

1   Linda Tuhiwai Smith, *Decolonizing Methodologies: Research and Indigenous Peoples* (London: Zed Books/Dunedin, New Zealand: University of Otago Press/New York: St. Martin's Press, 1999), 24.

of the Canadian arts market, what forms of resistance and actions are necessary to position Indigenous artists more centrally? For example, despite the number of established Indigenous composers in Canada and North America (Barbara Croall, Brent Michael Davids, Tara-Louise Montour and John Kim Bell, to name a very few), arts organizations are still excluding them in favour of non-Indigenous composers, commissioning new music with Indigenous content and text but hiring Western/non-Indigenous composers to set it. A case in point: in 2015 the Vancouver Foundation awarded City Opera a grant of $127,000 towards the development of a new work called *Missing*.[2] Acclaimed Métis playwright, performer, director, producer, and screenwriter Marie Clements was commissioned to create a libretto, but City Opera did not solicit Indigenous composers to create the music, opting instead to commission Brian Current, a non-Indigenous composer/conductor. Other examples include the Royal Winnipeg Ballet's commissioning of Christos Hatzis to write *Going Home Star—Truth and Reconciliation*, with story by Joseph Boyden;[3] the National Arts Centre's commission *I Lost My Talk*, composed by John Estacio and based on a poem by Rita Joe; and Opera in Concert's production of *The Ecstasy of Rita Joe*, text adapted and composed by Victor Davies. These examples perpetuate the image of the non-Indigenous male composer as the authority on music creation and production, simultaneously delegitimizing Indigenous traditions of music transmission.

Similar absences are notable in the education and training of young musicians. According to Canadian composer and academic Juliet Hess, "the marginalization of indigenous music and knowledges in the academy is fraught with intense issues of inequity

---

2   "MISSING Public workshop," City Opera Vancouver, http://cityoperavancouver.com/missing-women, accessed January 21, 2019.

3   In December 2016, the Aboriginal Peoples Television Network (APTN) published an article by Jorge Barrera questioning award-winning author Joseph Boyden's claim of Indigenous ancestry. The article listed numerous interviews in which Boyden had stated he was descended from a variety of nations, including Métis, Mi'kmaq, Ojibway, and Nipmuc. Barrera also cited a July 21, 1956, *Maclean's* article written by Dorothy Sangster in which Boyden's uncle, Earl Boyden, under the name "Injun Joe," admitted to impersonating the Ojibway to sell tin-can drums to tourists outside Algonquin Park in the 1950s.

and injustice."[4] Following Hess, our work, both on stage and in the classroom, responds to these realities and issues, and consequently we attempt to redistribute and recalibrate the scales so as to give Indigenous knowledge and cultural expression equal space in the Western–Indigenous knowledge paradigm. Understanding that Indigenous methodologies flow from traditional knowledge, allied to but distinct from Western qualitative approaches, our process draws from autoethnography and decolonizing methodologies to record and analyze elements of our work.

Theorist Margaret Kovach explains, "autoethnography, an approach with its foundations in ethnographical research, brings together the study of self (auto) in relation to culture (ethnography). Within this approach, self-reflection moves beyond field notes to having a more integral positioning within the research process and the construction of knowledge itself."[5] Self-reflection has been a critical process for our work, allowing us to interrogate and challenge issues of inequity and marginalization prevalent in musical practice and presentation. The process compels us to examine and self-critique our own artistic practice, thereby building new pathways for intercultural collaboration and storytelling. As scholars Kathy Absolon and Cam Willet opine, "one of the most fundamental principles of Aboriginal research methodology is the necessity for the researcher to locate himself or herself. Identifying, at the outset, the location from which the voice of the researcher emanates is an Aboriginal way of ensuring that those who study, write, and participate in knowledge creation are accountable for their own positionality."[6] We begin with our individual narratives to provide some context for our backgrounds, which, needless to say, inform our artistic development and collaborative process.

....

4   Juliet Hess, "Unsettling Binary Thinking: Tracing an Analytic Trajectory of the Place of Indigenous Musical Knowledge in the Academy," *Action, Criticism & Theory for Music Education* 14, no. 2 (2015), 55.

5   Margaret Kovach, *Indigenous Methodologies: Characteristics, Conversations, and Contexts* (Toronto: University of Toronto Press, 2009), 33.

6   Kathy Absolon and Cam Willet, "Putting Ourselves Forward: Location in Aboriginal Research," in *Research as Resistance: Critical, Indigenous, and Anti-oppressive Approaches*, eds. Leslie Brown and Susan Strega (Toronto: Canadian Scholars' Press, 2005), 97.

SPY'S NARRATIVE

Until my adulthood and following formal academic training and further life experience, I did not fully understand the impact of music and theatre in redressing historical injustices, empowering Indigenous communities, and restoring and preserving Indigenous knowledge and culture. I have come to realize that this understanding involves multiple worlds (Indigenous/non-Indigenous; music; theatre; pedagogy; history of colonization/decolonization) and necessitates re-examining the spaces in which oppression and power intersect. This is done by questioning how we begin to restore a balance in these spaces and how we re-examine what stories are being told, by whom and how. While my mother taught me who I am and about the land from where I come, I have worked hard to reclaim my cultural knowledge and familial history, which, like many with Indigenous ancestry, have been systemically suppressed through generations. These are the dimensions I now examine, both critically and creatively, using methodologies that support decolonizing power dynamics in the realm of art and culture.

My venture into music and performance did not follow a clear path. Nonetheless, my experiences were invaluable to my upbringing and training. As a child of Anishinaabe descent in northeastern Ontario, it was not easy to access formal music or theatre training. Unlike our counterparts in urban areas, we could not hop on a bus or streetcar to go to music lessons or classes, nor could we rely on affluent parents to drive us to the nearest conservatory for exams and recitals. Regardless, I found outlets in my small town that provided a degree of training that opened up alternate ways of thinking and working in the fields of music, theatre, and performance.

I picked up music around the age of nine, first acoustic guitar and then violin/fiddle. Largely self-taught on guitar, I found a violin teacher from a local orchestra, whom I paid with newspaper route money. The pursuit of music, theatre, arts, and literature resonated with me, as it allowed me to express my views and perceptions of the world through creative outlets. Admittedly, my early works in music and theatre, whether a short play or a song composed for a talent show, were clearly in a developing voice and I learned that talent and skill required time and space to become authentic. I knew early on that this was to be my career and life's trajectory; however, what I did not know was how it would look or what it would entail, never imagining that I would critically examine social justice issues, colonialism, decolonization, and Indigenous narratives through theatre, music, and opera. I was simply more focused on jamming with friends, learning new chord progressions, playing in battle-of-the-bands competitions, and trying out new riffs in a bar band. In the back of my mind I knew that, when the time was right, I would tell stories of substance and meaning, although I had yet to understand the implications of storytelling and the responsibilities associated with that role.

CATHERINE'S NARRATIVE

My Jewish parents fled anti-Semitism in communist Hungary in the 1970s, spent two years in an Austrian refugee camp before landing in Montréal, and finally settled in Toronto. While much of Canada's Hungarian refugee intake occurred in the 1950s, during and after the failed Hungarian revolution, my parents were minors and their families chose not to leave at that time. I have few family stories about their lives growing up, but I remember one in which my teenaged father was shot in the knee while searching for bread. The family on my mother's side included professionally trained and working musicians, but I did not know them. My access to music was through creative play at home until grade four, when I entered the school's rather limited music program. The school had few instruments and an itinerant music teacher who came once or twice a week for a couple of hours. In grade seven I gained access to regular music programming and full-time instructors, and in high school I did extracurricular music most weekdays, either at school or in district ensembles. This training contributed to my development, as access to private instruction was not available until, at the age of fifteen, I was taken in by my grade-seven music teacher. The Magowans have become my chosen family and have supported me throughout my musical development.

My choice of instrument, the bassoon, also contributed to my ability to access formal musical training. It is an expensive instrument to acquire for someone without means. Few public schools have bassoons in any playable condition, and fewer music teachers know how to assemble one or teach a student how to play it. My adoptive mother is a professional bassoonist; she provided me with an instrument and lessons, and she prepared me for a university entrance audition. Having trained for only eighteen months, I was not the most able player at my audition. However, because very few bassoonists auditioned in my year, I was awarded a full scholarship. Competition for other orchestral instruments is higher. Although I was an advanced flute player, I would not have had the same experience had I instead auditioned on that instrument. I began as the greenest student in my university class; the discrepancy was both in my abilities on the instrument and in my understanding of theoretical concepts. Discouraged and frustrated, I worked hard and eventually transferred into an intensive orchestral training program.

DISRUPTING PEDAGOGY AND PEDIGREE

There are issues, we both argue, around the social constructions of pedigree and heritage in music education, performance, and production in Canada. To have a career in the arts, there is an expectation that one must begin formal conservatory training at an early age. Certainly, many music schools' advertising prominently features tiny violins or legs dangling from piano benches in cavernous music halls. In his book, *Raising Musical Kids: A Guide for Parents*, Robert Cutietta recommends, "age appropriate music study can start as soon after birth as possible. Most experts would suggest beginning some sort of systematic music experiences no later than eighteen months. . . . Obviously, the first nine years of life are a critical window of opportunity for your child's musical future."[7]

However, the reality is that private instruction, and the complementary theory classes that are also encouraged, is expensive and subsidies are hard to come by. There are, however, programs in some urban centres meant to bridge this economic gap, including the introduction in Canada of the Venezuelan program, El Sistema. However, this does not address the issue of geography. Musical learners in suburban or rural areas may not have educators near them. This makes travel yet another barrier to music education. Many public schools do offer music instruction, but this is often the extent of formal music education to which some young learners have

7   Robert A. Cutietta, *Raising Musical Kids: A Guide for Parents*. (Oxford: Oxford University Press, 2001), 22.

access. Cutietta argues that, "although playing in band is excellent for learning musical concepts and ensemble playing skills, your child still needs the individual attention that can only be provided by a private lesson."[8] The common belief is that, without private instruction, students who get their music education strictly through the school curricula are at an early disadvantage. Certainly, musical education and expression in primary grades is often rudimentary and students frequently do not have access to actual instruments until grades four or five. Some primary programs do introduce smaller instruments such as ukuleles and recorders, instruments that have seen a recent resurgence in folk and Baroque music, but compared to their peers, who have benefitted from several years of private instruction on orchestral instruments, the discrepancy is apparent. It is also worth noting that public schools often do not have string instruments such as the violin, viola, or cello, making access to education on these instruments a significant challenge for those without the means for private instruction.

The lack of access to private music education and the deficiencies in services provided by public education compound the problem, creating a serious divide between those who have and those who do not by the time young people reach adulthood. Even if this discrepancy is not discernable in actual ability, it is an underlying current felt in interactions with peers. Jeanne Lamon, acclaimed violinist and former musical director of Tafelmusik, began her formal violin training at the age of seven. She claims, "in the Western world it's one of the few places where you still have a mentor, like you have teachers and private lessons, and *there really is no other way.*"[9]

Compounding issues of access to formal music education are inequities in the representation of women and members of marginalized groups as mentors and teachers in both the public school system and private music institutions. Female composers are also underrepresented in performing and learning institutions, and non-Western musical curriculum is frequently condensed into a single unit, a one-semester course, or an extra ensemble credit. Hess posits in regards to music in schools, "in labeling 'Other musics' as

....

8   *Ibid.*, 142.
9   Ann Shin and Cathy Gulkin, directors, *The Four Seasons Mosaic*, film (Toronto: Tafelmusik, in association with Bravo and CBC, 2005). Emphasis added.

optional, their status was affirmed as marginal, inscribing a hierarchy of knowledges, musics, and epistemologies."[10]

COLLABORATORS' NARRATIVE

While neither of us have had formal education in composition, we have always been creative musically. While we did not have the same access to music education as many of our colleagues, we have gained much by taking different paths. Most notably, we are not bound by the same rules that are enforced in formal training. Therefore, we are able to explore musically, always pushing the envelope.

Our collaboration began in 2006 with our first full-length opera, *Giiwedin* (produced in 2010). How that process would look was yet to be figured out, but from it developed a new form of working together. Before beginning to write music, we discussed how to incorporate decolonizing methodologies by starting with our own histories and discussing what we each might bring to the piece. Although our starting points were different, issues of diaspora and loss of culture and community emerged between us. We shared these themes musically, finding them both complementary and challenging. Understanding that both our ancestors suffered cultural erasure and intergenerational trauma, we consistently integrate decolonizing methods into our collaborative process. For example, we implement strategies drawn from Linda Smith's argument that Indigenous methodologies are successful in approaching issues of "cultural protocols, values and behaviours."[11] We examine these facets in our own collaborative practice through involvement of community (through workshops), reciprocity (how we develop musical idioms), and by encouraging differing worldviews (the way we engage both Indigenous and non-Indigenous artists). We implement a built-in, constant feedback loop that allows us to sound out and expand our ideas, provide constructive criticism, and avoid the isolation characteristic of the working methods of most composers. Through our own musical creation, we constantly explore new methods and continually reassess the meanings and implications of intercultural collaboration in relation to the stage. In *Giiwedin*, for example, we experimented

---

10   Hess, "Unsettling Binary Thinking," 58.
11   Smith, *Decolonizing Methodologies*, 15.

by composing musical material together, trading and responding to independently composed motifs. In another work, *Deux Poèmes sur la Formation des Glaces*, we independently developed music, then co-edited to merge voices. Recently, we have experimented with improvisational techniques on our respective instruments (Spy on guitar and fiddle; Catherine on bassoon and flute), using call and answer, theme and variations, and visualizations. These methods were also successfully employed in *Bike Rage, Spin Doctors for clarinet, violin and piano*, and the vocal chamber work, *Sojourn*.

Our aim, as research practitioners, is to apply methodologies to decolonize, thereby disrupting hierarchical structures prevalent in Eurocentric music and artistic creation and bringing forth marginalized or erased histories. In two operas we began with multiple narrative lines, focusing not only on what is communicated in the text, but on that which is found in the contexts that do not necessarily end up in the libretti. Drawing from a variety of musical traditions and aural aesthetics, we consider how music can best support the story's arc, characters, and overall message.

In some cases, we turn to the land to ground ourselves and connect with specific elements of projects often located in northern Ontario. When composing music based on natural elements, for example, we studied large bodies of water near Spy's ancestors' lands in the northeast of the province. Exploring rock formations and Indigenous knowledge transfer, we camped and conducted research near Petroglyphs Provincial Park. Preparing to write about ice, we took long winter excursions on the land around Sudbury. These interactions with land are important to our preparations and help to balance the spiritual, intellectual, emotional, and physical. Given our cultural differences, taking these additional steps helps establish a common understanding of the reclaiming of land through musical composition and storytelling. Such embodied research is core to our processes of decolonizing.

We are collaborative composers and have, through the course of our working relationship, come to realize that our artistic practice is atypical in the current landscape. While composer–lyricist/librettist relationships are still relatively common in current popular music and classical vocal music, there are few recent examples of two composers working together to create one musical work. Having said that, there are notable historical examples of cross-cultural composer duos. For example, in 1913 *The Sun Dance Opera*—a collaboration between Sioux violinist, activist, librettist, and composer Zitkala-Ša (also known as Gertrude Simmons Bonnin) and composer William F. Hanson—premiered at the Salt Lake City Theater. The story was based on the Plains sun dance and featured an Ute cast in its premiere production. In 1950, *Tzinquaw* was labelled the first Native opera and sold out during its initial five-night run in British Columbia.[12] The work was a collaboration between Frank Morrison, a music teacher in Duncan, BC, and his student, Abel Joe, who sang the lead tenor role. Tellingly, Frank Morrison is credited as the sole creator of the work,[13] although Abel Joe was involved in the creation of *Tzinquaw*. According to the opera director Alison Greene: "Abel Joe asked Morrison to write a musical theatre piece about the legend of the Tzinquaw, the Thunderbird, using the piano transcriptions of the Cowichan songs."[14] Greene considered a remount of the work, but abandoned the pursuit upon listening to an archival recording, realizing that the traditional Cowichan sections sounded "colonized, by the Western tastes and standards of the man responsible for creating it."[15]

Understanding that racism and stereotypes are often embedded in cultural forms in subtly entrenched ways has pushed us to re-examine and strategize ways to decolonize such expressions in our music and performance. Sometimes decolonization entails outright resistance to particular modes of musical expression, refusal to accept the commodification of music, and the downright subversion of certain sounds and textures. For example, we have been asked to incorporate Native drums into our instrumentation and orchestration. Whether or not it is appropriate to use such instruments to denote Indigenous sounds, we avoid falling into obvious musical tropes

12 James Hoffman, abstract, "Tzinquaw: A Site of Postcolonial Performance in British Colombia," http://faculty.tru.ca/jhoffman/tzinquaw.htm, accessed January 23, 2019.

13 See listing on Canadian Music Centre at: https://www.musiccentre.ca/node/30924, accessed June 21, 2018.

14 Alison Greene, "Too Much White Man in it: Aesthetic Colonization in *Tzinquaw*," in *Opera Indigene: Re/presenting First Nations and Indigenous Cultures*, eds. Pamela Karantonis and Dylan Robinson (New York: Ashgate Publishing, 2011), 233.

15 *Ibid.*, 231.

and aesthetic trappings. While there may be instances where such instrumentation is appropriate, it is necessary to reflect on and critique such musical expressions to determine if it serves the work or simply satisfies the ear of the colonizer. Unfortunately, this practice is evident in the recent work of several non-Indigenous composers. For example, Catherine was in rehearsal for an orchestral concert, when the guest conductor, who was also the composer of the work, described how one section depicted "war whoops" from a traditional Indigenous dance. To further illustrate, he brought a flat palm to his mouth repeatedly, making a sound typical of the Hollywood westerns of an earlier generation. This single orchestral work, commissioned for its premiere performance in the early 2000s, has been reworked for band, orchestra, brass ensemble, clarinet choir, as well as sold on compact disc and broadcast. One must ask: who benefits from this work's continued programming given its problematic representation of Indigenous communities?

Such a practice exemplifies a troubling trend of Indigenizing classical music by taking works written by European composers and resetting them into Indigenous contexts or inserting Indigenous content into them. For instance, in 2004 the Tafelmusik Baroque Orchestra commissioned Academy-Award-winning film composer Mychael Danna to rework Vivaldi's *Four Seasons* concerti, blending aspects of north-Indian classical music and eighteenth-century Chinese music with traditional Inuit throat singing. At first blush, the concept sounds revolutionary and reflective of Canada's multiculturalism; however, the inclusion of Inuit expression is brief and might be excluded without any detriment to the work, unlike the Chinese pipa and Indian veena, which form a greater contribution. In addition, the documentary film chronicling the rehearsal process and subsequent performances showed the Inuit performers positioned behind the orchestra, unlike the Chinese and Indian soloists, who are front and centre. Arguably, this placement was due to the Western musicians' inability (or unwillingness) to adapt to the Inuit performers' method of learning music orally. Inuit artist Sylvia Cloutier describes a rehearsal with Tafelmusik in which she and the throat singing ensemble Aqsarniit explained how their method differed from the Western model of reading notation. She recounts, "at one point I just said, just tell me when to come in and I'll feel it, you know?"[16] The exchange, which highlights the difference between Aqsarniit's oral approach and Tafelmusik's notated musical approach, is described by Juliet Hess as a product of formalized musical education. She argues, "the curriculum documents across Canada focus largely on Western classical music and Western notation-based musical study. As such, teaching the curriculum in its current incarnation actually reinforces dominant power relations."[17] In this instance, the Tafelmusik musicians were able, and willing, to work a different way and the situation was resolved. Jeanne Lamon, artistic director at the time, notes that the two groups quickly went from having trouble communicating musically to performing the work perfectly. She observed that Aqsarniit's process was "very different from our way to approaching music-making."[18]

CONCLUSION

Many of the country's established arts and culture organizations were founded at a time when Indigenous cultural practices were outlawed and Indigenous people did not yet have the right to vote. However, while arts councils are now creating initiatives that aim to address inequities, Indigenous arts organizations are still not afforded a fraction of the resources regularly bestowed on established non-Indigenous organizations. Furthermore, Indigenous arts organizations that are recipients of funding have not seen the amount they are awarded change to reflect inflation or the economic landscape.

In 2005, Canadian Métis playwright, performer, director, producer, and screenwriter Marie Clements authored a report for the Canada Council of the Arts (CCA) that illustrated the discrepancy. She writes: "In 2004–2005, Aboriginal theatre companies made up 3.0% of the total number of companies in the operating grants program, but accounted for 1.8% of funding awarded through the program."[19] In dollars, this means that of the $18,339,800 in operational

16 Shin and Gulkin, *The Four Seasons Mosaic*.
17 Juliet Hess, "Decolonizing Music Education: Moving Beyond Tokenism," *International Journal of Music Education* 33, no. 3 (2015), 2.
18 Shin and Gulkin, *The Four Seasons Mosaic*.
19 Marie Clements, *The Developmental Support to Aboriginal Theatre Organizations Study* (Ottawa: The Canada Council for the Arts, 2005), 15, www.ipaa.ca/files/dsato-study-final-pdf.pdf.

funding that CCA awarded in that year, only $331,750 was allocated to Indigenous companies.

In the *Aboriginal Artistic Leaders' Summit: Report and Analysis*, author Candace Brunette notes that "Longstanding companies have to apply to up to 20 different grants annually (including grants with strict contribution agreements) in order to survive. Since these companies create the foundation of the Aboriginal performing arts sector, and smaller Aboriginal companies heavily rely on them, their instability undermines the Aboriginal performing arts sector as a whole.... This reality leaves the Aboriginal performing art sector in a constant cycle of depression and dependency. In an ideal situation, mainstream Canadian institutions would support Indigenous artists, providing them the autonomy to create their own work."[20]

In the last decade, there have been developments made through such documents as the 2008 *United Nations Declaration on the Rights of Indigenous Peoples* (UNDRIP), and the 2015 *Truth and Reconciliation Commission of Canada: Calls to Action*, which serve as guidelines for how artists and cultural organizations should engage with Indigenous topics and communities. Ten years after the CCA's own 2005 report, which drew attention to discrepancies in funding, the organization announced a re-examination of their policies through the Creating, Knowing and Sharing program, via a YouTube video released in December 2015.[21] However, in a report written by Brittany Ryan, entitled *Freedom to Engage: An Indigenous Approach to Ways of Being, Knowing, and Doing in the Performing Arts* and produced in the same year, Curtis Peeteetuce, former artistic director of the Saskatchewan Native Theatre Company (Saskatoon) states,

> I am a playwright, an actor, and a director. It can be very hard on our organization. I have worn those three hats in our productions just because we need to make the work happen. . . . SNTC, we still receive the same amount of

20 Candace Brunette, *Aboriginal Artistic Leaders' Summit: Report and Analysis* (Toronto: Indigenous Performing Arts Alliance, 2007), 3, www.ipaa.ca/files/ipaa-leadership-summit-report-pdf.pdf.

21 Canada Council for the Arts, "Creating, Knowing and Sharing: The Arts and Cultures of First Nations, Inuit and Métis Peoples," https://www.youtube.com/watch?v=a5KlsEHroGo, accessed March 6, 2018.

funding we've received 10, 15 years ago [even though] the economy has boosted and things have become more expensive since then. So, we had to find creative ways to "go under the radar" and ... my work wearing numerous hats just goes under my Artistic Director wage. It hurts me because I often do a lot of good work for free. It is very hard to swallow that but that's the way it is right now.[22]

Compounding this is the continuing absence of Indigenous representation on Canadian stages, both in hiring practices and in programming, which are frequently structured following European models. This leaves Indigenous artists to do the work of telling their stories and overseeing the logistics involved in production with inadequate institutional support. This inattention depletes community resources and is a barrier to the success of Indigenous arts in Canada. Our own experience has been that non-Indigenous organizations are averse to supporting intercultural projects unless the projects easily fit into their production structures and funding frameworks, leaving artists such as ourselves with the responsibility to both create work and produce it independently.

While we have been mindful of minor policy amendments, our experience is that meaningful change will require a shift from within institutions that have, for decades, dominated the Canadian arts and culture landscape. This will involve a careful consideration of what work is being created and produced, and a redistribution of resources to allow Indigenous organizations to do their work.

The question that remains is how do we as a nation effectively address entrenched misrepresentations and under-representations of Indigenous people in arts and culture. The arts councils must continue to work toward balancing their funding models so that Indigenous arts organizations are as supported as established non-Indigenous production companies. This will require channelling significant resources towards capacity building, capital investments,

....

22 Curtis Peeteetuce, quoted in Brittany Ryan, *Freedom to Engage: An Indigenous Approach to Ways of Being, Knowing, and Doing in the Performing Arts* (Toronto: Indigenous Performance Arts Association, 2015), 39, www.ipaa.ca/files/freedom-to-engage-draft-05-02-2015-pdf.pdf.

and operational and project funding. This level of investment will enable Indigenous arts organizations to adequately present their own stories to Indigenous and non-Indigenous audiences alike.

REFERENCES

Absolon, Kathy, and Cam Willet. "Putting Ourselves Forward: Location in Aboriginal Research." In *Research as Resistance: Critical, Indigenous, and Anti-oppressive Approaches*, edited by Leslie Brown and Susan Strega, 97–126. Toronto: Canadian Scholars' Press, 2005.

Barrera, Jorge. "Author Joseph Boyden's Shape-shifting Indigenous Identity." APTN *News*. December 23, 2016. http://aptnnews. ca/2016/12/23/author-joseph-boydens-shape-shifting-indige-nous-identity/. Accessed June 22, 2018.

Berlin, Irving, composer and lyricist. *Annie Get Your Gun*. New York: 1946.

Brunette, Candace. *Aboriginal Artistic Leaders' Summit: Report and Analysis*. Toronto: Indigenous Performing Arts Alliance, 2007. http://ipaa. ca/wp-content/uploads/2009/08/IPAA-Leadership-Summit-Report.pdf. Accessed June 22, 2018.

City Opera Vancouver. "MISSING WOMEN Public Workshop." City Opera Vancouver. http://cityoperavancouver.com/miss-ing-women. Accessed January 21, 2019.

Clements, Marie. *The Developmental Support to Aboriginal Theatre Organizations Study*. Ottawa: The Canada Council for the Arts, 2005. www.ipaa.ca/files/dsato-study-final-pdf.pdf. Accessed June 22, 2018.

Cutietta, Robert, A. *Raising Musical Kids: A Guide for Parents*. Oxford: Oxford University Press, 2001.

Dénommé-Welch, Spy, composer and librettist, and Catherine Magowan, composer. *Deux Poèmes sur la Formation des Glaces*. Toronto: 2011.

——. *Bike Rage*. Toronto: 2012.

——. *Giiwedin*. Toronto: 2010.

——. *Sojourn*. Hamilton: 2016.

——. *Spin Doctors for Clarinet, Violin and Piano*. Toronto: 2014.

Estacio, John, composer, and Rita Joe, author. *I Lost My Talk*. Ottawa: 2016.

Gabriel, Mike, and Eric Goldberg, directors. *Pocahontas*. Buena Vista Pictures, 1995. Film.

Geronimi, Clyde, Wilfred Jackson, and Hamilton Luske, directors. *Peter Pan*. Walt Disney Productions, 1953. Film.

Greene, Allison. "Too Much White Man in It: Aesthetic Colonization in *Tzinquaw*." In *Opera Indigene: Re/presenting First Nations and Indigenous Cultures*, edited by Pamela Karantonis and Dylan Robinson, 231–44. New York: Ashgate Publishing, 2011.

Hatzis, Christos, composer, and Joseph Boyden, storywriter. *Going Home Star—Truth and Reconciliation*. Winnipeg: Royal Winnipeg Ballet, 2014. Ballet.

Hess, Juliet. "Decolonizing Music Education: Moving Beyond Tokenism." *International Journal of Music Education* 33, no.3 (2015): 1–12.

——. "Unsettling Binary Thinking: Tracing an Analytic Trajectory of the Place of Indigenous Musical Knowledge in the Academy." *Action, Criticism & Theory for Music Education* 14, no. 2 (2015): 53–84.

Hoffman, James. Abstract. "Tzinquaw: A Site of Postcolonial Performance in British Colombia." http://faculty.tru.ca/jhoffman/tzinquaw.htm. Accessed January 23, 2019.

Kovach, Margaret. *Indigenous Methodologies: Characteristics, Conversations, and Contexts*. Toronto: University of Toronto Press, 2009.

Morrison, Frank, trans. *Tzinquaw: A Musical Dramatization of the Cowichan Indian Legend: The Thunderbird and the Killer Whale in Four Scenes*. Vancouver: 1950.

Ryan, Brittany. *Freedom to Engage: An Indigenous Approach to Ways of Being, Knowing, and Doing in the Performing Arts*. Toronto: Indigenous Performing Arts Alliance, 2015. http://www.ipaa.ca/files/freedom-to-engage-draft-05-02-2015-pdf.pdf. Accessed May 7, 2018.

Sangster, Dorothy. "The Double Life of Injun Joe." *Maclean's*, July 21, 1956. https://www.macleans.ca/archives/the-double-life-of-injun-joe/. Accessed May 7, 2018.

Shin, Ann, and Cathy Gulkin, directors. *The Four Seasons Mosaic*. Toronto: Tafelmusik, in association with Bravo and CBC, 2005. Film.

Smith, Linda Tuhiwai. *Decolonizing Methodologies: Research and Indigenous Peoples*. London: Zed Books/Dunedin, New Zealand: University of Otago Press/New York: St. Martin's Press, 1999.

Somers, Harry, composer, Mavor Moore, and Jacques Languirand, librettists. *Louis Riel*. Toronto: Canadian Music Centre, 1967. Opera.

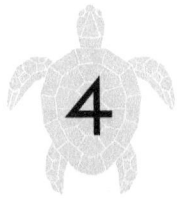

4

MAKING OUR OWN BUNDLE: PHILOSOPHICAL REFLECTIONS ON INDIGENOUS THEATRE EDUCATION

Carol Greyeyes

The term bundle in Northern Plains Indigenous cultures could refer to something, large or small, containing simple everyday items bundled together and wrapped in hide or cloth. Or a bundle could also be a collection of special objects, gathered over generations for use in ceremony or healing: sacred bundles, society bundles, medicine bundles. Items in a bundle can be used to educate, to heal, and to provide essential elements and teachings for ceremony. Certain bundles can unify and make connections: they remind you of the past, of who you were and who you are now, of stories, songs, or the way of things. Over the last three to four decades since the 1960s, in Canada, Indigenous artists and educators, of which I count myself as one, have been creating a new sort of bundle, a conceptual one. We have taken the Eurocentric art form of theatre, and the way it has been taught in mainstream institutions, and made it our own. By borrowing elements and ideas, by collaborating, by adapting various techniques and discarding others, artists and educators have contributed to what we might call an Indigenous Theatre Education Bundle.

As a theatre artist and teacher for over three decades, I have had the privilege of being a participant and witness not only to the emergence of the Canadian Indigenous theatre genre, but also to the development of a culturally affirming Indigenous theatre praxis and education. In this chapter I will unpack items from this metaphorical bundle to show how, from my perspective, the bundle came about. As I symbolically remove an item, I will not only explain its significance and provenance, but I will also include some of the sociopolitical contexts that influenced them. In addition, each item I unpack will be preceded by excerpts from the teaching philosophy statements embedded in my course syllabi to show how the objects have contributed to my ideas on Indigenous theatre education. Although this philosophy is dynamic and ever evolving, the basic ideas contained in it have been derived from the experiences and understandings that I have reached by making the Indigenous Theatre Education Bundle.

> *I endorse the adage that says: even though the view from the top of the Mountain of Truth is the same, there are infinite paths to the top. Therefore, I encourage students to be pathfinders—to find their own path to Truth.*

The first item in my metaphoric bundle is not an object, but it is the general idea of making a bundle—not the Indigenous Theatre Education Bundle itself, but rather an improvisational theatre exercise in which one is assembled. The way it works is that diverse objects are collected together, and then an item is selected from the bundle to trigger a significant memory or story based on the object by whoever chooses the item. My first encounter with this improvisational exercise was in 1982, after I had completed a bachelor of fine arts (BFA) with a major in theatre performance at the

Department of Drama, University of Saskatchewan. I was invited to participate in a theatre project at the Native Survival School in Saskatoon.[1] The school provided an alternative, culturally based curriculum for First Nations and Métis students. This experimental theatre project was led by Ruth Smillie, then artistic director of Persephone's Youtheatre, and Kelly Murphy, an English teacher at the school, with Métis author Maria Campbell and me as co-facilitators. The plan was to use popular theatre techniques with the upper-year students to develop a collective theatre piece that they could perform. One of the foundational exercises we used to elicit their stories was called the medicine bag game. I still remember all of us—teens and teachers—sitting on the floor of the classroom in a big circle. Our medicine bag, a large hockey bag, was placed in the centre. Every time we went around the circle to select an item, I was filled with anticipation as to what item people would choose and what the associated story might be. The stories ran the gamut from tragic and raw to rolling-on-the-floor funny, but all were deeply felt and bravely shared. The project was called Story Circles because of the collective process used to develop the production. From those authentic and richly imaginative stories came the basis for the final script, performed by the students before an enthusiastic local audience at the end of the school term. Although no one was certain how the experiment would turn out, Story Circles was a rousing success. The project engaged, encouraged, and empowered the student participants—students who had previously struggled in mainstream educational programs—thus proving its value to the administration. This recognition meant that the project continued as a regular part of the school's programmatic offerings for a number of years.

The reason the Story Circles project had such an impact on me was that I had not had any previous experience with collaborative theatre processes. My university training did not include improvisation or popular/community theatre techniques, nor could the approach to teaching acting be described as collaborative. We were trained to be interpreters of text and to follow orders given by the

....

1   The Native Survival School was renamed as Joe Duquette High School in 1989 and as Oskāyak High School in 2006. "History," Oskāyak High School, https://www.gscs.ca/studentsandfamilies/schools/OSK, accessed January 23, 2019.

director. The notion that I, or any other student, might have something of value to contribute to the educational process was foreign to me. We were meant to be receptacles of information, not generators of it. Not only was this pedagogical approach used in all my other university classes, from biology to English, there was also an emphasis on British and European cultural content. For example, on the drama department's main stage, the plays on which I cut my acting teeth were all written by English or American playwrights. Similarly, in theatre history we studied playwrights such as Shakespeare, Ibsen, Shaw, and Sophocles; no Saskatchewan or even Canadian plays were included. Even our Saskatchewan ways of speaking, our local accents and expressions, were not valued. At the time, however, I wasn't aware of the omissions. I simply thought that this is what theatre was—Shakespeare and Noel Coward plays, Broadway musicals, Arthur Miller's *The Crucible*, and Anton Chekhov's *Three Sisters*. Arguably, it was a very sound theatre training program, for which I was and am still grateful, but it did create a desire for something more. However, I didn't know what I was missing until my experience at the Native Survival School.

The popular/community theatre and collective-creation techniques that I discovered while working on the theatre project at the Native Survival School caused a shift in my thinking about theatre and teaching methodologies in significant ways. First, I realized that our own stories and perspectives were interesting and valuable, and that hearing our own voices through this style of storytelling connected people at a deep level. In addition, I discovered the effectiveness of a collective play-making process, which was the methodology used to create the theatrical piece. The use of a circle in that process and the experience of being included as an equal in a circle were quite revolutionary ideas to me. Finally, although I wasn't aware of it, this early community theatre project marked a beginning to the leitmotif of my life's work—finding voice and connecting, through art.

The Story Circles project was also a good example of how larger sociopolitical changes were impacting education in First Nations communities, the province, and the country. The creation of the Native Survival School in 1980 was a response to Indigenous self-determination and sovereignty in education. In 1972, The National Indian Brotherhood produced a seminal policy paper calling for

"Indian Control of Indian Education."[2] The Canadian government adopted it in 1973, but in Saskatchewan, even before the paper was published, we had already begun to develop the foundations for our own Indigenous educational institutions. The Federation of Saskatchewan Indians (FSIN), a provincial political body, led this movement towards Indian control of its educational institutions. Although the FSIN was created to protect the treaties and treaty rights, their mandate also included the goal of "fostering progress in economic, educational and social endeavours of Indian people."[3] In 1972, one year before the federal government had even adopted the paper, the FSIN established the Saskatchewan Indian Cultural College in Saskatoon, and it became the foundation for other Indigenous training programs and educational institutions in the province. Two of the largest of these institutions were the Saskatchewan Indian Federated College at the University of Regina, and the Indian Community College in Saskatoon, which both opened in 1976. These two colleges were created with a view to not only control education for Indigenous students and combat the cultural isolation that Indigenous students faced in mainstream education systems, but, perhaps more importantly, to preserve and revitalize First Nations cultures.[4]

....

2   National Indian Brotherhood/Assembly of First Nations, *Indian Control of Indian Education: Policy Paper Presented to the Minister of Indian Affairs and Northern Development*, 1973, http://www.oneca.com/IndianControlofIndianEducation.pdf, accessed December 2, 2017.

3   Indigenous treaties in Canada are constitutionally recognized agreements between the Crown and Indigenous peoples. Most describe exchanges in which Indigenous groups agree to share some of their ancestral land interests in return for payments and promises. Treaties are sometimes understood, particularly on the Indigenous side, as sacred covenants between peoples that establish the relationship linking those for whom Canada is an ancient homeland with those whose family roots lie in other countries. Thus, treaties form the constitutional and moral basis of alliance between Indigenous peoples and Canada. Anthony J. Hall, "Treaties With Indigenous Peoples in Canada," *Canadian Encyclopedia*, Historica Canada, http://www.thecanadianencyclopedia.ca/en/article/aboriginal-treaties/, accessed February 12, 2017.

4   Doug Cuthand, "Indian Control of Indian Education—A Brief History," *Saskatchewan Indian* (September 1988), 18, http://www.sicc.sk.ca/archive/saskindian/a88sep18.htm, accessed February 12, 2017.

I regard the process of learning as holistic; the mind,
emotions, body and spirit need to be engaged. These
aspects of human nature are all equally valuable
ways to understand and to build meaning, and they
need to be integrated in the learning process.

The next item in the bundle is the crest and logo of the Indian Teacher Education Program (ITEP). This crest symbolizes the purpose of ITEP, which is to provide a pedagogically and culturally appropriate post-secondary education degree program for First Nations students. The logo is a black eagle, wings outspread, on a field of red and soaring up towards a yellow rising sun. Above the sun are the words *Indian; Teacher; Education; Program*—all set within a red circle.

ITEP was also established as a strategic response to the call for "Indian Control of Indian Education"[5] in 1972 and 1973 at the University of Saskatchewan. Logically, if First Nations were to have control of education for their children, large numbers of well-trained Indigenous teachers would be required to meet those educational goals. Therefore, ITEP was created to educate future teachers. Not a separate institution like the Saskatchewan Indian Cultural College or the Saskatchewan Indian Federated College, ITEP was based in the College of Education and followed the curriculum set out for a standard bachelor of education degree. Despite it not being an autonomous institution, ITEP still tailored its programming and course content to the cultural and pedagogical needs of Indigenous students. Thus, ITEP was one of the first teacher training programs in Canada to blend and integrate Indigenous cultures into a mainstream degree-granting institution. This integration is symbolized on the crest by the eagle, which is set in the middle and balances both the top half and the bottom half of the logo. The eagle could be interpreted as a bridge between the past and the future. ITEP has its roots in an Indigenous cultural past, but the teacher training that students receive in the college ensures its graduates can also meet the educational needs of their students as they progress to other educational programs and institutions in the future.

....

5   National Indian Brotherhood, *Indian Control.*

When I became an ITEP student in the mid-1980s, the director at the time was Dr. Cecile King. A great advocate for Indigenous languages, Dr. King (Anishinaabe) was a wonderful role model and champion for Indigenous languages, cultural development, and preservation. Due to this emphasis on Indigenous cultures and the inclusion of an Indigenous perspective, ITEP represented a second major step in changing or decolonizing my thinking about education and learning in general. I discovered that an Indigenous cultural perspective—ways of understanding, learning, and doing things—was just as valuable and certainly more relevant to me as the dominant culture and mainstream perspective. During ITEP, not only did I discover a new perspective and pedagogy, but because the curriculum also included the political and legal history of the First Peoples of Canada, the treaties, Native rights, government policies, imposed systems of government, and the historical and political contexts for our current educational systems, I understood, for the first time, why things for First Nations Peoples in Canada were the way they were. It did and does continue to astound me that I had no knowledge of this history, despite being in the middle of a second post-secondary university degree. The history and information were simply never taught. It wasn't included in the curriculum in either my primary or secondary school education, nor was it in any of the BFA courses from my first degree. In many ways, my education in education taught me much more than just how to teach in a classroom.

ITEP represented another real watershed moment because, not only did I have shifts in understanding and perspective, I also flourished academically. ITEP marked the first time that I ever graduated from anything "cum laude." Perhaps it was the pedagogy. Or maybe it was because I felt accepted and respected. During my course of study, I was treated as if I represented a valuable point of view around the circumference, as on the ITEP logo. So, when the opportunity eventually came for me to help develop theatre training for Indigenous students, I had a very good paradigm to follow with regards to culturally based curriculum and pedagogy. Additionally, in Dr. King I had a wonderful mentor to turn to whenever I doubted or had questions.

Knowledge is a circle and it is democratic; all heads are the same height and whatever position you have in the circle is unique and has a valuable perspective. Not only do we contribute from our perspective in the circle, but we expand our collective knowledge in the process of watching others learn.

The importance of intellectual freedom, of being an equal and valued part of a group, and of a democratic learning environment leads to the next item: a well-worn paperback book, entitled *Improvisation for the Theater*, by Viola Spolin. First published in 1963, Spolin's approach to theatrical training was similarly based on those concepts.

My first real contact with *Improvisation for the Theater* came in 1984. I was working for Catalyst Theatre in Edmonton. Catalyst Theatre's mandate at the time was "to promote and practice the use of theatre for public education and as a catalyst for social change."[6] I was part of a team of theatre professionals, both Indigenous and non-Indigenous, who were embarking on a community theatre project in the northern Cree community of Wabasca-Desmarais. Before we left, however, we spent a week developing our curriculum, which was comprised of theatre exercises, games, activities, and play-making strategies for the project. Most of the games and exercises came from Spolin's book and I had great resistance to them. I thought they were culturally insensitive and inappropriate. In my youthful arrogance I was unable to see past the language and the form to the actual content of the exercises. Now I understand why they were chosen and why they worked so well. It was because the underlying principles that inform them are respectful and democratic. Spolin makes several statements clarifying these ideas and her teaching philosophy in the preface to the book's second edition. In an interesting dovetailing between her philosophy and that of ITEP, the following statement of Spolin's could also be represented visually by the same circle that surrounds the ITEP logo:

6   Anne Nothof, "Catalyst Theatre," in *Canadian Theatre Encyclopedia*, Athabasca University, http://www.canadiantheatre.com/dict.pl?term=Catalyst%20Theatre.web, accessed January 13, 2017.

Players see themselves as an organic part of the whole, becoming one body through which all are directly involved in the outcome of playing.[7]

The next key idea she stressed could also explain in part my success in the ITEP program, if the word "player" were replaced by "student":

Being part of the whole generates trust and frees the player for playing, the many then acting as one.[8]

This "acting as one" could be a guiding principle in many human endeavours, not just instructing theatre. Spolin describes a democratic classroom and creative process, stressing

the need for players to see themselves and others not as students or teachers but as fellow players, playing on terms of *peerage*, no matter what their individual ability. Eliminating the roles of teacher and student helps players get beyond the need for approval or disapproval, which distracts them from experiencing themselves and solving the problem.[9]

Although the playing field is levelled by a principle of peerage, it is nevertheless the role and responsibility of the teacher to create a democratic, respectful environment in which students have the freedom to discover, problem-solve, and create. Spolin writes that the classroom's "living, organic, non-authoritarian climate can inform the learning process and, in fact, is the only way in which artistic and intuitive freedom can grow."[10]

Based on my own experiences as a student and as a professional theatre artist, I can attest to the critical importance of having a non-authoritarian, non-competitive climate in which to learn

7   Viola Spolin, *Improvisation for the Theater: A Handbook of Teaching and Directing Techniques*, 2nd ed. (Evanston, IL: Northwestern University Press, 1983), xv.
8   *Ibid.*
9   *Ibid.* Emphasis added.
10 *Ibid.*, xv–xvi.

and share. In fact, an equitable, respectful approach to teaching any subject is essential, and even more so when we are asked to take risks and expose our innermost selves. Therefore, despite my early dismissal of the book, Spolin's pedagogical approach has been one that I have adopted and continue to use. Occasionally I have adapted the forms of the exercises to make them a bit more culturally appropriate, but the core ideas in *Improvisation for the Theater* still hold an important place in my theatre bundle.

Success is sometimes measured in tiny increments. If students can experience a shift of just a millimeter in their understanding, they have accomplished much.

The next item is a dark-blue wool vest with round brass studs in a chevron pattern down both sides of the vest's front. It was a costume piece worn by the late Gordon Tootoosis when he portrayed Chief Poundmaker in Ken Mitchell's play, *The Young Poundmaker*. Tootoosis' character was that of an actor hired to play the role of Poundmaker in a play within a play. Although set in 1985, it was meant to commemorate the events of a century earlier—the Battle of Cutknife Hill in 1885, and Poundmaker's arrest and subsequent trial for treason. The chief and council of Poundmaker First Nation had commissioned the play because they wanted to bring attention to this little-known part of Saskatchewan history. Someone (maybe Tootoosis himself) had convinced them that if they did a play about it and performed it for the public, everyone could learn Chief Poundmaker's story from the Battle River Cree perspective. This version was, as you can well imagine, very different from the official Canadian version of events.

Since there were no Indigenous theatre companies in Saskatoon at that time, the play had to be independently produced with a non-Indigenous director and playwright, and in early spring 1985, *The Young Poundmaker* had its world premiere at the Sands Hotel in Saskatoon, Saskatchewan. I was cast to play Tootoosis' character's sister, and although there was a large cast (including a role played by actor Tantoo Cardinal), almost all my scenes were with Gordon Tootoosis. He was already famous in Saskatchewan because of his film work.[11] "Sure, he has natural talent and a good look for the camera," I arrogantly thought as we began rehearsals, "but those attributes just don't cut it for acting on stage." I knew he had not had any formal theatre education, whereas I had completed four years of what I considered rigorous training. Furthermore, I had two whole years as a professional theatre actor under my belt (with a union card to prove it!), so despite the fact that he was my elder, I had an attitude of superiority. Looking back, I was embarrassingly patronizing: I was going to show this uneducated movie actor how it was really done. Fortunately, I have no memory of saying anything disrespectful, but I do remember what I secretly thought and what my perspective was. That perspective did a 180-degree turn, because during the *The Young Poundmaker* Tootoosis gave me a lesson in acting I have never forgotten. Neither before nor since have I ever acted with someone so totally in the moment and listening. People often talk about Tootoosis' presence, something that may be confused with charisma, but being really present, in an acting sense, is more accurately described as having all of one's attention focused in the moment. Up to that point, every actor that I had worked with had been just waiting for me to finish my lines so that he or she could speak his or her lines. With Tootoosis, even though I had several lengthy monologues in our scenes together, I always felt he was listening to me with every part of his being. With that kind of focus, you cannot help but be dragged into that same moment. The generous and total attention he gave me has made me a better performer.

Why, despite not having any formal training, Tootoosis was such a focused and powerful performer is the reason that Poundmaker's vest is included in the bundle. It all goes back to his upbringing: he and his siblings were raised by his father, Senator John B. Tootoosis, in a traditional way (which is to say an uncompromisingly rigorous

---

11   My first memory of Gordon Tootoosis was when he played Almighty Voice in the film *Alien Thunder* (1974) with Donald Sutherland and Chief Dan George. This was a major feature film shot right here in Saskatchewan, and it caused a big stir not only for the community, but also for me as a budding actor. Hollywood had come to Saskatoon! I remember standing in the winter cold outside the Bessborough Hotel in downtown Saskatoon for hours, watching them shoot scenes from the film.

fashion) in the Cree language, the Cree value system, and its cultural praxis. With this strict early training, Tootoosis learned how to listen and be present in a way that non-Indigenous education does not formally teach. Evidence for this theory may be found in the language. For example, in Cree there are many words for 'listen.' This is a good indication of the value placed on listening in the culture. There is, for example, *nitohta*, to mindfully hear; *nâkasohta*, to hear selectively, but not in a derogatory way, "more in a wise way, as in to hear the lesson given in a story"; and *nistohta*, to listen with three foci: mind, heart, and ears.[12] Active listening, as a specific skill or acquired technique, was not something I remember ever being taught in my formal education. Perhaps it was because we had a literary educational culture—reading, writing, and arithmetic—and not an oral one, which led to such passivity in our oracy. We could tune out and not pay attention to what was being said or demonstrated because we assumed we could read about it later. This became a habitual learning pattern for me. Instead of paying attention to what was happening in the moment, I believed I could simply access the information in a book at another time—usually just before writing an examination at school.

Then I came up against my mosôm (grandfather), Joseph Greyeyes, who tried to teach me the Cree language. Although he had only a grade three in formal education, he had been raised in a traditional Cree way: "you have two eyes and two ears, but only one mouth, so you must watch and listen twice as much as you speak," as the old saying goes.[13] Therefore, my mosôm would expect that when he showed me how to do something, or if he told me a new Cree

12 Darlene Auger, Cree instructor, "Cree Listening Question," (class lecture, Dram 211: Indigenous Performance Methods, University of Saskatchewan, Saskatoon, SK, August 27, 2016). This information was also subsequently shared in an email to the author on August 27, 2016.

13 My grandfather, like many others, was sent to St Michael's Residential School in Duck Lake, Saskatchewan, as a young child. After his being stuck in grade three for three years and never advancing, they finally gave up and sent him back home to Muskeg Lake Reservation. In a rare conversation about his residential school experiences, he told me that he "hated that damn book"— apparently, he was only taught from one textbook in all the years he was in grade three. Because he'd just had one book during all those years, he had memorized the entire thing.

word, I would only need to be shown or told once. I quickly learned that if I didn't pay attention the first time, it would not be repeated. However, without notes or something written to refer to, I found I retained very little. I had not been trained to pay attention, to quiet my mind and thoughts, and to simply listen or observe what was happening. While thinking about Tootoosis and his highly developed and focussed listening skills, I remembered my mosôm's method of teaching. Then I understood why Tootoosis could be so present—it was due to his Cree cultural upbringing. That is my theory, and the powerful acting lesson the untrained Tootoosis gave me became an essential life skill that I use in my own acting and relationships to this very day. It is also a story and lesson that I continue to pass on to my acting students when we begin to develop active listening skills in the acting studio.

My job is to guide students to discover and make their
own connections to the content or subject and therefore
establish a process of personalized learning. I believe that
if students are autonomous and take responsibility for
their learning, they not only become intrinsically engaged
and motivated, but they also experience a strong sense of
success and accomplishment that lasts long into the future.

A round hand drum made of deer hide stretched over a wooden frame and laced with sinew across the back is what comes out of the bundle next. It is one of many such drums made during the Centre for Indigenous Theatre's summer program called Native Theatre School (NTS) during the time I was artistic director. The history of the Centre for Indigenous Theatre (CIT) goes back to 1974. To put it on the Indigenous education timeline, it was only a few years after ITEP and SICC were created in Saskatchewan that James H. Buller established the Ontario-based Native Theatre School.[14] A Cree, also

---

14 The NTS was based at Kimbercote Farm, halfway between Kimberly and Heathcote, Ontario.

from Saskatchewan, Buller believed that if First Nations students could have access to professional training in theatre arts—acting, playwriting, directing, and design—Native theatre would develop and flourish across the country.[15] Ideologically, NTS was a response to "Indian Control of Indian Education,"[16] but specifically in the theatre arts. Over the decades, the NTS summer program trained many renowned Indigenous theatre artists and made significant contributions to the burgeoning Indigenous theatre scene in Canada during the 1970s and 1980s. Even if many of the NTS graduates did not continue on in theatre, they became performers in other genres like dance or music, or became filmmakers, performance artists, writers, or radio and television producers. Thus, Native Theatre School was a springboard for First Nations artists to share their cultural identities, realities, and visions with the rest of the country, and the world.

Building on James Buller's and the ITEP model, CIT also established the Indigenous Theatre School (ITS) in 1998. By then, numerous Indigenous-controlled educational programs, colleges, and institutions had sprung up across the country, and they had either developed their own culturally specific curriculums and pedagogies or adapted them from mainstream programs. Similarly, NTS and ITS sought to develop training that was pedagogically appropriate and used culturally affirming curriculums while providing Indigenous students with excellent pre-professional performance training. To that end, ITS offered a curriculum that was a blend of culturally based courses such as Indigenous Singing and Indigenous Dance, Indigenous History and Culture, along with courses that you could find in most mainstream theatre training programs, such as Clown, Neutral Mask, and so forth. We also hired Indigenous instructors and non-Indigenous teachers, all experts in their specific performance or theatre practice, such as pow wow dance, and speech and text analysis.

Before we launched the full-time ITS program, the CIT board members, the cultural director, and me as the artistic director/principal, sat down to brainstorm the company's mission statement. This statement included the values we wanted for the company, but also

---

15 Centre for Indigenous Theatre, "About," http://indigenoustheatre.weebly.com/about.html, accessed February 12, 2017.
16 National Indian Brotherhood, *Indian Control.*

for ITS and the other programming we offered. It was important to root our courses in authentic Indigenous cultural perspectives, and not be mere imitations of non-Indigenous training programs. What resonated so strongly in those discussions was a reiteration of the circle as an Indigenous pedagogical approach. Granted, the circle as a concept or even as a symbol does not belong exclusively to Indigenous people, but it is the clearest representation of the non-hierarchical and equitable perspective that most Indigenous peoples espouse. I can still see our cultural director, Lee Maracle, jumping up from her seat and drawing a big black circle on the flip chart, then launching into her interpretation of what a circle meant in the context of CIT's pedagogical approach and mission statement.

What evolved from that was what I will call the Circle Principle. When a group is gathered together and you are in a circle, all heads are the same height—no one is at the head or the bottom—and all are equals. It signifies that everyone has a valuable perspective and something to add. If the circle concept sounds familiar it is because the ITEP logo is a circle too, with points equally distributed on the circle's circumference. Further, the Circle Principle builds on what I had learned from my experiences of collective creation, the Story Circle at the Native Survival School, and from Spolin's democratic ideas used to teach improvisation in Wabasca-Desmarais. As Spolin says, "being part of the whole generates trust and frees the player for playing, the many then acting as one," and "this living, organic, non-authoritarian climate can inform the learning process and, in fact, is the only way in which artistic and intuitive freedom can grow."[17] It was during my time at CIT that I had an experience that reinforced the Circle Principle in an unexpected but powerful way. It happened one summer during NTS. In addition to teaching, acting, and directing the CIT student productions, I also sat in on most of the other classes, especially during summer school. It was during a voice class that I saw how the Circle Principle really worked. Our instructor, Jani Lauzon, had given the class an assignment to collaboratively create an original song. Jani had left the room so they could work on their own, and I was casually observing (probably catching up on paperwork) from a discreet distance so as not to interfere in their creative process. To make the group song, they went around the

---

17   Spolin, *Improvisation*, xv–xvi.

circle and each student contributed a melodic phrase of their own creation. The next step was to put the separate pieces together. This was the hard part because it required a lot of give and take on the part of the students' egos. They had to meld their separate melodies and voices together to create the whole. But they did it, and once all the phrases were put together they began rehearsing the entire song from start to finish. Midway through, however, one of the students stopped the song. "Wait! Someone is singing it wrong," she said. So they started over. Then she stopped them again. This time, a few other students could also hear what she was hearing. To discover what was wrong and who the guilty party might be, they decided to go around the circle and have every student sing the song. About halfway around the circle, they found the person who had been singing it wrong. What they were objecting to was not the melody, because she had that right, but it was the notes and the tone of her singing. So they sang her part for her and she tried to sing it back for them. It sounded the same as before. They tried coaching her to imitate their sound and sing it like them, but she could not, or would not. Part way through the second try, she stopped and paused for a moment to collect her thoughts. Then she carefully explained that she was from Vancouver Island (Kwakiutl) and, among her people, the way she sang (low and slightly flat) was considered a "good sound, a beautiful sound." The others were all from east of the Rockies, and many of them sang with a high, open-throated sound of the Plains, which was generally considered by the group to be the right way to sound. There was another pause as the other students processed this new information. It was fascinating to watch them shift their previous viewpoint and make room for this new idea. In the end, their change in perspective and their acceptance came because she had explained her sound and provided reasons for why she sang the way she did. When they took up the song again, their voices blended together and the song sounded wonderful despite her not changing the way she sang. It was just a mental shift in perspective that allowed them to accept and accommodate differences. It was for me a wonderful example of unity through diversity and that, in a circle, all heads are the same height.

There is one more story connected to CIT and specifically with the hand drum itself. The story is about one student's transformation, and it cemented my belief in the importance of connecting

Indigenous students to their culture. It was about a NTS student who came to the school in rural Ontario, who had been adopted and raised by non-Indigenous parents far from her biological family and community. Although she looked Indigenous, she had very little knowledge of her First Nations background and heritage, which, if I remember well, was Cree from Saskatchewan. When she first arrived at NTS, she was timid and withdrawn. Despite her desire to connect to her Indigenous culture, she seemed overwhelmed at times. Perhaps it was just being at the theatre school with all the drama exercises that caused her to withdraw even more. She was so quiet and contained, physically stiff and awkward—what we refer to as being out of your body—that, when it came to assigning roles in the final production, I gave her a silent role so she would not be required to speak.

Perhaps it was due to the cultural stimulation of summer school, or perhaps it was just the right time for this student to explore her Indigenous identity, but after NTS was finished, I heard that she had gone back to Saskatchewan to investigate her Cree roots. Four years later, the very same student showed up to take summer school again, but this time it was held in Saskatchewan on the Wahpeton Dakota First Nation. I barely recognized her. She was somehow much taller than I remembered, much more graceful, and she smiled and laughed more often. She was no longer timid or afraid. For the final student production, she not only featured in many of the scenes, but she opened the show with her own song, using the hand drum she had made during her first stay at NTS. As she walked towards the stage from behind the audience, holding the drum high and with her clear, powerful voice filling the auditorium, tears filled my eyes. What a transformation! She was like the bird on the ITEP logo, soaring upwards on powerful wings. Obviously, CIT or NTS can't claim that those five weeks at summer school made her into a proud Indigenous woman; she had to do that work herself. But I do know that because of the Native Theatre School program, we opened a door to her cultural heritage so she could experience the beauty of Indigenous culture with like-minded students.

*I feel that learning and teaching is a recipro-
cal process, a collaborative and collective journey that we all agree to go on together.*

The last item out of the bundle is a little cloth toy mouse—*apâkosîs* in Cree. The little toy mouse had originally been part of our *maski-hkiy maskimot*, our story bundle. The bundle was a large canvas bag filled with various items that we had collected for an Indigenous Theatre Performance Methods course. Held for the first time in the summer of 2016, the course is part of the new *wîcêhtowin* Aboriginal Theatre Program at the University of Saskatchewan.[18] The course is designed to teach an Indigenous language through performance training methods, and for this iteration we used the Cree language, Y-dialect. Mouse or *apâkosîs* was the name used by Darlene Auger, one of our Cree instructors.[19] In an elegant completion of a circle, this Cree language expert was a former drama student in the Wabasca-Desmarais community theatre project. In this course, we did an exercise I had learned nearly forty years ago, at the Native Survival School Story Circles project. We used the *maskihkiy maskimot* or the medicine bag game in the standard way—to help students create performance pieces. This time, however, the game had been adapted to suit our goals for this class, and the performance pieces had to be done entirely in the Cree language.

The course that *apâkosîs* (Darlene Auger) helped to teach, Indigenous Theatre Performance Methods, is a required course in the *wîcêhtowin* Aboriginal Theatre Program (ATP). ATP is a new two-year certificate program in theatre performance for emerging First Nations and Métis theatre professionals. Launched in the fall of 2015 in the Department of Drama at the University of Saskatchewan, the *wîcêhtowin* Aboriginal Theatre Program combines Indigenous

---

18 After a year's hiatus between 2017 and 2018, the program, now renamed the *wîcêhtowin* Theatre Program (WTP), reopened in a revised format in the fall of 2018.

19 To teach animal names in Cree during the immersion unit of Indigenous Performance Methods, everyone had to select an animal identity, which then became that student's Cree name for the entire course.

cultural knowledge with contemporary theatre practices. Building on the work of its predecessors, such as NTS and ITS and James Buller's original vision for the Native Theatre School, ATP offers courses in all aspects of theatre: acting; playwriting; collective creation; stage management; set, lighting, and sound design; and costume design, while integrating an Indigenous cultural praxis. The program culminates in a world premiere of a new work created, designed, and performed by ATP participants.

In developing ATP, the challenge, as it was with ITS, has been to ensure that it would be based on an Indigenous world view and set of values. From the very start we wanted to develop an educational program that included Indigenous cultural knowledge in a way that was not merely superficial or generalized. Experience has taught me that you cannot teach culture without teaching from where it resides—in language. Therefore, when ATP was first designed, it was imperative that Indigenous language be included in the curriculum. To that end, the Indigenous Theatre Performance Methods course was created to provide ATP students with the basic language skills needed to create performance work. This performance piece and the process used to develop it would therefore be rooted in an Indigenous language and, by extension, its world views and cultural praxis. For the initial pilot of the Indigenous Performance Methods course, we decided to use Plains Cree Y-dialect because ATP is based in Saskatchewan where most First Nations are Cree. Capitalizing on the fact that the Y-dialect is the most common Indigenous language here, we knew we would have a large pool of Cree language instructors and cultural resources.

With the ATP students' final presentation of their performance pieces—entirely in the Cree language—the Indigenous Performance Methods course achieved one of ATP's fundamental objectives: to celebrate and promote Indigenous experiences and culture. It did these things by providing theatre students with foundational Cree, as well as a performance opportunity at the culmination of the class that allowed them to learn about Cree culture and develop a basic understanding of its world view. To meet these objectives and achieve an even broader impact, it was decided that the students' final presentation would be a public one. Typically, final presentations in first- or second-year drama classes are done only for the instructor and a few faculty or students. By widening our circle to an invited audience of family, friends, university members, and other community members, we sought to celebrate and promote Indigenous experiences and culture beyond the confines of the classroom and the drama department. Why invite and perform for an audience that is neither Cree, nor Cree-speaking, and therefore cannot understand what was being said? The reason is because the *wîcêhtowin* Aboriginal Theatre Program is not just a form of "Indian Control of Indian Education,"[20] which is to say culturally appropriate pedagogy and curriculum for Indigenous students; ATP is also a way to Indigenize the entire university and the communities that the institution serves. Ideally, *wîcêhtowin* ATP is a program that not only maintains and revitalizes Indigenous cultures for Indigenous people, but also shares these cultures with everyone. I believe that Indigenous languages and cultures need to be alive and thriving for all our sakes, not only for Indigenous peoples. Therefore, we will continue to create and perform new work in Indigenous languages, so we can share the beauty of our place in the circle with everyone. After all, the name of the program is *wîcêhtowin*—a Cree word, a noun and process; we live together in harmony, we help each other, we are inclusive.

Although we continue to build our 'Indigenous Theatre Education Bundle,' I end on *apâkosîs* and the *wîcêhtowin* Aboriginal Theatre Program because ATP represents an integration of the lessons and experiences that have gone into making this metaphoric bundle. One of the most exciting developments is how the *wîcêhtowin* Aboriginal Theatre Program influences and impacts the drama department, the University of Saskatchewan, and perhaps education in general. There are indications that ATP is subtly transforming the department. It will be interesting to see the long-term effects of the program on the participants, the institution, and on the broader community—both Indigenous and non-Indigenous.

As for the Indigenous Theatre Education Bundle, even now there are hints of additions: not only as ATP continues to grow and develop, but as other post-secondary training programs start up and evolve as well. Since the bundle is dynamic, items already in it are continually being reused, restored, and reinvented as we build contemporary performance training informed by and rooted in an

20 National Indian Brotherhood, *Indian Control.*

Indigenous perspective. There will be new items added, and new carriers of the bundle, I have no doubt, but for me it has been an honour and privilege just to be included in its making. As the current coordinator of ATP, I shall carry it with me, to be used from time to time whenever I need guidance or inspiration. Hopefully, I will put into it as much or more than I take out. I am and will be eternally grateful to all those who have so generously helped create the Indigenous Theatre Education Bundle with me (truly *wîcêhtowin* in practice): former teachers, students, cultural practitioners, artists, elders, and masters—Indigenous and non-Indigenous.

REFERENCES

Auger, Darlene, Cree instructor. "Cree Listening Question." Class lecture, Drama 211: Indigenous Performance Methods, University of Saskatchewan, Saskatoon, SK, August 27, 2016.

Centre for Indigenous Theatre. "About." http://indigenoustheatre. weebly.com/about.html. Accessed February 12, 2017.

Cuthand, Doug. "Indian Control of Indian Education—A Brief History." *Saskatchewan Indian* (September 1988): 18. http://www.sicc.sk.ca/archive/saskindian/a88sep18.htm. Accessed February 12, 2017.

Hall, Anthony J. "Treaties with Indigenous Peoples in Canada." In *Canadian Encyclopedia*. Historica Canada. http://www.thecanadianencyclopedia.ca/en/article/aboriginal-treaties/. Accessed February 12, 2017.

National Indian Brotherhood/Assembly of First Nations. *Indian Control of Indian Education: Policy Paper Presented to the Minister of Indian Affairs and Northern Development*. 1973. http://www.oneca.com/IndianControlofIndianEducation.pdf. Accessed February 12, 2017.

Nothof, Anne. "Catalyst Theatre." In *Canadian Theatre Encyclopedia*. Athabasca University. http://www.canadiantheatre.com/dict.pl?term=Catalyst%20Theatre. Accessed January 13, 2017.

Spolin, Viola. *Improvisation for the Theater: A Handbook of Teaching and Directing Techniques*, 2nd ed. Evanston, IL: Northwestern University Press, 1983.

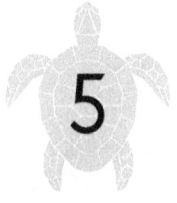

5

CONVERSATION WITH DANIEL DAVID MOSES, AUGUST 2016

Annie Smith and Daniel David Moses

Daniel David Moses (Delaware), poet, playwright, essayist, and editor, was a keynote presenter at the Performing Turtle Island gathering in September 2015 at First Nations University of Canada and the University of Regina. His talk focused on the play project he was then working on, *Crazy Dave Goes to Town*, based on the memoir, *Crazy Dave*, by Indigenous writer and educator Basil Johnston (Chippewas of Nawash Unceded First Nation, 1929–2015). Moses teaches playwriting at Queen's University in Kingston, Ontario, and, at the time of the interview, he was beginning a year-long sabbatical. Moses published his first volume of poetry in 1980 and began his career as a playwright in 1988. He has co-edited a number of anthologies of work by Indigenous writers. His own work has been included in anthologies and periodicals. For a list of his primary publications, please see the Addendum.

This edited conversation, conducted in two telephone interviews during the summer of 2016, picks up on Moses' current interests and discusses his process as a playwright. As a Euro-Canadian theatre director, I am curious about his play 'wrighting' and how he understands the development of Indigenous theatre and performance in Canada.

CONVERSATION

A. In terms of your play development process, you talk about finding a story you need or want to tell. Going back to the city plays[1] and *Coyote City* (1988), what was the story you needed to tell?

D. *Coyote City* came about when I was part of a writers' circle with Lenore Keeshig-Tobias, poet and storyteller from the Chippewas of Nawash Unceded First Nation. One day she showed up with "Coyote and the Shadow People," a story from the Nez Percé. It had been collected by one of their own people who had been trained as an anthropologist and so was exquisitely told. It moved me and I thought, "I need to do something with this story." It told of the limits of love, life, spirits, and the afterlife. This was a very different world from the city of Toronto where I lived at that moment—a very material, unspiritual place. It became my struggle to make the connection between the story, which came from a time that included spirits, to a time in which we might joke or whisper about ghosts but we don't see them in our daily lives. Instead, the supernatural gets pushed off into religion or horror movies. One day, I got lucky. I came across a little paperback collection of stories about phone calls from the dead. I realized that something from our modern material world—phone calls—could help me make that cultural connection. Looking at the phone call as a metaphor, it was a way of retelling the story in a contemporary context.

A. You found a tangible way to bridge between cultures and past and present.

D. I am a modern person. I look and see a world that's been reshaped by science and technology. I can't deny that real force. We are

---

1   The four "city plays", beginning with *Coyote City*, explore the experiences of an Indigenous family living in the city and their connection to the spirit world that underlies a shifting urban reality. The other three plays in the cycle are *Big Buck City* (1991), *Kyotopolis* (1993), and *City of Shadows* (1995).

in a dilemma in the world now because many of us try to hold on to the old beliefs. But that is impossible because contemporary culture insists there are very real unseen things that are not spirits, X-rays, DNA, dark matter, that we've come to understand through science.

A. Before the Enlightenment, the natural world, philosophy, religion, and science were not separated. There was not a contest between these different world views. Everything was viewed holistically. We have moved away from that. Do you think that the kitsch of Hollywood, with its vampires, angels, and people coming back from the dead and haunting us, is an attempt to integrate the supernatural with the material?

D. Yes. Most zombie movies are useless in that effort. However, there's a movie out right now called *Swiss Army Man* (directed by Daniel Kwan and Daniel Scheinert, 2016) with Daniel Radcliffe and Paul Dano. A man, a castaway on an island, is about to commit suicide. Then a dead man washes up on the beach and the castaway develops a relationship with the corpse. The dead man comes back to life gradually. The plot reflects the Christian resurrection and it is played for comedy and fart jokes. But it's also very serious. When I saw it I thought, "Well, this is more like it; this is a more useful examination of the division between life and death."

A. Do you think you would ever want to tackle that as an idea—that we don't understand the reality of death?

D. One thing I hope to work on is a piece that I began on my last sabbatical. It sprang from an incident in which I had gone down into the Toronto subway. I was waiting for the train when the woman next to me on the platform—a young woman dressed in cut-off jean shorts and a summery flower-printed blouse, flip flops, a baggy purse—walked forward and right off the platform! She crashed down to the tracks, like she didn't know what she was doing. A bunch of us on the platform panicked. Was the train coming? How were we going to get her out of there? A couple of guys jumped down to lift her up and I knelt on the edge to pull her out. She had hurt herself and we waited for the ambulance. The incident stayed with me because you do not normally run into that sort of thing. In reflecting on the incident, I connected it with two things. One was the image of Sky Woman, from the Iroquois creation story, who fell to earth through a hole in the sky. I am not sure why I made the next connection, but the other incident was the grotesque beheading of a twenty-two-year-old Canadian, Tim McLean, that happened in 2008 in a Greyhound bus west of Portage la Prairie, Manitoba. The beheader, an immigrant, was psychotic. In those two events is the beginning of a play and I want to see where it goes. I've gathered some information about the immigrant: he was Chinese. The victim was a carnival barker from Alberta who I mistakenly thought was Métis. There's a story there, but I don't know yet what it is about. Unlike the play based on the Nez Percé story that came to me fully formed, with this one I feel like there is a beginning, but the rest is coming to me in staged images. It is a different process and I am interested in that. So far, I have found a mother and father for the young man who was killed. We see them from overhead as they lie sleepless in bed. I think I've also found the young man's ghost. That is as far as I have gone.

A. Is this a different process for you?

D. Yes. Another example of process is this: last year I read Paul Kane's journal. He was the Irish-born Canadian painter who went across Canada, two trips in the years 1845 to 1848, funded by the Hudson's Bay Company. There's a collection of his paintings in the Royal Ontario Museum in Toronto. I picked up his book to see what one might see through his eyes. He was one of the first Europeans to look with an artist's gaze at Native people. The book is mostly anecdotal, not much use narratively, but he collected one complete story when he was stopping over on Manitoulin Island in Lake Huron. I was reading this story when I thought, "This is exactly like the stuff I do. All I've got to do is add one thing and I've got myself a play!" The thing that intrigues me is the character at the centre of the story, a powerful warrior. But his jealousy is overwhelming; he commits a murder, killing an innocent man. At the centre of the Iroquois political foundation myth, the story of how the confederacy was formed, there is a monster chief, Tadodaho. He is a cannibal monster who is redeemed and becomes the moral centre of that political universe after encountering Hiawatha and the Peacemaker.[2] We don't seem to believe in redemption anymore. I'm wondering, is it possible to think in those terms in our modern society? The other theatrical example of redemption is Shakespeare's play, *The Winter's Tale*. The king in that play is one of these powerful monsters. Think about that dilemma—what is your duty in being a man and what happens when you fall into the monstrous?

A. How do you live with yourself after you have committed terrible crimes, when you come to understand what it is that you have done?

D. Yes. How do you be human? How do your fellows forgive you if you've acted monstrously? That is the theme that I'm hoping to explore in these new pieces. The short plays I should be able to write this year. I believe I will write some prose about this, as well. I also have a habit of writing poetry.

A. One of your plays I found most troubling is *Brébeuf's Ghost*. What was your process in coming to that play; what drew you into it?

D. The story in the play was created during the writing process. The impulse was this: I was visiting Nipissing University in the fall one year and was given a tour of the campus. The university is in the Canadian Shield, on the edge of the city of North Bay, Ontario. You can look out from the heights and see a lake with islands in it. It has never happened to me before, but I got weird vibes from those islands. I started asking, "What's the story here? What happened in these places?" I came home with a book of local history from which I took a few of the strange incidents that ended up in the play. Once I figured out when it all happened and why, I was able to place them historically. They were events that happened on the edge of that conflict between the Iroquois and the Huron, the English and the French, at the time of first contact, the fur trade,

---

2   During the fourteenth century, the Peacemaker, a Huron, chose Hiawatha, a Mohawk leader, to translate his message of unity from the Great Spirit for the five warring Iroquois nations. This message not only succeeded in uniting the tribes but also changed how the Iroquois governed themselves. His words became a blueprint for democracy that would later inspire the authors of the United States Constitution.

and Black Robe missionaries. It happened long ago in a world in which the local Anishinaabe were known as shamans—they had powerful magic. The missionaries too had their own powerful spirituality. Imagine what an issue the communion service would be to Indigenous people whose greatest demon is the cannibal skeleton. A ceremony that says, "Here, take, eat my body" makes Christianity look very dark. It created a compelling, conflicted energy that reminded me of Shakespeare's Scottish Play. So I reread it and used its structure to start shaping my own drama. I did that for the first three or four scenes and the overall form. By then my own story started taking off. It was another world, so long ago—a very strange place to us. They just did another production of *Brébeuf's Ghost* with students at York University this past winter (2016) with Algonquin director Yvette Nolan. I hadn't looked at the text for a long time. When I saw it on stage, I thought, "This is so strange, so wild. How did I ever write this?" But it worked.

A. The play came out of a place, of being at Lake Nipissing and seeing the islands. On the Canadian West Coast, there is no Windigo, no cannibal spirit. There are stories and ceremonies around cannibalism among some of the Coast Salish peoples, but you must be part of a community to have access to them. You must be initiated into them. But you don't feel the presence of the Windigo on the West Coast in the same way as you feel it in the eastern part of the country because winter is simply not the same experience.

D. The way their reality is layered, among the West Coast peoples, seems different to me. For example, in the few stories I've read or have been told, their heroes go on journeys under the sea.

A. There is a wonderful story about Raven, a Nuu-chah-nulth story called "Ko-ishin-mit and the Shadow People," told by George Clutesi Sr. in his book, *Son of Raven, Son of Deer*. "Ko-ishin" is Raven and "mit" is son, so, "son of Raven." In the Nuu-chah-nulth stories, the animal people and the human people are together. The animal has human characteristics and the human has animal characteristics. It's not the same thing as shape-shifting: they coexist. Ko-ishin-mit is very greedy and his wife Pashook, the Squirrel, is very busy. She does not think a whole lot and does everything Ko-ishin-mit asks her to do. Ko-ishin-mit hears spirits talking about a deserted island where there is vast wealth. He convinces Pashook to go with him in his canoe to the island. They discover an abandoned village with cedar boxes full of treasure. He starts to pack them down to the canoe, but when he tries to drag the loaded canoe into the water, it won't move. This is because the spirits of that place are very angry. They cast a spell on Pashook so she cannot move. Ko-ishin-mit becomes terrified and unloads the treasure and leaves it behind in order to rescue Pashook. The story mixes the humorous and the sinister. The spirits play tricks on the trickster. In the eastern Canadian stories there is a different reality, a different way of thinking.

D. Stories can be different if they're put to different uses. The story of Sky Woman is part of a creation story, and the story about Tadodaho is a myth-into-history story. This is an example of stories with different purposes but coming out of the same culture.

A. What else can you share about how you develop scripts?

D. I gather as much information as I can and hope at some point to start writing. That usually allows me to get a first draft. At that point, I'll start talking to my director about it.

A. You work with Colin Taylor, the African Jamaica-born Canadian theatre director and producer in Toronto. Do you feel that your relationship is collaborative, or do you bring something to him when you figure the play is ready to go?

D. I'll write stage images that might take some effort to figure out—a character spontaneously combusting or a battle with shamanic orbs on shifting ice floes, things that he will need to worry about rendering way ahead of time. He will point out current cultural things I should know about his influences: W.G. Sebald's *Austerlitz*, or Christopher Logue's *War Music*. I would not have found those European artists on my own. For the actual production, the process is collaborative. He has more focus on realizing the production, on getting it to happen on stage. A lot of playwrights talk as if they know exactly what the play is going to look like on the stage. I'm usually only aware of the characters, of the action, and of an overall look to the piece. For the moment-by-moment specifics, I'm often surprised and always delighted by what Colin and the actors and designers come up with.

A. You and Colin Taylor have formed a production company.

D. Yes. We're hoping to do a production of *Brébeuf's Ghost* for the Canada 150 celebration. We've got a lot of support behind it. It depends now on whether the money comes through. It has such a big cast.[3]

A. What is the name of the production company?

D. It is called Arts & Science Performance Company. We want to foreground our skill set and contemporary lives, not necessarily just our cultural backgrounds. We will be doing my plays and the plays of other transcultural people in the city.

A. You use the term transcultural referring both to yourself and immigrant artists. Can you talk about that?

D. We are all theatre people living in this country. We are all working within the Canadian aesthetic culture. Generally, we have a sense of the history of colonialism, so that gives us an understanding of each other's stories of conflict. We have all experienced similar struggles. But it's also the question of: Can we be Canadian? Do we have a place here, or are we still the Other, always from elsewhere? I still feel that, despite my knowledge and relative success, maybe I should be back on the reserve. I feel that I should be put in my place.

A. Why do you feel that?

D. These are all learned attitudes. I grew up before being Indian was fashionable. When I first started to think about writing First Nations stories, my father's mother, a schoolteacher and a lady, warned me, "That Indian stuff—it'll just get you into trouble." When I look back at my parents and their generation, most of them lived large parts of their lives off the reserve and had careers as nurses, musicians, and civil servants. They weren't honoured

---

3 Many national and provincial arts and culture funding bodies made special project funds available for theatre companies and other arts entities to create projects to celebrate Canada's 150th anniversary in 2017. There was a particular emphasis on projects with connection to Indigenous stories and history. This coincided with the impetus towards reconciliation following the publication of the Truth and Reconciliation Commission of Canada's final report in 2015.

to the level they deserved. It makes me still question the values of the mainstream.

A. The term mainstream, as it relates to theatre culture, differentiates professional theatre from alternative theatre, fringe theatre, ethnic theatre, applied theatre, and all of these ways of working in theatre and performance that are tributaries of the main stream. There are so many different ways of representing human experience in their commonalities, as you mentioned in talking about shared colonial history. My question is: Do the tributaries have to be in opposition or subservience to a mainstream? Is the concept of mainstream even valid?

D. Well, we will see if we get the money for our Canada 150 project.

A. Speaking of funding, if you get the funding for *Brébeuf's Ghost*, will this be its first professional production?

D. Well, we are now up to four student productions of a large-cast play involving shamanic magic, spectacle, and an obscure pre-Canadian moment.[4]

A. This raises the question about the 1 percent of theatre in Canada that is considered professional while there is so much amazing non-professional work being done. Why do we only value work done by professional theatre? Are not student and non-professional productions equally or more important?

D. Yes. As one of my students said, "I love this. It's like Sword and Sorcery [an epic fantasy cooperative board game], but with Indians!"

A. What are your thoughts about touring within Canada?

D. Because of the limited number of venues, touring is hard to do. Limited performance space is an issue in Canada. Because of the expense, it is necessary to form partnerships. In the past the money has been so meagre; there was hardly enough for the local artists in any city without flying in outside artists on tour. In the

----

4 The play has been performed at York University, 2016; Queens University, 2003; Centre for Indigenous Theatre, 1999; and University of Windsor, 1996.

past we always had a hard time planning years ahead when we were not sure the next year's funding was secure.

A. Is that just a matter of political will or do you feel that Canada is too regionalized to be able to actually create a national-tour model that works?

D. Native Earth Performing Arts, Canada's oldest professional Indigenous theatre company, over the last decade did a remount of *Almighty Voice and His Wife* (2009). They were able to tour it all across the country. This last winter (2016) they did a tour with *Huff*, Cliff Cardinal's one-man play. Apparently they are going to do it again in this coming season because they didn't hit all the places that wanted it.

A. Living in northern Alberta, I had no access to touring productions. They just didn't come there.

D. Those Native Earth tours were done with one- and two-actor plays. You can pack them in a trunk. Anything bigger than that, it becomes a real challenge to travel.

A. The other claim you made is that the theatre community in Canada has no interest in Indigenous work. Can you speak about that?

D. There just has not been enough education around Indigenous work. The audience does not see it as Canadian. Maybe it is the hangover of the old education, the story that said Indians would simply die out and not be a problem anymore. That is not coming true. For the past four or five years I have taught a First Nations playwrights course at Queen's University. The students say, "I didn't know about this. I didn't know about that. Why wasn't I taught this in high school?" They lack any knowledge of the historic issues around the plays, let alone the plays themselves.

A. In Vancouver, when I was a graduate student, it was somewhat better. For example, when Michelle La Flamme (University of the Fraser Valley) and I created the first course at the University of British Columbia (UBC) on Indigenous Theatre (2004), it was an exciting moment. Students did not know there was so much amazing Indigenous work, but there was a context for it because Vancouver's Firehall Arts Centre did (and does) many plays by

Indigenous playwrights.[5] This meant that there were Indigenous artists who could come to speak to the class. For example, performance artist Rebecca Belmore gave us permission to view a video of her street performance, part of the installation *Vigil*, commemorating the missing and murdered Indigenous women of Vancouver's Downtown Eastside, which was exhibited at the Morris and Helen Belkin Art Gallery on the UBC campus in 2002. Dana Claxton, Hunkpapa Lakota filmmaker, photographer, and performance artist, did a presentation of her video work. There were many resources we could tap into, which made that course exciting. Greg Young-Ing (UBC, Okanagan, Opsakwayak Cree Nation in Northern Manitoba) and I did a course together the next year (2005) on Indigenous performance. These were successful courses because we had access to so much material. Indigenous actors Margo Kane and Sophie Merasty and performance artist Archer Pechawis came to class and we went to the Talking Stick Festival.[6] There was a great wealth of material in Vancouver compared to other places in the Canada.

An understanding I have had about Indigenous poetics is that Indigenous artists are creating not just for themselves, in the tradition of the Western artist, but also for their community. Is that a differentiation for you?

D. I start working on pieces because I have a problem I want to address, I have an issue, I have something I'm curious about. The way I solve it usually comes back to my cultural background and that will open it up to the community. I think any artist has to start with his or her own questions and impulses. I trust the theatrical process to find the wider politics in the personal experience.

A. Do you identify as a two-spirited person and does that make a difference for you?

---

5   In 1985, the Firehall Arts Centre "established itself as one of the first theatre companies to incorporate aboriginal and culturally diverse artists within its practice." (firehallartscentre.ca)

6   The first annual Talking Stick Festival, hosted by Full Circle: First Nations Performance in Vancouver, BC, was held in 2001 and has grown in scope to become a mecca for Indigenous performers and artists from across Canada. The festival includes performances, exhibits, discussions, workshops, panels, feasts, and more.

D. There are moments that I do, although I do not usually think politically. Identity politics? I just want to be me. But if that's the language I need to use to connect with the questioner, I'm willing to give it a try. The idea of two-spiritness is part of my history and has shaped my sensibility. Doubtless, younger people are more adept in identifying these ideas in the current culture. I think I need to google the meaning of cisgender. I seem to have missed that memo.

A. There is an assumption that a person who is two-spirited can be viewed as a mediator between people who are male gendered and people who are female gendered—as somebody who can bridge between those perspectives. Is this how you understand it?

D. Or between many perspectives. Make a list of social dichotomies—race, class, musical genres—and two-spirited individuals are more likely to be able to bridge them. We are considered to be good babysitters because we have both young and mature natures: innocence and wisdom.

A. In your writing, your characters are just who they are. This is also true of characters created by Cree two-spirited playwright and novelist Tomson Highway. They are wonderfully male and wonderfully female and wonderfully two-spirited. I wonder if that's a particular gift that a two-spirited writer can bring that other writers cannot.

D. Anyone can get in touch with their two-spiritness. It is a matter of being willing to imagine the Other. That is why we still think about Shakespeare: his women characters are worth the effort. As for other writers in the canon? I've been looking through William Butler Yeats of late and so few of his poems rise above his Irish political/historical moment. That is part of the reason we rarely do his plays: they are full of clichéd archetypes. In this world, at this moment, we need to connect with the Other. That is the issue for younger writers. They have a hard enough time imagining themselves clearly without having to imagine the Other.

A. Tracey Lindberg asked you, in "Interviewing Daniel David Moses: 2015," how working in the academy has impacted your writing.[7] You said there's sort of a balance in the work. It does mean you have less time to write, but there are also benefits to working with students. Do you feel that has informed your work as a writer?

D. It has allowed me to wander off in directions I might not have chanced on or chosen otherwise. Take Yeats, for example. I think I have a basic set of impulses and curiosities that I had before I came to the University and they are what has allowed me to find the things that I want to say yes to, to think about and question.

A. How do you feel about the idea of the writer as translator? In Tracey Lindberg and David Brundage's book, *Daniel David Moses: Written and Spoken Explorations of His Work*, Randy Lundy and Tracey Lindberg write about the writer as translator. Lundy says: "Language truly is a translation. . . . It is an expression of both our desire to know and the world's desire to be known, to have us know, simply because we too are part of the whole."[8] Do you think of yourself as a translator?

D. The metaphor I use is negotiator. I am always trying to make language mean the same thing for both of us. This does not necessarily work, but that is part of the game, part of trying to figure out how language communicates ideas. We are all different people and at different places in space/time and it makes sense that we do not understand things exactly the same way. That is part of the fun of trying to communicate through distances and from a variety of moments in time.

A. What are the elements of language that you work with to make that negotiation?

D. Language is abstract and our lived experience is concrete. That is why we employ rhetoric and metaphor. I use images to suggest connections and parallels, and that is what gets the imagination

---

7 Tracey Lindberg, "Interviewing Daniel David Moses: 2015," in *Daniel David Moses: Written and Spoken Explorations of His Work*, eds. Tracey Lindberg and David Brundage (Toronto: Guernica Editions, 2015), 381–405.

8 Randy Lundy, "So What's Indian About Your Poetry, Anyway?," in *Daniel David Moses*, eds. Tracey Lindberg and David Brundage, 151.

engaged. The rhetoric engages the emotions. If one is lucky and/ or smart, the work also gets the moral imagination engaged.

A. What do you mean by the moral imagination?

D. The stuff that connects to how we behave, with kindness or without, towards each other as human beings.

A. Do you feel that it is a cultural negotiation or a human-experience negotiation?

D. It is a bit of both. I feel like there are a lot cultural assumptions that I grew up with on Six Nations Reserve near Brantford, Ontario, that are valid as ways of behaving in the broader world. For example, in the first humanities course I took in university, I became the designated denier in the room. The professor would make some blanket sort of statement—"Competition is essential to civilization"—and everybody else in the room would nod and take notes. But I would say, "I don't I believe that. That's not how we do it where I come from. We cooperate."

A. And then what happened in the room?

D. Things would get stirred up and the professor would be happy about that. If I lost the argument, I would still end up with a good mark because I was contributing to developing a dialogue beyond habitual thought.

A. Is that something you try to get your students to do?

D. Students who take courses in writing don't need that sort of encouragement because the nodding in response to blanket statements is not part of who they want to be. Students who are interested in learning about First Nations playwrights are generally willing to listen to other points of view. That is the benefit of teaching creative, upper-year courses.

A. The negotiation is working on so many different levels. To me, that negotiation is what makes theatre so valuable.

D. How much can I do before the audience refuses to suspend its disbelief? That's the life of it—the embodiment of those differences in action. Sometimes that conflicts with our ideas about who we are and who we want to be.

A. When you write as a poet, are you still working within the space of an imagined audience?

D. Perhaps it is more a space of cultural history. I'll find myself thinking, "I don't know what a particular word means." Out comes my dictionary. Well, I'm mostly correct, but the meaning could also go off in a different direction. Then I shift it slightly. That's the beauty and the challenge of the language.

A. When you write poetry, do you read it out loud to yourself?

D. Yes. That is the centre of my aesthetic. If I cannot make it as clear, concise, and musical as possible, then I'm not writing in my own best voice. I'm writing in a voice that is lazy, clichéd, or formulaic. I believe in revision.

A. Do you ever record yourself reading and then listen to it?

D. I did that early on, but now I am more removed from my own voice. The revision process allows me to find my way back to it.

A. Is rhythm important?

D. Yes. In theatre it is important to find a rhythm to your own voice as a playwright, your own way of using the language. It is also important to find different rhythms for the individual characters.

A. As a director you have to help the actors find the rhythm of the piece as a whole. When the rhythm begins to establish itself everyone says, "Oh, this is what's going on."

How is your current sabbatical shaping up for your writing projects?

D. For the moment, I've stopped writing poetry because I've met the deadlines I'd agreed to. I am now in that space before I can start writing a play, a space where my mind gets chaotic. Until I can grab ahold of something else, I am spiritually uncomfortable. I cannot concentrate on other things for very long. Mind you, this morning I may have started something. We will see if the inspiration continues. Until I'm sure I have a grasp on something, I am lost.

A. What do you do in that lost space? Do you have things to help you work through it?

D. I trust that it is part of the process. A lot of the decision-making is unconscious. I have got all this information in my head and I am looking for a form and I know what the forms, what the possibilities are or might be. In this way, I can make some decisions, but until the impulse becomes clear, when I can wake up each morning knowing what I'm going to work on, it feels chaotic.

A. How do you work your way through the chaos?

D. I read interesting things in the meantime. For example, this morning I picked up the latest *National Geographic* and I read the first two or three short articles. Suddenly, an idea occurred to me and I turned the computer on and wrote for an hour.

A. What was the idea?

D. It was an idea about my Chinese immigrant characters that I referenced earlier deciding to come to Canada. What did they really know about this country that would attract them? I cannot assume they were only fleeing their homeland. Something here must have made it seem a good destination. Because the characters are contemporary, it must have been something beyond the old idea of the Gold Mountain. And then I wondered, "Do they still teach Chinese children about Norman Bethune?" I'm not sure if this detail will stay in the play, but I did find something Mao had written in honour of the man that I may use.

A. You have said that current Indigenous women playwrights, Jani Lauzon, Monique Mojica, and Tara Beagan, have not received the same attention that your work and that of Tomson Highway, Floyd P. Favel, and Drew Hayden Taylor has received.

D. The mainstream is still focused on guys. Meanwhile, I'll go to a Native arts event and there will be no women presenting. I want to know where they are, because they're supposed to be there.

A. I began to understand how patriarchy operates when I was working for the Nuu-chah-nulth Tribal Council where I attended years of tribal council meetings that followed the colonial model of governance required by the Department of Indian Affairs. They were dominated by elected male chiefs. Before that, I had accepted the colonial model of governance as a given. Being in an

Indigenous context allowed me to see the inequities and injustice of colonial systems of governance. Indigenous cultures have their own vibrant realities but still have to negotiate the restrictions and forms of the larger culture that 'gatekeeps' money and access.

I am curious about the historical and thematic movement in Indigenous theatre. What is the difference between plays by Indigenous women writers and Indigenous male writers? Have women had to reach further into themselves because of the many forces arrayed against them?

D. Of the first generation of Indigenous playwrights, the woman who made a splash was Monique Mojica with *Princess Pocahontas and the Blue Spots* (1991). It wasn't a personal play. It was based on historical knowledge. In it she found ways to theatricalize and ceremonialize the oppression of our women under colonialism. It was one of the most respected works of that first generation of plays. In a way, I feel like she established a model that the other women have had to strive to live up to.

A. Another Indigenous woman, Shirley Cheechoo, a co-founder of De-ba-jeh-mu-jig Theatre on Manitoulin Island, was writing and performing her own plays. They were more autobiographical and were not readily accessible until 2003.[9]

D. Cheechoo is a multidisciplinary artist, painter, film producer, and writer. In the last decade, she has also established the non-profit Weengushk Film Institute for at-risk youth on Manitoulin Island in Ontario.[10] She has worked in so many different art forms. Perhaps that is the reason her theatre career is not as well remembered.

A. In the first generation of plays is Margo Kane's *Moonlodge* (1990) and *Tales of an Indian Cowboy* (2003). These plays are autobiographical, as is Maria Campbell and Linda Griffith's collaboration, *Jessica* (1996), based on Campbell's book *Halfbreed* (1973). My response to Mojica's *Princess Pocahontas and the Blue Spots* was that she was

---

9 Cheechoo's play, *Path with No Moccasins* (1991), was published in *Staging Coyote's Dream Anthology*, vol. 2, eds. Ric Knowles and Monique Mojica (Toronto: Playwrights Canada Press, 2003).

10 Weengushk Film Institute, http://weengushk.com, accessed November 2, 2017.

telling not just the historical stories of so-called country wives such as Pocahontas and La Malinche, but also the experiences of my sisters who have been betrayed by white men.[11]

D. The past is very present when dealing with these issues. Perhaps we have not yet achieved a post-feminist culture.

A. When you consider Jani Lauzon and Tara Beagan, do you feel there is a continuum of work by women playwrights?

D. I see Lauzon and Beagan as individuals. Jani has just started producing her own plays in the last four or five years. She had worked with established playwrights Monique Mojica and Michelle St. John and their company, the Turtle Gals, creating collaborative pieces, but now she is bringing all her knowledge as an individual performer to it—the last thirty years working as an actress, singer, and puppeteer. Part of what she wants to explore is her mixed ancestry. For example, in *A Side of Dreams* (2014) she places a gigantic dream catcher on stage that serves as a base for acrobatics. That is very stageworthy material. Beagan is from the younger generation of Indigenous playwrights. She has read a lot and is not afraid of mainstream theatre. For example, she wrote a piece that was inspired by *Desire Under the Elms* and another that was an adaptation of *Miss Julie*. Seeing it, I understood why that creaky old classic play might still mean something. She has also written commissioned pieces for other small theatres, as well as work that comes out of her own family experience. She acts and is a writer/director. These are very different impulses.

A. These women writers are multifaceted in that they explore their artistry in multiple ways in theatre. This brings a different flavour to their work. It is presentational and very theatrical.

----

11 Country wives were Indigenous women who made alliances with Europeans during the period of colonization in North America. These relationships had a firm, practical foundation. For example, by marrying an Indigenous woman, fur traders strengthened trade ties with her Native relatives. However, country wives were more than diplomatic pawns or unpaid servants. They were women who played a major role in Canadian history, occupying a unique position between two cultures. A. Gottfred, "Femmes du Pays: Women of the Fur Trade, 1774–1821," *Northwest Journal*, http://www.northwestjournal.ca/ XIII2.htm, accessed November 2, 2017.

D. Tara's first noticed piece was *Dreary and Izzie* (2005). It had the issue of fetal alcohol syndrome as its background, but it was really a story about being a young woman, responsible and searching for her life and love.

A. Is it important, instead of thinking of a continuum in the development of female Indigenous playwrights, to focus on individual artists?

D. There must be something happening in the broader culture that they are part of—that we are all part of—but it can only be articulated by the individual expression that each artist brings. That is what makes it interesting. It has always been my assumption that the feminine had a very strong place in traditional cultures. Part of the way we define our indigeneity is by giving the feminine its place in the human experience. For example, Tomson Highway talks about how the Cree language has no gender. That is another way of allowing both sexes to be in the culture without necessarily giving one gender pride of place. People frequently look at the traditions of the Iroquois in contrast to the mainstream's patriarchy and say, "Oh, they're so matriarchal." It's more about a balance between male and female rather than one or the other having the power. However, it is hard to break those habits of hierarchical assumption.

A. Yes. The matriarchal/patriarchal is an anthropological construct. Years ago, at the National Native Theatre Symposium in Montreal in 2000, participants were invited to the traditional longhouse at Kahnawá:ke' Reserve. We were divided by gender and we went into the Longhouse through the women's entrance and the men's entrance. Yet it was not about dividing us up, it was about balance.

D. At the Banff Playwright's Colony I watched a performance based on our traditional dances. I saw men doing women's steps and vice versa. I thought, "That just doesn't look right." I was happy that they were willing to think about these traditions but it seemed they were only learning the forms, they weren't learning the meanings.

A. Do you think the impulse for movement in the body comes from a different place in men and women?

D. Our bodies are differently weighted. When you try to put on the moves of the other sex, it plays as comic.

A. Your family is Delaware and immigrated to Six Nations, where you were given land and a place to live. Is your family still connected to your Delaware roots in the States?

D. We have been in Canada for generations and have only a few threads of knowledge about those roots. I have written a radio play called *My Grandfather's Face* that epitomizes the situation.[12] The face in the piece is a lost Delaware medicine mask. Although my family is mostly integrated into the Six Nations scene, I'm officially Delaware—that's from my father's father. I also have Mohawk, Cayuga, and Tuscarora grandparents. I was given an anthropological text that described the Delaware longhouse. It pointed out some of the differences between it and the Iroquois longhouse, and I found it strangely familiar. Our family has been Christian for five or six generations, if you count my cousins and their children. A lot of that Delaware history is just 'by the way.'

A. Is that a reflection of how, as we have moved over generations, our connections become severed?

D. The Six Nations is a contemporary culture, largely Christian, but with a strong awareness of Longhouse traditions. I think it has a quarter or fifth Longhouse adherents and everybody else believes in versions of Christianity—Anglican, Baptist, Presbyterian. A number of them are contemporary non-believers. But our attitudes are very much formed by our traditions. I remember the first time I visited a white person's house where the woman was treated like a servant. I thought it was creepy. We were a bunch of healthy teenage boys sitting around watching sports on television while the mother was working in the kitchen doing the ironing. As busy as she was, she took a moment to come and serve us soda pop. I thought, "This is just not Canadian." I guess I was wrong.

A. Within Canada there are so many different traditions that have translated to a new place. Métis playwright Maria Campbell

---

12 Daniel David Moses, *My Grandfather's Face*, in *Daniel David Moses*, eds. Tracey Lindberg and David Brundage.

comments that audiences in Saskatchewan, where your play *Almighty Voice and His Wife* is set, would not understand it because it is an urban play.[13] Do you see this as a problem?

D. This is the dilemma of needing to see the play performed. If you only read it and don't feel the emotional effect that performance gives, you only get the ideas and not the stirring of the psyche. You can write a play, but it needs to have the embodied performance of the space/time of the stage to really do its job. If the audience sees the piece, they'll get it.

A. At this point in your career, where do you want to land? Do you need to create that space?

D. If we can just have a space to make our world, to do our work, that's all we can do. Most of the non-Indigenous writers and their audiences don't think they really need us. It's so hard to change their minds, and life is short. But as the world warms up, they do seem to be paying more attention to some of our older ideas.

A. The largest part of it is lack of exposure. The first time I heard Tomson Highway read from *Dry Lips Oughta Move to Kapuskasing*, I was at the Stein Valley Festival in 1989. I stopped in my tracks hearing his maniacal voice speaking in English and Cree, calling the shots of the hockey game scene. That moment was like being struck by lightning. I knew that there was something happening here that was different from any theatre I had seen or read, and I knew it was vitally important for me, as a non-Indigenous person, to learn more. So I continue to learn. I believe that your work and the work of other Indigenous playwrights has had a huge impact on theatre in Canada, in the new forms that are being explored, in the stronger connection to community, in the desire to tackle social issues. These changes are happening in large part because of the impact Indigenous theatre has made and continues to make in Canada. Thank you for the wonderful conversation, laughter, and for sharing so much of your process as a writer.

....

13 Maria Campbell, Tracey Lindberg, Brenda Macdougall, and Greg Scofield, "Identity, Identification, and Authenticity in *Almighty Voice and His Wife*: A Round-Table Discussion," in *Daniel David Moses*, eds. Tracey Lindberg and David Brundage, 278.

ADDENDUM: SELECT WORKS BY DANIEL DAVID MOSES

Plays

Coyote City. Toronto: Playwrights Guild of Canada, 1988.

Belle Fille de L'Aurore. Toronto: Playwrights Guild of Canada, 1989.

The Dreaming Beauty. Toronto: Playwrights Guild of Canada, 1990.

Coyote City. Stratford, ON: Williams-Wallace, 1990.

Big Buck City. Toronto: Playwrights Guild of Canada, 1991.

Almighty Voice and His Wife: A Play in Two Acts. Stratford, ON: Williams-Wallace, 1992.

Almighty Voice and His Wife. Toronto: Playwrights Guild of Canada, 1992.

Kyotopolis. Toronto: Playwrights Guild of Canada, 1993.

The Indian Medicine Shows: Two One-act Plays. 1995. Reprint, Toronto: Exile Editions, 2002.

City of Shadows. Toronto: Playwrights Guild of Canada, 1995.

The Witch of Niagara. Toronto: Playwrights Guild of Canada, 1998.

Big Buck City: A Play in Two Acts. Toronto: Exile Editions, 1998.

Coyote City and City of Shadows: Two Plays (Necropolitiei). Toronto: Imago Press, 2000.

Brebreuf's Ghost (A Tale of Horror in Three Acts). Toronto: Exile Editions, 2000.

Almighty Voice and His Wife. 2001. Reprint, Toronto: Playwrights Canada Press, 2009.

Kyotopolis: A Play in Two Acts. Toronto: Exile Editions, 2008.

Collections of Poetry

Delicate Bodies. Vancouver: blewointment, 1980. Reprint, Sechelt, BC: Nightwood Editions, 1992.

The White Line. Saskatoon: Fifth House Publishers, 1990.

Sixteen Jesuses. Toronto: Exile Editions, 2000.

River Range, Poems. Comp. David DeLeary. Dir. Colin Taylor. Independent, 2009. CD.

A Small Essay on the Largeness of Light and Other Poems. Holstein, ON: Exile Editions, 2012.

Nonfiction

Pursued by a Bear: Talks, Monologues and Tales. Toronto: Exile Editions, 2005. Print.

For a comprehensive bibliography of works by Daniel David Moses see: Tracey Lindberg and David Brundage, eds., *Daniel David Moses: Spoken and Written Explorations of His Work* (Toronto: Guernica Editions, 2015), 425–64.

REFERENCES
Campbell, Maria et al. "Identity, Identification, and Authenticity in *Almighty Voice and His Wife*: A Round-Table Discussion." In *Daniel David Moses*, edited by Tracey Lindberg and David Brundage, 275–94.

Cheechoo, Shirley. *Path with No Moccasins*. In *Staging Coyote's Dream Anthology*, vol. 2, edited by Ric Knowles and Monique Mojica, 1–41. Toronto: Playwrights Canada Press, 2003.

Gottfred, A. "Femmes du Pays: Women of the Fur Trade, 1774–1821." *Northwest Journal*, http://www.northwestjournal.ca/XIII2.htm. Accessed November 2, 2017.

Lindberg, Tracey. "Interviewing Daniel David Moses: 2015." In *Daniel David Moses*, edited by Tracey Lindberg and David Brundage, 381–405.

Lindberg, Tracey, and David Brundage, eds. *Daniel David Moses: Spoken and Written Explorations of His Work*. Toronto: Guernica Editions, 2015.

Lundy, Randy. "So What's Indian About Your Poetry, Anyway?" In *Daniel David Moses*, edited by Tracey Lindberg and David Brundage, 131–64.

Moses, Daniel David. *My Grandfather's Face*. In *Daniel David Moses*, edited by Tracey Lindberg and David Brundage, 406–21.

PART II
PERFORMANCE IN DIALOGUE WITH THE TEXT

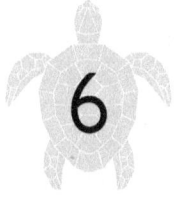

6

PERFORMING THE BINGO GAME IN TOMSON HIGHWAY'S *THE REZ SISTERS*

Jesse Rae Archibald-Barber

n *The Rez Sisters*, Tomson Highway uses the bingo game to stage a metaphysical clash between Christian and Cree-Ojibwa spiritual traditions. The main comedic action of the play depicts the trials and tribulations of seven Cree and Ojibwa women who travel to Toronto to play "the biggest bingo in the world."[1] On a serious level, Highway dramatizes how the women deal with social ills, domestic violence, and death on their reserve. Highway's overall concern is the way the women struggle to maintain a traditional identity within a colonial system that has been imposed on them. His goal is to restore to the community a sense of the immanent presence of Nanabush, a trickster-transformer being that provides

---

1   Tomson Highway, *The Rez Sisters* (Saskatoon: Fifth House, 1988). All quotations from the play and the accompanying page references in brackets refer to this edition of the play.

a way of interpreting the play's social concerns from an Indigenous perspective.[2]

The ambivalent and arbitrary nature of the bingo game further relates to the broader underlying colonial conditions that still reso-nate in modern society. To this point, Highway represents the bingo game as revealing the predicament of modern life as a closed system without transcendence while also offering the possibility of tran-scendence and consolation through it. In this way, Highway crystal-lizes the metaphor of the game as both trap and freedom.

The entrapping aspect of the game is that Highway's charac-ters play a Western game that in turn represents layers of Western systems, such as the colonial political system, the Christian reli-gious system, and, we might even add, theoretical systems such as postcolonialism and post-structuralism. Janice Acoose addresses the problem of applying these last theories to Indigenous works: "forces of Western literary criticism and its accompanying critical language. . . enact another form of colonialism."[3] However, Acoose is also aware that attempting to move out of the Western paradigm risks "essentialising Indigenousness."[4] In turn, Acoose advocates that Indigenous writers and performers "define our own critical methods and language, and resurrect our respective cultural epis-temologies and pedagogies."[5] However, this can still create an ironic problem, as it critically involves what Jeannette Armstrong calls the "deconstruction of colonialism."[6] Armstrong goes on to say: "Aboriginal literary voices also support the reconstruction of a new order of internal culture and a relationship that transcends colonial thought and practice."[7] The ironic condition revealed here is that

....

2 Nanabush (also called Nanabozho or Nênapohš) refers specifically to the Ojib-wa, or Anishinaabe, trickster. The Cree name for this figure is Wîsahkîcâhk.

3 Janice Acoose, "A Vanishing Indian? Or Acoose: Woman Standing Above Ground?," in *(Ad)dressing Our Words: Aboriginal Perspectives on Aboriginal Litera-tures,* ed. Armand Garnet Ruffo (Penticton: Theytus, 2001), 37.

4 *Ibid.,* 38.

5 *Ibid.,* 47.

6 Jeannette Armstrong, "Aboriginal Literatures: A Distinctive Genre within Canadian Literature," in *Hidden in Plain Sight: Contributions of Aboriginal Peoples to Canadian Identity and Culture,* eds. David R. Newhouse, Cora J. Voyageur, and Dan Beavon (Toronto: University of Toronto Press, 2005), 183.

7 *Ibid.*

"Aboriginal peoples see the world through two separate realities."[8] The result is that one is often bound by these Western systems when attempting to move outside of them and open up the conditions needed to restore Indigenous traditions.

Alternatively, the liberating aspect of the game is that the deconstruction and transcendence of the colonial system are precisely what Highway's play involves. Highway uses a Western dramatic form, tragicomedy, but transforms it by giving it the Indigenous spiritual centre of Nanabush. While Highway's characters struggle against the violent legacies of colonial policies and institutions, he ultimately restores the legitimacy and effectiveness of Indigenous consolatory symbols and uses these to modify Western metaphysical assumptions that underlie the traditional colonial tropes of consolation. In other words, Highway attempts to restore the possibility of Indigenous spiritual immanence by challenging the initial colonial substitution of Christian forms.

THE STRUCTURE OF THE GAME AND
THE POST-STRUCTURAL SYSTEM

Throughout *The Rez Sisters*, Highway uses the structure of the bingo game as a metaphor for the modern human condition, or, more specifically, the modern Indigenous condition, with all the concomitant legacies of colonial history, including the loss of culture, language, and identity. The bingo game is a system that is based on chance, where each game is essentially an arbitrary sequence of numbers in a closed system—a closed system because, although the sequence of numbers (or signs, elements, experiences) varies with each cycle, nothing new is added or removed from the system, and thus it is only the same numbers or elements that are shuffled around each time the game repeats. In terms of modern philosophy, this is the epitome of the reduction of traditional metaphysics to a closed system emptied of transcendent meaning. This is why Highway attempts to restore a sense of spiritual immanence: without it, the closed system by analogy reduces life to an arbitrary sequence that repeats itself with minor variations of the same essential elements and from which there is no escape or transcendence. Moreover, from

8   *Ibid.*, 184.

a post-structural perspective, the bingo game represents a decon-structive allegory of 'the text' as a closed system in which signs circle around and meaning is endlessly deferred. My interpretation here, furthermore, also applies to the existential predicament of Highway's characters, as they are bound up in a reserve system that separates them from their traditional origins or identities, repeating the pat-tern of the game where the fulfillment of their hopes is always just out of reach.

Highway represents these issues explicitly in the dialogue and ac-tion of the play. In the opening scene, Pelajia laments that her people have lost their traditions: "the old stories, the old language. Almost all gone" (5). The bingo game and all its constituent parts and patterns have overwritten the characters' traditional culture, as is indicated by the loss of fluency in their own language: "was a time Nanabush and Windigo and everyone here could rattle away in Indian fast as Bingo Betty could lay her bingo chips down on a hot night" (5). With the potential loss of her ancestral world, Pelajia further complains that there are "no jobs," and that there is "nothing to do but drink and screw each other's wives and husbands" (6), acknowledging how re-lationships too have become variable, shuffling around like elements in the game. On a deeper level, Pelajia laments how her people have "forg[otten] about our Nanabush" (6), or, in other words, the spiritual centre of a shared sense of the divine in their lives. Instead, now their culture hero is Bingo Betty (16–18), a legendary bingo guru who learned how to maximize playing the game. Thus, the characters are caught up in a game that provides excitement and hope, but is also problematic. The serious concern is that the characters have lost the ability to affirm their identities in their own tradition, which was based on a spiritual immanence in nature, having been overtaken by an arbitrary and material form of 'salvation.'

The bingo game is based on sequence, repetition, and permuta-tion, and in the play, it follows a circular yet escalating structure. This structure also informs the ways in which the game puts Cree-Ojibwa and Christian spiritual traditions into conflict, and this structure can be seen in the manner that Highway further develops the dia-logue and action and, thematically, in the ways the game supplants traditional religious practices. The sisters express how the church has become a diminished presence in their community and how the repetition of their local game has also become unfulfilling: "That old priest is too slow and sometimes he gets the numbers all mixed up and the pot's not big enough" (14). The sisters want the game to be more stimulating, the patterns more dynamic, and the prizes more rewarding: "The numbers at those bingos in Espanola go faster and the pots get bigger by the week" (15). They also base their identities on their mastery of the game. As one sister says: "I'm good at bingo. . . . I'm gonna go to every bingo and I'm gonna hit every jackpot between here and Espanola" (5); another sister says: "The bingo in Espanola is bigger. And it's better. And I'll win. And then I'll go to Sudbury, where the bingos are even bigger and better" (13). Finally, with a "revolution[ary]" cry of "Wasy women want bigger bingos!" (15), the sisters' desire for bingo threatens to fully displace the church from the community: "We'll march up the hill, burn the church hall down, scare the priest to death, and then we'll march all the way to Espanola, where the bingos are bigger and better" (15). However, although the ascending levels of the game may suggest that the system is open and thus allows for freedom or something better, any kind of transcendence through the game remains illusory, as the system is still closed, and all the sisters can really do is expand the idea of bigger and bigger bingos, until they reach "THE BIGGEST BINGO IN THE WORLD!" (27).

Although it is just a game, it has consequences in real life as the boundary between the game and life blurs and the game becomes the dominant pattern that structures the sisters' desires and aspirations. In the section where several sisters describe in turn how winning the game will improve their lives, each monologue reveals the nature of the game as based on sequence and repetition, exposing how their lives, like the text, have become permutations of the same discourse or series of experiences (27–36). Thus, the sisters are trapped in a pattern, playing the same game over and over again, in a sequence that keeps repeating and inflating with minor variations until they reach the ultimate system, where the jackpot becomes their only hope.

The bingo jackpot represents the central goal of the game. In a sense, the jackpot is what Jacques Derrida would call the "transcendental signified,"[9] the centre that governs and gives meaning to the

....

9   Jacques Derrida, "Structure, Sign and Play in the Discourse of the Human Sciences," in *Writing and Difference*, trans. Alan Bass (Chicago: University of Chicago Press, 1978), 280.

system and ends the constant deferral of each sequence. To win the jackpot is to achieve the "full presence" of the centre, which allows one to escape "being caught by the game."[10] However, even when characters win the jackpot, it does not mean they escape the game: with each repetition it becomes clear that the jackpot is merely a temporary prize that becomes just another element in the next sequence, a resource to continue playing more games. This leads to what Derrida calls a "series of substitutions of center for center."[11] The problem is that if this substitution for centre never stops, if one can never truly escape the deferral of the system, then in reality there is no centre origin, or end to the game. In other words, the centre does not lead outside the system and therefore it cannot provide an escape from the game. This is why, in the play, the sisters' hopes are always pushed just out of reach, just as the centre of meaning in a system of signs "has always already been exiled from itself into its own substitute."[12] The serious concern is whether it is ever possible to transcend the closed circle of signs—or the game. Is there an outside? Or does Highway's treatment of the game reveal the human condition as one of being trapped in a system reimprinting itself over and over within a range of possible variations? It is here we see, within the tradition of modern tragicomedy, how Highway represents his characters as trapped in an endless cycle, waiting for an absent figure to reveal a greater purpose to their lives.

CHANCE AND DIVINE WILL

Before we address the climax of the play, where Highway breaks out of this Western interpretive system, it will be helpful to briefly explore the connection between chance and spirituality. Kathryn Gabriel argues that for traditional Indigenous cultures "gambling has nearly always been a sacred activity, inextricably bound together with myth, legend, and ritual."[13] Alyce Cheska further confirms that traditional Indigenous games "were officially sanctioned

---

10 *Ibid.*, 279.

11 *Ibid.*, 280.

12 *Ibid.*

13 Kathryn Gabriel, *Gambler Way: Indian Gaming in Mythology, History and Archaeology in North America* (Boulder, CO: Johnson, 1996), 5.

by the gods and culture heroes."[14] In this context, traditional games of chance also foster a relationship with the environment, and this direct relation with nature further provides the root connection that traditional games of chance have with myth, spiritual beliefs, and cultural practices. When these games are played in a ceremonial context, the playing field becomes a sacred place in nature where the four directions, significant landmarks, and the arrangement of the cosmos provide the boundaries of the playing field. Traditional games of chance speak to the uncertain and random aspects of life and the universe, at their origins and in what people face on a daily basis, and this is why these games are sanctioned by a society's highest spiritual authorities and cultural figures.

In contrast, from a Christian point of view, one would not characterize human life as a game or lottery, as God's creation is not based on chance. Events are not arbitrary or random because there is a greater design to existence. Thus, Christian missionaries saw Indigenous games of chance as governed by 'pagan' gods and deities who are ambivalent about the fate of human beings. Subsequently, in order to aid conversion to Christianity, missionaries commonly encouraged Indigenous villagers to abandon their games. As Jesuit Paul Le Jeune complained, back in the seventeenth century: "We give them Instruction or Catechism in our cabin, . . . for we have as yet no other suitable Church. This often was the most we can do: for their feasts, dances, and games occupy them that we cannot get them together as we would like. . . . [T]hese Savages are great gamblers, . . . [sometimes they] do nothing but gamble in our cabins."[15] Yale Belanger further explains: "First Nations gaming was generally presented as an idolatrous pastime in which lazy individuals hoped to improve their living conditions through games of chance that usually ended with the participants losing their possessions."[16] Furthermore, like the Catholic missionaries, the Protestant churches also condemned this form of labour and wealth redistribution: "The

---

14 Alyce Cheska, "Native American Games as Strategies of Societal Maintenance," in *Forms of Play of Native North Americans: 1977 Proceedings of The American Ethnological Society*, eds. Edward Norbeck and Claire R. Farrer (St. Paul: West, 1979), 237.

15 From *The Jesuit Relations*, quoted in Yale Belanger, *Gambling with the Future: The Evolution of Aboriginal Gaming in Canada* (Vancouver: Purich, 2006), 28.

16 Belanger, *Gambling with the Future*, 27.

Puritan ideal of succeeding through hard work was antithetical to the gambler's hope of obtaining a livelihood by participating in games of chance."[17] The oppressive effects of these views cannot be overstated, as they underpin the colonial policies that eventually led to the reserve system and the banning of Indigenous games, cultural practices, and economics in the nineteenth century. Belanger summarizes:

> The Potlatch and the Sundance were outlawed in 1885 and 1894, respectively, as were the games associated with each event. The transformation of First Nations religious ideology and practice was considered essential if the assimilation of First Nations into Canadian society was to succeed. Most games were outlawed, as was any form of wagering. No longer could games be used as a mechanism of wealth distribution. Nor could they be used as a means of promoting inter-tribal contact, predicting future events, asking for spiritual guidance, or even as simple entertainment to promote tribal unity. By this time, historic gaming practices were considered both illegal and immoral.[18]

Hence, the interdiction on Indigenous games of chance was part of the larger process of displacing the social and spiritual core of their cultures.

Indeed, it is noteworthy that in *The Rez Sisters* the characters are not playing a game of chance within their own cultural traditions, but are rather obsessed with bingo, a Western game that acts as a metaphor for a Western system in which the Indigenous characters are caught. At the same time, the critical point here is that Highway uses this contradictory condition as a site to decolonize the system that dominates the characters' lives. This works on several levels. In terms of the game itself, the general principle of drawing lots and the concept of repeating sequences are inherent to traditional Indigenous games of chance. As Stewart Culin states in his seminal survey: "The ultimate object of all Indian games of chance is to determine a number or series of numbers, gain or loss depending upon

---

17 *Ibid.*, 31.
18 *Ibid.*, 38.

the priority in which the players arrive at a definitive goal."[19] In other words, although Indigenous games of chance primarily involve the casting of lots and guessing games with sticks, and not numbered balls as is the case with bingo, the general concept of the repeating sequence is the same, as casting lots creates a series of random figures that are marked on a counting board. Furthermore, on a social level, Cheska notes, "in spite of the acceptance of Anglo games by Native Americans, the social processes traditionally sustained by game participation continue to be preserved."[20] This point is clearly demonstrated in the play as the bingo game becomes the central unifying force that brings the sisters together. Thus, although the bingo game represents a Western colonial system, the principles of the game are not foreign to the Indigenous characters, and indeed it becomes something the characters are easily, even unconsciously, able to infuse with social and spiritual significance.

On a critical level, however, there is still the issue of how the bingo game works as a metaphor for the reduction of the human condition to a closed system without transcendence. If the wheel of fortune is an ambivalent and pitiless wheel and the only real salvation lies outside the wheel, then, as the deconstruction of the sign system shows, the centre or jackpot cannot lead outside the system and therefore cannot lead to spiritual consolation, but only to a material salvation that falls into the next shifting sequence. This Western perspective removes spirituality from the system. However, in the play these principles have never been divorced from each other, and indeed the sisters are able to operate within this system because they are industrious in raising capital and organizing their trip to the biggest bingo, and they act on a root principle from their spiritual tradition when they arrive. During the climactic game, Nanabush, the Bingo Master, reinforces the connection between chance and spirituality as he is the very process of play and substitution within and beyond the game. Nanabush, as both transcendental signified and shifting signifier, is what 'ruptures' the system, and, as we will see, this is what enables Highway to restore a sense of spiritual immanence and transcendence to the sisters' lives.

19 Stewart Culin, *Games of the North American Indians*, vol. 1, *Games of Chance* (1907; repr., Lincoln: University of Nebraska Press, 1992), 44.

20 Cheska, "Native American Games," 239.

THE CULTURAL SUBSTITUTION

At the climax of the play, Highway enacts a substitution of the central figure in the Christian tradition for the central figure of the Cree and Ojibwa traditions. As the sisters begin playing the biggest bingo in the world, the ultimate game, they are seated in a parody of Leonardo Da Vinci's *The Last Supper*, symbolizing the culmination of a scriptural narrative, reaching the end of a series. The figure of Christ, here, is replaced by the so-called "dozy pagan" (39), Zhaboonigan, a sister who embodies a Native version of the Holy Fool. Zhaboonigan, whose name means "needle" (48), also crystallizes the play of appearance and reality throughout the work as her character mirrors the double aspect of the text as both tragic and comic. Even though the woman's outward facade has been ravaged, she still possesses a kind of second sight for, unlike the other sisters, she (along with Marie-Adele) is able to immediately perceive Nanabush. She is central to the substitution of the centre, the 'needle' that pierces both cultural systems, and she now sits *at the table's center banging a crucifix Veronique has brought along for good luck* (102), ironically bringing divinity and luck back together. At this point, Nanabush manifests as the Bingo Master, with glitzy attire and a booming voice, and the sisters play the game zealously, working themselves into a fury when they need only one more number to win the jackpot. However, the final number never comes, and in their frenzy the sisters end up *attacking the bingo machine* (102), destroying that which has governed their lives.

However, it is during this catharsis that the continual deferral of the game does finally end as the sisters perceive the system of control that has entrapped them, and they purge the game from the play. This also allows them to perceive the Indigenous spiritual figure, at least for a moment, as the Bingo Master, who represents God, now transforms into the nighthawk-Nanabush. Thus, at the climax of the play, Highway enacts an absolute substitution of the central figures in each cultural mythology. The substitution reveals that Christ and Nanabush essentially fulfill the same role in offering the characters the possibility of spiritual salvation, but at the same time the point of Highway's restoration of Nanabush is that, from the sisters' perspective, Christ belongs to a foreign system, as there is already a figure at the centre of their culture that fulfills the same spiritual role. Nanabush the Trickster represents the ability to transform one's life, and this ability allows the characters to transcend the systems that have oppressed them.

On this point, returning to Western literary theory, the game depends on a centre, even though its nature does not allow for one. According to Derrida, the centre can never achieve full presence, and as we saw with the illustration of the problematic nature of the jackpot, the 'transcendental signified' does not really stand beyond the system but becomes just another element, or signifier, that falls into the next sequence. Indeed, nothing can ever really become the 'transcendental signified,' and pursuit of it simply belies a logocentric desire to substitute centre after centre, like chasing the jackpot in game after game. However, Nanabush resolves this contradiction, as he is both a part of the game and beyond the game—he is "the free hole in the middle of the card" (101), which is the one constant element in every sequence, and thus he transcends the random variations of the system. In this way, Nanabush is not caught within the limits of Derrida's theory and escapes "being caught by the game."[21] Rather, at the climax of the play we have experienced a paradigm shift outside of Western theory: from Highway's Indigenous perspective, the full spiritual presence at the centre of the play is not only possible, but essential to the system. Nanabush is the "free hole" in the centre, through which the Aboriginal spiritual stem allows the characters to escape the endless deferral and go beyond the arbitrary construct of the game, as well as beyond the limits of Western colonizing theories.

This dynamic nature of Nanabush further redeems Marie-Adele's death at the tragic climax of the play. Along with Zhaboonigan, Marie-Adele can see Nanabush and she welcomes him as the master of the game. However, Nanabush the Trickster is the agent of the tragedy, separating that which dies from the play, leading Marie-Adele off stage, into the spirit world. The tragic perspective is that death is the only way to escape the closed system; only death ends the repeating sequence of the game. But Nanabush is also the agent of comedy, and comedy here is redemptive. By recognizing Nanabush, Marie-Adele sees that there is a reality beyond the game, and she "waltz[es] romantically in the arms of the Bingo Master" (103), who transforms into the nighthawk-Nanabush. Thus she dances at the

---

21 Derrida, "Structure, Sign and Play," 279.

end of the game, the end of the series, where Nanabush restores an Indigenous consolation to the sisters' lives.

This transition from Christian to Indigenous traditions and the breaking down of colonizing systems is reinforced by the code shifting between English and Cree, which also reveals the limits of language systems in relation to spiritual transcendence. Marie-Adele switches from English to Cree early in the play, when Nanabush is present but invisible (19), and during her death scene, when he becomes visible (104). With her actions, the words are made somewhat understandable for an English audience, and their sense is made clearer as they blend with English, even though the grammar is broken and the sequences are fragmented. Indeed, the code shifting and fragmentation of dialogue represent the return of language to its root forms, especially in relation to a spiritual experience. Language breaks down when it confronts death, and it is the silence between words that paradoxically becomes more pronounced. The result of this code shifting is that Indigenous spirituality is not assimilated to notions of Christian transcendence; rather, Cree-Ojibwa traditions indigenize Christian transcendence as the sisters sing an Ojibwa funeral song at Marie-Adele's grave: "Wa-kwing, wa-kwing, / Wa-kwing nin wi-i-ja"; "(Heaven, heaven, heaven, I'm going there)" (105).

THE SPIRITUAL CENTRE AND THE TRAGICOMIC GAME

Pelajia's eulogy at Marie-Adele's funeral becomes the central speech that unifies the play's tragic and comic perspectives, providing greater insight for the characters, as she compares their lives to the game: death is "the big jackpot" (105). She laments the arbitrariness of their situation: "What choice do we have? When some fool of a being goes and puts us Indians plunk down in the middle of this old earth, dishes out this lot we got right now" (105). The "lot" is a number drawn from the game; it is also a parcel of land, like the reserve; and it also carries the sense of one's destiny in life. Indeed, the lot the sisters have received underscores the bitter irony that, if their lot is their destiny, as it turned out, in the sweep of history, the land was, like the jackpot, only temporarily theirs. Thus, the game board becomes a version of the divided land and, in particular, the reserve that they find themselves on as a result of colonization. At the same time, it is during this funeral that the characters become the most self-conscious of their conditions and the limits of the game. One must be inside the game and have a thorough understanding of every permutation of the system, for it is this that allows the sisters to decolonize their condition: "I figure we gotta make the most of it while we're here" (105). It is in this self-conscious moment when the Trickster gives them the power to transform their lives and transcend the game that Highway restores the Indigenous sense of spirituality and the view of death as part of a continuing cycle or transformation: "See you when that big bird finally comes for me" (105).

As the denouement ensues, the play casually falls back into its natural, circular sequence, ending where it began, on Pelajia's roof. The props, the characters, and the dialogue are slightly rearranged, but the basic pattern remains as the characters return to their basic concerns—the roof, the road, the toilet. This reveals the central predicament of tragicomedy: the sisters are bound up in their existential condition, and yet they focus on the mundane things of life. This is because, as the play replays its cycle, the remaining characters are still in the middle of the endlessly repeating series, waiting for an absent figure to return meaning to them. At the same time, Highway goes beyond this tragicomic condition and there is a sense of renewal after the catharsis. On a political level, Pelajia no longer wants to abandon the reserve, but instead wants to become chief in order to renew the community. On a spiritual level, the sisters also have a new awareness of their own mortality; although they still cannot see Nanabush, there is now a sense that they are at least searching, indicating that, although they live in a world very much dominated by the Western concept of the game, the older tradition still informs their lives.

Thus, Highway uses the structure of the game to dramatize the predicament of finding oneself inside a system outside of which one cannot think. As a response, Highway displaces the central symbols of Christianity and restores an Indigenous spiritual tradition with a Trickster figure that existed prior to the system the characters find themselves in. In this way Highway opens the possibility of transcending Western systems. In the play, chance is not divorced from spirituality—rather, it actually might be a great expression or emanation of the divine through the figure of the Trickster, whose split-second appearance dancing *"merrily and triumphantly"* (108) re-deems the arbitrary nature of the game, at least for the glimpse of a moment. Indeed, the arbitrary moment is itself the opportunity for transcendence—and Indigenous transformation.

REFERENCES

Acoose, Janice. "A Vanishing Indian? Or Acoose: Woman Standing Above Ground?" In *(Ad)dressing Our Words: Aboriginal Perspectives on Aboriginal Literatures*, edited by Armand Garnet Ruffo, 37–56. Penticton: Theytus, 2001.

Armstrong, Jeannette. "Aboriginal Literatures: A Distinctive Genre within Canadian Literature." In *Hidden in Plain Sight: Contributions of Aboriginal Peoples to Canadian Identity and Culture*, edited by David R. Newhouse, Cora J. Voyageur, and Dan Beavon, 180–6. Toronto: University of Toronto Press, 2005.

Belanger, Yale. *Gambling with the Future: The Evolution of Aboriginal Gaming in Canada*. Vancouver: Purich, 2006.

Cheska, Alyce T. "Native American Games as Strategies of Societal Maintenance." In *Forms of Play of Native North Americans: 1977 Proceedings of The American Ethnological Society*, edited by Edward Norbeck and Claire R. Farrer, 227–48. St. Paul: West, 1979.

Culin, Stewart. *Games of the North American Indians*. Vol. 1, *Games of Chance*. 1907. Reprint, Lincoln: University of Nebraska Press, 1992.

Derrida, Jacques. "Structure, Sign and Play in the Discourse of the Human Sciences." In *Writing and Difference*, translated by Alan Bass, 278–93. Chicago: University of Chicago Press, 1978.

Gabriel, Kathryn. *Gambler Way: Indian Gaming in Mythology, History and Archaeology in North America*. Boulder, CO: Johnson, 1996.

Highway, Tomson. *The Rez Sisters*. Saskatoon: Fifth House, 1988.

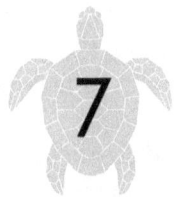

A PRAYER FOR RITA JOE

Yvette Nolan

n June 1969, the National Arts Centre opened in Ottawa with two weeks of performances. Bilingual—in English and French—with a mandate to produce and present dance, music, opera, and theatre, the National Arts Centre was realized because of the desire of a community for a good concert hall and the excitement and resources around Canada's centennial celebration in 1967. Although construction of the edifice was behind schedule by two years, the National Arts Centre was indeed a centennial project,[1] and its Studio Theatre opened with another centennial project, *The Ecstasy of Rita Joe*, which had been commissioned by the Vancouver Playhouse and premiered there in 1967.[2]

In 2008 I received a call from Peter Hinton, who was three years into his tenure as the artistic director of English theatre at the National Arts Centre. Peter wanted to revive the play to celebrate

----

1   G. Hamilton Southam, when fighting for funding as the costs rose and the construction dragged on, called it "the Government's only Centennial project in Ottawa." Quoted in Sarah Jennings, "Art and Politics," in *The History of the National Arts Centre* (Toronto: Dundern Press, 2009), 43.

2   *The Ecstasy of Rita Joe* that opened the NAC in 1969 was a remount of the Vancouver Playhouse production, with only four minor roles (policeman, teacher, witnesses) recast and the direction credited to David Gardner.

the centre's upcoming fortieth anniversary, but was not willing to undertake a production without an Indigenous director.

Somewhat tentatively, he asked me if I knew the play and if I had any feelings about it. I did, I told him. And I did have strong feelings about *Rita Joe*, all kinds of feelings, complicated and often contradictory.

My first engagement with *The Ecstasy of Rita Joe* was not the play proper, but the ballet, which had been commissioned by the Royal Winnipeg Ballet and premiered there in 1971, choreographed by Norbert Vesak. As a ten-year-old ballet student, I was eligible for season tickets, and sitting in the audience at the Centennial Concert Hall with my Algonquin mother, I saw for the first time, my (hi)story onstage. Never mind that Ana Maria de Gorriz and Salvatore Aiello played Rita Joe and Jaimie Paul; to me they were Indian lovers who came to the city and struggled to survive. The ballet used the music of Ann Mortifee, who had created the role of the Singer in the original production, and the voice of Chief Dan George, who played Rita Joe's father, David Joe. Chief Dan George's voice surrounded us in the concert hall, held us all. I had never heard an Indian man's voice that loud before.

The words that Chief Dan George says, which migrated from the play to the ballet, became touchstones for my mother and me: "When Rita Joe first come to the city, she told me the cement made her feet hurt," we used to say to each other. Sometimes, after a particularly hard day, my mother might say, "the cement makes my feet hurt."

It would be another fifteen years before I saw a play by an Indigenous writer. Tomson Highway's touring production of *The Rez Sisters* and Margo Kane's one-woman *Moonlodge* both came to Winnipeg, courtesy of Popular Theatre Alliance of Manitoba, and again, I was shocked to discover a part of myself onstage. But *Rita Joe* was first.

At the inaugural Canadian Theatre Conference in Saskatoon in 1998, the theatre scholar Robert Wallace suggested that *The Ecstasy of Rita Joe* was the first truly Canadian play, commissioned as it was for the centennial of Confederation in 1967 and being about the intersection of two cultures and the fallout of that cohabitation. George Ryga, awarded the commission, instead of writing a celebratory play about nationhood, looked around and took stock of where we were as a country. What he showed us was not pretty.

I knew that a 2009 production directed by an Indigenous woman would be radically different from the 1969 iteration. I suspected that it would even be dramatically different from the 2007 production at The Firehall in Vancouver under Donna Spencer's direction.[3]

The first and most profound change was to the Singer. I asked Michelle St John, the former Turtle Gal, to play the role of the Singer. The stage directions introduce the Singer thus:

> At the front of the desk is a lip on stage right side. The SINGER sits here, turned away from the focus of the play. Her songs and accompaniment appear almost accidental. She has all the reactions of a white liberal folklorist with a limited concern and understanding of an ethnic dilemma which she touches in the course of her research and work in compiling and writing folk songs. She serves too as an alter ego to RITA JOE. (15)[4]

Well, that was not going to work. If the purpose of the National Arts Centre production was to shift the white gaze, there would be no white liberal folklorist on the stage.

I seized on the idea that the Singer serves as Rita Joe's alter ego. I looked at the words that the Singer sang, which were Ryga's lyrics. I looked at the last few lines of the play, when the Singer has the penultimate word:

> Oh, the singing bird
>   has found its wings
> And it's soaring!

---

3   Programmed in part to celebrate the twenty-fifth anniversary of The Firehall, which is located in Vancouver's Downtown East Side, Donna Spencer's production maintained Ryga's convention of "a white, liberal folklorist" Singer, casting Tracey Power. And while Donna Spencer is a woman deeply invested in diversity and inclusion, she is white; none of my research has ever unearthed evidence of any other Indigenous director at the helm of a professional production of *Rita Joe*.

4   Unless otherwise noted, all quotations from *The Ecstasy of Rita Joe*, and the accompanying page numbers in brackets, are taken from the following edition: George Ryga, *The Ecstasy of Rita Joe* (Vancouver: Talonbooks, 1970).

My God, what a sight
On the cold fresh wind of morning! . . . (125)

Throughout the play, the Singer sings Rita Joe's heart. This final song is the expression of Rita Joe's spirit leaving her body, joining the Mystery. Fine then, that was how we would approach the Singer. Michelle St John and I entered into a discussion about who the Singer was, how she interacted with Rita Joe. For reasons that we still do not understand, the deer keeps asserting itself to us, Michelle Olson and me, appearing in the choreography for previous work we had done together—*the place between*—and separately—*The Unnatural and Accidental Women*. When I raised the idea of the deer and its connection to spirit with Michelle St John, she sent me two stories and a poem about deer: *Deer Dancer* by Joy Harjo (Creek/Cherokee); *The Deer Women* by Ella Cora Deloria (Lakota/Dakota); and *Deer* by Deborah Miranda (Chumash/Ohlone-Costanoan Esselen). The designers too were excited by the connection, and so the spirit of the deer made its way into the costume of the Singer and the choreography of the play.

We recruited Jennifer Kreisberg, the Tuscarora singer and composer, to co-compose the music for our production. Jennifer and Michelle began to reach out to Secwepemc speakers to help translate some of the lyrics into the language that would have been Rita Joe's mother tongue.

We did not expect resistance. We were shocked when we were told by the administration at Western Canada Theatre, the co-producer, that Ann Mortifee, the original Singer and composer of the music for the original production, considered her music an integral part of the play and that any production must use it.

I do not know how the conflict was resolved, or what it cost the National Arts Centre or Western Canada Theatre. Once I expressed my resolve that this *Rita Joe* would have new Indigenous-composed music, the theatres' administrations worked to make it so, and I am grateful to this day for their support. But it was the first pushback we got on the idea of an Indigenous-led *Rita Joe*, and to this day the irony makes me shake my head.

Jennifer and Michelle wrote music that Michelle would sing onstage, but there were also songs that were sung by members of the company. In a scene when the Old Woman and Eileen Joe are

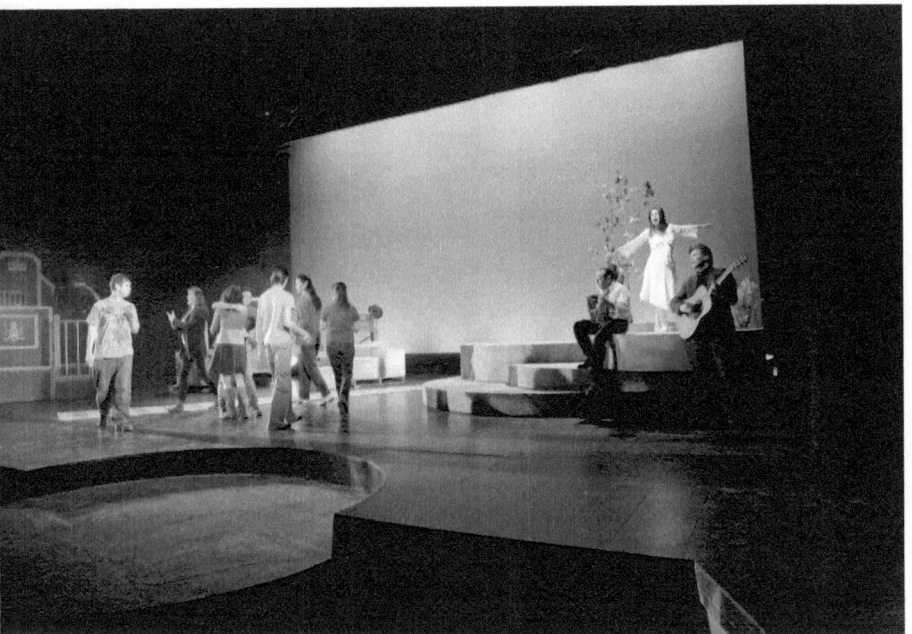

Figure 7.1 The company in the National Arts Centre/Western Canada Theatre Company's production of *The Ecstasy of Rita Joe*, 2009. Credit: Barbara Zimonick

washing clothes (59), the women sang "Bad Seed" with the Singer. In the final moments of the play, Rita Joe stepped out of her murder and walked into the entire community, and they sang together, the dead and the living, the whites and the Natives.

We also began the play with the entire company singing, but in this case they did not sing a Kreisberg/St John composition, but a Buffy Sainte Marie song, "Little Wheel Spin and Spin." Originally released in 1966, Sainte Marie had recorded a softer, more melodic version in 2009 and released it on the album *Running for the Drum*. The song is about how things do not change, and it seemed a fitting way to launch the show, with the company being introduced in choreography by Michelle Olson, meeting each other in groupings that we will see later in the play: Jaimie Paul and David Joe, the Magistrate and Rita Joe, Jaimie Paul and the "Young Indian Men," all singing "Little wheel spin and spin / Big wheels turn around and around."

Sadly, *The Ecstasy of Rita Joe* is not a period piece. All the challenges that Rita Joe faces in 1967 still exist in 2009, still exist now.

In my estimation, George Ryga got a lot of *Rita Joe* right. He knew the poverty and despair that so many Indigenous people confronted when they moved to the city. He identified the racism, both overt and insidious, that Indigenous people dealt with on a daily basis. He traced the system that criminalizes the poor and the marginalized. With his 1967 centennial play, he challenged the mainstream, the settler population, Canadians, to actually see the relationship they had with the first people of this land.

The making visible that George Ryga made manifest in 1967 did not endure, or else how could we be here now, with almost 2,000 missing and murdered Indigenous women? How, indeed, could we have arrived at a shorthand phrase—"missing and murdered Indigenous women"—with its own twenty-first-century hashtag, #MMIW?

I did not consciously set out to Indigenize *The Ecstasy of Rita Joe*. The structure of Ryga's play, the structure that so many find so problematic, seemed to me to lend itself to an Indigenous worldview, to Indigenous theatrical storytelling. Short scenes strung together in a non-linear fashion, characters slipping in and out of timelines, calling to each other across time and space—this was all very like the storytelling we had already undertaken at Native Earth in productions such as *The Unnatural and Accidental Women*, *A Very Polite Genocide*, and *Giiwedin*.

The stage directions that are published in the script describe the first production's set, of course, and while a twenty-first-century production was in no way obligated to recreate that first stage, the description offered clues about the conversation between the text and the stage forty years earlier and informed the discussion we now had in 2008: "A circular ramp," "elevation," "wrapping"; "No curtain is used during the play"; and the use of lighting "for isolating scenes from the past and present in RITA JOE's life" (106).

I was blessed to work with Phillip Tidd and Catherine Hahn as the designers on the production. In September 2008 we met in Vancouver to jam on ideas. Although Phillip was contracted to design the set and Catherine the costumes, the ideas generated at the first jam session were the result of three minds working together. We talked about the way the scenes flowed into each other, the balance of the city and Rita Joe's home community, the train that eventually claims Jaimie Paul. Phillip's set was bisected by the murderous train

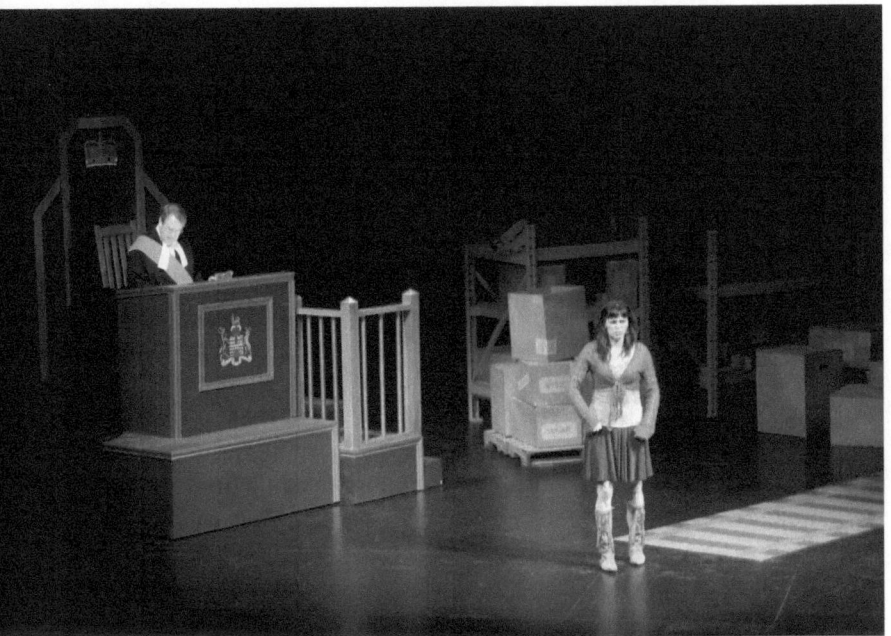

Figure 7.2 Layne Coleman and Lisa C. Ravensbergen in the National Arts Centre/
Western Canada Theatre Company's production of *The Ecstasy of Rita Joe*, 2009.
Credit: Barbara Zimonick

tracks; the cityscape stage right, the "rez" stage left. The city side
of the stage was all squares and blocks; the Magistrate's desk was
elevated on a platform that raised him two feet above the deck—and
Rita Joe. To his right, the box where the witnesses testify against Rita
Joe was enclosed in railings. Mr. Homer's "Centre," just left and up-
stage of the Magistrate, was a set of six-foot shelving units, stacked
with boxes of donations and supplies marked with "Pea Soup Mix"
and "Sugar". There were lots of boxes of Sugar, that insidious tool of
colonization, that handmaiden of diabetes. We called Mr. Homer's
space The Trading Post, where Jaimie Paul and the other Young
Indian Men come to trade on their poverty and hunger with Mr.
Homer, who dispenses stew and second-hand clothes.

By contrast, the "rez," Rita Joe's home community, was all circles: five circular discs stacked irregularly on each other, creating
a series of elevations. On the top circle was a stump that sprouted
new growth, a young sapling growing out of the old tree. The small-
est circle, attached to the rest but off to one side, was the Singer's

spot, her own spirit place, where she sat on a length of a felled tree, surrounded by her drum and a tuft of sage that the set designer had harvested from the hills around Kamloops, leaving tobacco in acknowledgement and thanks. From this spot the Singer oversaw the action of the play, part of the community but not interacting with them, always watching Rita Joe, in the city as in the community, over time and space.

The other major playing space was what we called 'the rez in the city,' Jaimie Paul's room, the city streets that Jaimie Paul inhabits with his crew, the Young Indian Men, the space that David Joe comes to when he comes to retrieve Rita Joe from the city. Like the "rez," the rez in the city is made of circles, but they are cut out, depressions instead of elevations, dropping ten inches at a time, just as the "rez" risers rose in ten-inch increments, a kind of negative image of Rita Joe's home.

Catherine Hahn's costumes were timeless, neither anchoring us in the past century, nor cementing us in the present. The urban Indigenous characters looked like they had dressed themselves out of Mr. Homer's donations, the policeman looked like a policeman, the Magistrate like a judge, the priest like a priest in sports jacket and Roman collar. The Singer, now identified as a deer spirit, was clothed in white with deerskin, knee-high moccasins that she ended up sewing herself.

We came into the room to begin the work. We had been very, very careful in the casting. I suspected that the rehearsal process would be challenging for everyone, for a number of reasons, and I wanted to create a room that began in a good way, populated with artists who wanted to be there because they were invested in the telling of the story. Artists who were generous and kind and patient. Artists who could—who would be willing to—work across cultures. Artists who would know that they did not know everything and be willing to work in the unknowing for a while. Artists who would know that they did not know everything and would be willing and able and open to learn.

I was also aware of my own status—or lack of status—as a director. I am a woman, I am Indigenous, and while I was at the time the artistic director of Native Earth Performing Arts, the oldest professional Indigenous theatre in Canada, most people never saw the work at Native Earth. While I am a confident director, I also practice

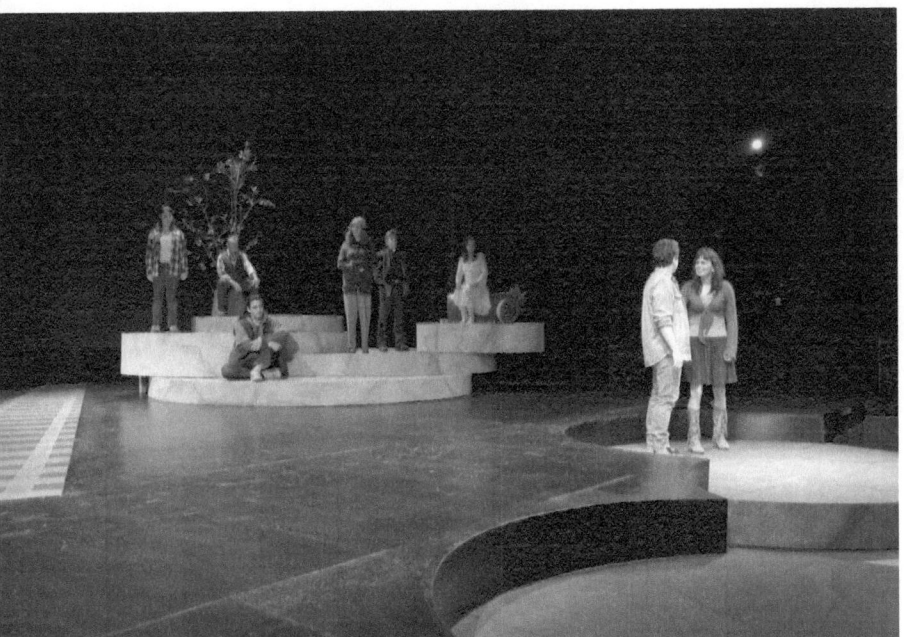

Figure 7.3 Falen Johnson, August Schellenberg, Jeremy Proulx, Renae Morriseau, Todd Duckworth, Michelle St John, Kevin Loring, Lisa C. Ravensbergen in the National Arts Centre/Western Canada Theatre Company's production of *The Ecstasy of Rita Joe*, 2009. Credit: Barbara Zimonick

a non-hierarchical, collaborative directing style which can be interpreted as irresolute; as my general manager at Native Earth often said, "Don't mistake her flexibility for weakness." I work closely with a choreographer, often the same choreographer, Michelle Olson (Tr'ondëk Hwëch'in), the artistic director of Raven Spirit Dance in Vancouver, and we work more as co-directors, the text and action and movement in constant dialogue with each other. But for actors who are trained to the director-as-dictator model of theatre making, the easy sharing of responsibilities, the comfort with not-knowing that Michelle and I manifest in the room can be spooky.

Peter Hinton had suggested a senior, highly respected actor for the role of the Magistrate in the co-production. While I was a huge fan of this actor and his work, having watched him for the past twenty-five years, I knew that he would not be directed by me, in the style in which I worked. I countered with suggestions of middle-aged actors who would be willing to enter into the process of my room, willing to dance, to sing, to be a part of a community, in spite of the weight of the role of the Magistrate. Each time an actor declined the role, because of scheduling conflicts or the vicissitudes of life, Peter would again suggest this actor. I understood his desire; the stature of the actor would lend this production gravitas, place on it his imprimatur, validate me. I was tempted, for I would have loved to have worked with so experienced an artist, but I knew also that it would not work.

In the end I was thrilled to be able to cast Layne Coleman as the Magistrate. Layne had been around in the trenches of Canadian theatre for as long as I had been aware there was such a thing, a Canadian theatre, co-founding 25th Street Theatre in Saskatoon in the 1970s, serving as the artistic director there in the 1980s. By the time I got to Toronto in 2002, he was the artistic director of Theatre Passe Muraille, one of Canada's oldest and most influential alternative theatres. Most importantly, I knew Layne and knew him to be a good man, sensitive to the changing demographic of theatre-makers and conscious of the fact that Canadian theatres were not quick to embrace the change. I knew him to be aware of his own privilege and power. Further, as an actor who had been a part of early Canadian collective creations, I knew that he would be open to the organic, physical, music-infused process that *Rita Joe* would be.

While Peter had been strongly promoting his choice of actor for the role of the Magistrate in order to have some (albeit Canadian) 'star' power, we already had it in the person of August Schellenberg (Mohawk), who was to play David Joe, Rita's father. Forty years earlier, in the premiere production, Augie had created the role of Jaimie Paul. In the intervening years he had been a working stage and television actor and a movie star, playing everything from Willy's keeper, Randolph Johnson, in *Free Willy* (I, II, and III) to Sitting Bull in HBO's *Bury My Heart At Wounded Knee*.

The rest of the cast was gathered from all over the country: Lisa C. Ravensbergen (Ojibwe/Swampy Cree) and Kevin Loring (Nlaka'pamux), who were reprising their roles as Rita Joe and Jaimie Paul from the 2007 Firehall production, live in Vancouver, as does Renae Morrisseau (Saulteaux/Cree); Ryan Cunningham (Métis) and Telly James (Siksika) came from Alberta; Jeremy Proulx (Ojibwe/Oneida), Michelle St John (Wampanoag), and Falen Johnson (Tuscarora/Mohawk) all live in Toronto. Ottawa actors Todd

Duckworth and Pierre Brault played the Priest and Mr. Homer, respectively, and Vancouverite Darcey Johnson completed the company in the role of the Policeman.

PRODUCTION CREDITS

Creative Team

Director	Yvette NOLAN
Musical Director	Micah BARNES
Set Designer	Philip TIDD
Costume Designer	Catherine HAHN
Lighting Designer	Michelle RAMSAY
Choreographer	Michelle OLSON
Composers	Jennifer KREISBERG and Michelle ST. JOHN

Cast

Mr. Homer/Murderer	Pierre BRAULT
Magistrate	Layne COLEMAN
Policeman	Darcey JOHNSON
Young Indian Man/Witness/Murderer	Ryan CUNNINGHAM
Priest/Witness/Murderer	Todd DUCKWORTH
Young Indian Man	Telly JAMES
Eileen	Falen JOHNSON
Jaimie Paul	Kevin LORING
Teacher/Old Woman	Renae MORRISEAU
Young Indian Man/Murderer	Jeremy PROULX
Rita Joe	Lisa C. RAVENSBERGEN
David Joe	August SCHELLENBERG
Singer	Michelle ST. JOHN

Stage Management Team

Stage Manager	Kelly MANSON
Assistant Stage Manager	Samira ROSE

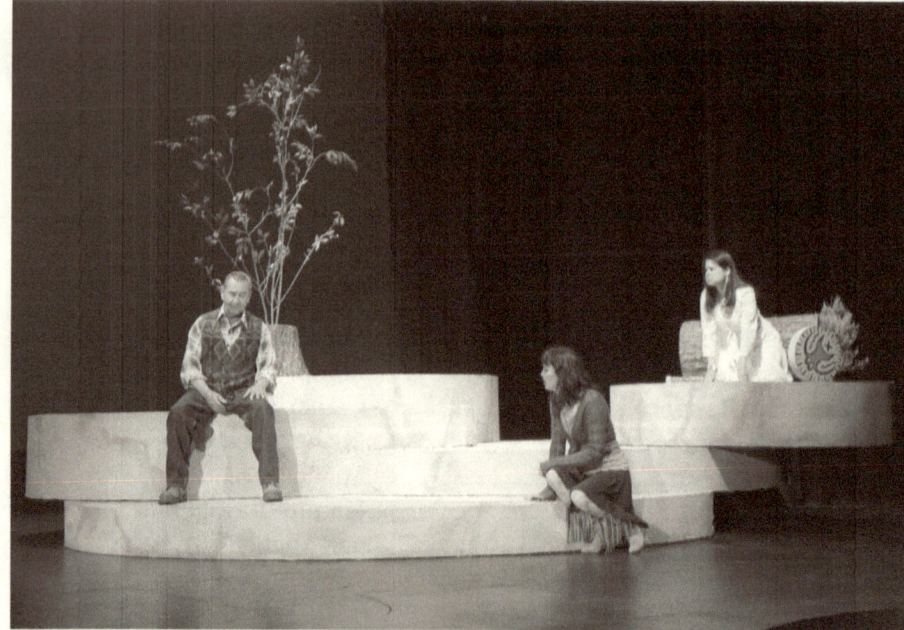

Figure 7.4 August Schellenberg, Lisa C. Ravensbergen, Michelle St. John in the National Arts Centre/Western Canada Theatre Company's production of *The Ecstasy of Rita Joe*, 2009. Credit: Barbara Zimonick

We began the work in the room at Western Canadian Theatre Company's home in Kamloops, BC. This could be Rita Joe's land, this swath of the BC interior that was home to the Secwepemc people. Although Rita Joe is not identified as belonging to any particular nation, the Magistrate tells a story about holidaying "in the Cariboo country" (18) and seeing a child that looked like her, which means she could be Nlaka'pamux, Stl'atl'imx, Secwepemc, Tsilqot'in, Dakelhne, if she were from the territory . . . . But George Ryga wrote much of *Rita Joe* at the table in his house in Summerland, in the Okanagan, home of the Siylx people, so she could have been Siylx as well. Still, our Rita Joe had to be from somewhere, not just anywhere, and so, for our purposes she was Secwepemc. Hence the decision to translate some of the lyrics into Secwepemc.

We began work in the room and it proceeded apace. We sang, under the skilful and generous musical direction of Micah Barnes. We danced and moved to Michelle Olson's choreography, building the opening entrance.

I thought we were doing fine, until one day, about ten days into the rehearsal process, one of the non-Indigenous actors snapped at me, "I am not used to workshopping an existing script! I know how to workshop a new play, but I didn't expect to be workshopping a script that's been around for forty years!"

In my memory the actor is supine on the floor, yelling up at me. I don't know if that is actually the way it happened, or if that is just my way of understanding the shift we were undertaking. Yes, he was right; we were workshopping the script. We were, by examining the play through a different filter, an Indigenous gaze, altering it. Whose theory is that, about the act of observing something changing it? The Heisenberg effect?[5]

George Ryga's empathy notwithstanding, the play was written from a position in the dominant culture. George Ryga could see the injustice and trace the systemic racism that contributed to Rita Joe's and Jaimie Paul's untimely ends and animate it on the stage for audiences to witness, but ultimately, his place in the story is separate from the experience of his characters. For the eleven Indigenous artists in the room, this was our story from the inside. Each of us knew the reality of being marginalized in our own country, on our own land, even though our experiences were widely disparate. Many of us were children of residential school survivors, some of us had been or had relatives who were street-engaged, many of us had direct experience with poverty and addiction issues, many of us had experienced some kind of interaction with the judicial system, and all of us—all of us—were living in cities, away from our home communities, where, sometimes, the cement made our feet hurt.

The actor who in my memory is yelling up at me, over whom I tower, was right. We *were* workshopping the script. We were in fact translating it, adapting it, shifting the gaze from a dominant culture to an Indigenous view.

Change is difficult. Sometimes we cling to our positions, of power or of weakness, of privilege or of victimhood. Sometimes what is known is more comfortable than stepping into the unknown.

---

5   The German Nobel-winning scientist Werner Heisenberg (1901–1976), one of the pioneers in quantum mechanics, posited that the very act of observing something changes it, a process also referred to as 'the observer effect.'

My mother used to tell a—a what? an adage? a cautionary tale?—about change: "I walk down the street, I see the hole, I fall into the hole. I climb out of the hole. I walk down the street, I see the hole. I walk around the hole. I walk down the street, I see the hole, I fall into the hole . . . ." Change is a process, not a fixed point at which we arrive.

When I agreed to direct *Rita Joe*, I was clear that I did not want to end the play with another dead Indigenous woman on the floor. So many of the works coming out of the Indigenous theatre community featured the rape and/or murder of Indigenous women that it was practically a trope. I am no exception; my play *Annie Mae's Movement*[6] about the Mi'kmaq warrior Anna Mae Pictou Aquash ends with her murder. Perhaps it is the most apt metaphor for the pillaging of a country and the people who were here, perhaps it is the howl of a people who have been silenced for so long by government acts and policies, but a survey of the Indigenous body of work offers an awe-inspiring list of women raped and/or murdered. Even when the play is a celebration of survivance, the stories of violence are still there; during the directing of the Turtle Gals' production, *The Only Good Indian . . .*,[7] I broke up the room by saying, innocently, "All right, let's take it from 'rape and mutilation' . . . ."

So, entering into the world of Rita Joe I knew that the play could not end with "her twisted, broken body" (124) on the stage. I did not anticipate the resistance I would meet in abstracting the rape and murder of Rita Joe.

The final four pages of the text are largely stage directions describing the beating and murder of Jaimie Paul, the rape, murder, and attempted "necrophillac rape" (124) of Rita Joe, and the funeral of the two. The final words are those of the Singer, as noted before, singing Rita Joe's soul soaring, followed by the words of Eileen, Rita's sister,

When Rita Joe first come to the city, she told me . . .
The cement made her feet hurt. (126)

---

6 First produced in 1998 by Hardly Art in Whitehorse, Winnipeg, and Halifax.
7 Produced by Turtle Gals Performance Ensemble in 2007 in Toronto.

My idea of Rita Joe's death was that she did not end, she was not destroyed, but rather passed over, from this world to the spirit world, to the place where the ancestors were, the place where the Singer existed, the place where loved ones were reunited, where communities were whole and healthy again. I wanted to see that; I wanted to show that to audiences, that we were not beaten, that we could not be beaten into disappearing, that we were still here, our ancestors were here, our spirits live on.

Michelle Olson and I worked the final scene over and over, trying different ways of raising Rita Joe. Eventually, Michelle created a beautiful/terrible scene in which the Murderers continue to assault Rita Joe; the four of them gathered around the imagined woman, but Rita Joe herself gets up downstage, awaking in another place. Turning, she sees the community, the dead and the living, the Singer amongst them. They begin to sing the Kreisberg/St John composition *Ascension*. Rita Joe walks to them, is met by the Singer, and the two of them walk up to the top level to join David Joe and Jaimie Paul. By now, the Murderers have fled, and the image we are left with is a whole community, Indigenous and not, singing together.

Coincidentally, I was working with Michelle Olson on another project when I was writing this chapter, and so had the opportunity to ask her about that moment.

> I use cosmology here—I wonder if it is worldview?—interesting to think about these two words. Anyways. It is worldview/cosmology that made us put the dramatic beats where they were . . . it is what made us change . . . "JAIMIE!!!" into "Jaimie?" This was the moment that changed everything . . . .

I had forgotten that critical change, a change in punctuation that translated into a change in attack and shifted the dramatic beat. Rita Joe was no longer a body savaged, but a spirit *invictus*, unconquered. The Murderers were still carrying out their attack, but Rita Joe's spirit was no longer part of it. Michelle had spoken to people who thought it was important that the audience see the men on the body of the woman, but Michelle asserts, "we placed Rita front centre stage, you could not deny her . . . ."

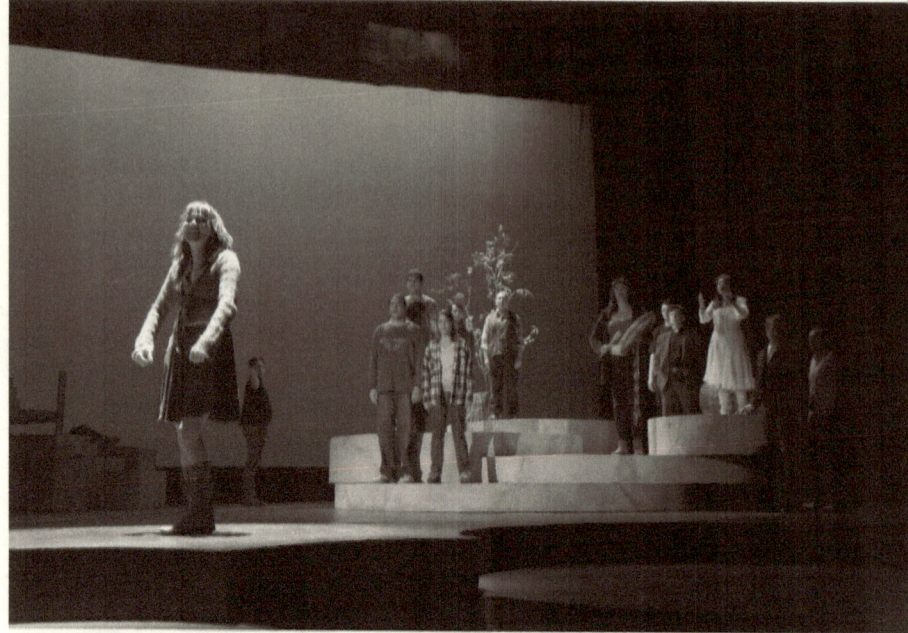

Figure 7.5 Lisa C. Ravensbergen, Kevin Loring, Jeremy Proulx, Ryan Cunningham, Falen Johnson, Telly James, August Schellenberg, Renae Morriseau, Darcey Johnson, Todd Duckworth, Michelle St. John, Layne Coleman, and Pierre Brault in the National Arts Centre/Western Canada Theatre Company's production of *The Ecstasy of Rita Joe*, 2009. Credit: Barbara Zimonick

Here then was the "ecstasy" of Rita Joe. At the beginning of the process, I had brought both the definition and etymology of the word to the company, as well as a photograph of Bernini's sculpture, *The Ecstasy of St Teresa*. For me, the idea of *extasis*—displacement—describes the entire experience of Rita Joe, buffeted from this memory to the next, transported between time and across space. In Bernini's sculpture the saint is being pierced by an angel, a point where the earthly and the divine meet; in the ending I envisioned, Rita Joe transcends the earthly, the mortal, stepping out of the corporeal and into the spirit.

The actors rebelled. Not all of them, but there was a definite schism in the company about the way we were staging Rita Joe's rape and murder. Some felt that by abstracting the violence we were pulling our punch, diminishing the horror of the violence visited on Indigenous women. Some felt that we were letting audiences who were complicit in the system that allowed—practically invited—this violence off the hook.

I disagreed. I felt that freeing Rita Joe from the brutalization she receives at the hands of the Murderers allows the audience to feel more than just guilt or horror, enables them to keep watching, rather than turn their faces away. After all, is that not how we had arrived at this moment in time where the Canadian people were able to not see the Indigenous people with whom they lived? Is that not how 2,000 Indigenous women were disappeared, because Canadians were able to turn their faces away? Out of sight, out of mind. Is that not what George Ryga had set out to do forty years earlier: force us all to look and to actually see what our relationships were?

I have another memory from that rehearsal period in Kamloops, but like so many memories it is fuzzy, missing details. I remember the story, but not the teller. I have asked a couple of colleagues if they remember, but they too remember only the story and cannot be sure who first told it. In the end, the facts are not critical; it is the truth that matters.

One morning, as the company gathered, pouring coffees and foraging for snacks, one of the senior actors said, very excited, "We met Rita Joe last night!" "What?" I said, and he proceeded to tell me about the young Indigenous woman some of them had met in the bar the night before and how she was Rita Joe. He told me details, and he was excited about the encounter, that this young woman had pretty much walked out of the pages of our play and into the bar, but I was shaken and sad. I imagined the young woman, come to the city from some community, feeling lonely and alien, looking for comfort and company in a bottle or a casual encounter. I thought about all the Rita Joes in all the bars and friendship centres and cheap hotels, on all the streets and corners of all the cities in this country we now call Canada.

I sent a quick prayer up for her, that particular Rita Joe, and turned to go into the rehearsal room to continue the work.

REFERENCES

Deloria, Ella Cora. "The Deer Women." In *Through the Eye of the Deer*, edited by Carolyn Dunn and Carol Comfort, 29–31.

Dunn, Carolyn, and Carol Comfort, eds. *Through the Eye of the Deer: An Anthology of Native American Women Writers*. San Francisco: Aunt Lute Books, 1999.

Harjo, Joy. "Deer Dancer." In *Through the Eye of the Deer*, edited by Carolyn Dunn and Carol Comfort, 29–31.

Jennings, Sarah. *Art and Politics: The History of the National Arts Centre*. Toronto: Dundern Press, 2009.

Miranda, Deborah. "Deer." In *Through the Eye of the Deer*, edited by Carolyn Dunn and Carol Comfort, 101–103.

Ryga, George. *The Ecstasy of Rita Joe*. Vancouver: Talonbooks, 1970.

8

CRADLING SPACE: TOWARDS AN INDIGENOUS DRAMATURGY ON TURTLE ISLAND

Dione Joseph

The history of dramaturgy can be traced back to the mid eighteenth century when its practice was focused on the complexities of translating texts—in particular mid-eighteenth-century and other classical plays—into theatrical performance. Within a Eurocentric paradigm, understandings of dramaturgy can be traced to secularization of the form in the sixteenth century and reflect the critical examination of a play's structure and organization as well as input into the development of the process of the play. The emphasis, within the world of the play, has almost without contention focused on developing the written text.

As Patrice Pavis explains, "dramaturgy is a rich, varied, confused and tormented landscape,"[1] but there is scope to examine the

---

1 Patrice Pavis, "Dramaturgie et postdramaturgie," in *Alternative Dramaturgies of the New Millennium in Arabo-Islamic Context and Beyond: Selected Papers from the 10th Annual Meeting of the Tangier International Conferences: Performing Tangier 2014,* ▶

subtleties of various approaches within an Indigenous dramaturgical space. In my conversations with Indigenous artists, I aim to locate specific theatre processes and practices within a dialogue that responds to dramaturgy as distinctively land-based. Using this premise, these practices contextualize the political, social, and spiritual development of Indigenous narratives. Subsequently, these are brought together under an overarching framework that allows specificity of individual practices and spaces to be valued and legitimized on their own terms. Cradling space, therefore, is a returning inwards to embrace the creative individual's work and its world in ways that are nurturing, holistic, and supportive. It is a process through which space is constructed both spatially and temporally to facilitate a deliberate and purposeful Indigenous understanding of bodies, minds, and spirits—and their intersections. However, conventionally, dramaturgy is generally conceived differently. Often, a dramaturge is a theatre specialist responsible for providing critical support and feedback to the playwright and, occasionally, to the director. The process can range from traditional forms of script advice to responding to other elements such as narrative arcs and plot, as well as providing context and history of earlier productions. Depending on the nature of the production, the dramaturge may also offer programme notes or develop audience-engagement plans. The role of the dramaturge also varies according to the requirements of the production, relationship with the playwright and/or director, and expectations of the company. Still, like all aspects of performance, including 'performing' any creative role (playwright, director, actor), there are multiple historical paradigms that stretch across time and space. Within a western European framework, dramaturgy owes its development to Gotthold Lessing and his *Hamburg Treatise*.[2] By contrast, other forms of dramaturgical input, intervention, and action have had their roots in non-text-related performance that take into account mime, puppetry, oral traditions, and mask work, as well as the effects of intergenerational legacies, diaspora, migrations, and fluid borders.

....

◂ eds. Khalid Amine and George F. Robertson (Tangier: Collaborative Media International, 2015), 15–21.

2   Gotthold E. Lessing, *Hamburgische Dramaturgie* (Hamburg, 1767; University of Duisburg, 2012).

Nevertheless, as the role of the dramaturge and the understanding of what constitutes the dramaturgical act have evolved, the notion of dramaturgy has also been contextualized to serve different forms of theatrical and performative storytelling. Grounded in an Indigenous worldview, this chapter proposes the notion of 'cradling space,' a conceptual and pragmatic understanding of dramaturgy to describe how different environments, specifically native lands, contribute to the development of land-based Indigenous narratives and performance. These practices, while increasingly articulated and described in the written form, are not simply adaptations of conventional dramaturgy, but rather practices that have developed outside the paradigms of the written text and address a different process, one that emphasizes relationships outside black words on white pages.

As a writer, director, and dramaturge from Aotearoa (New Zealand), my writing here is located within my larger and ongoing project to explore dramaturgy within culturally specific contexts. On two separate occasions I had the opportunity to be based in Saskatoon, Saskatchewan—for a period of five weeks in 2014 and ten days in 2015—as a performance scholar and practitioner. During my second visit, as a result of growing networks, relationships, and a deeper understanding of Indigenous performance traditions from the region, I invited Cree playwright and academic Kenneth T. Williams (George Gordon First Nation in Treaty 4 Territory) and Cree actor, playwright, and director Curtis Peeteetuce (Beardy and Okemasis First Nation) to join me in a face-to-face discussion on Indigenous dramaturgy in Saskatoon. These conversations, held over cups of tea, were also an exercise in cradling space, in allowing this concept to function simultaneously on two levels: as a verb to describe a non-linear engagement with text prioritizing alternative approaches to space and time; and also as an adjective descriptive of a more inclusive approach, one that values multiplicities, nuances, and subtleties to refute any notion of a pan-Indigenous dramaturgy.

The concept of an Indigenous dramaturgy is not new. For example, in 2013, Dr. Rachael Swain and Dalisa Pigram, artistic directors of Marrugecku, developed a research and development project called *Listening to Country*. Based in Broome, a coastal and pearling town in the Kimberly region of Western Australia, the project developed an ongoing set of questions about the nature and function of Indigenous dramaturgy for contemporary intercultural-Indigenous dance theatre. The description outlines that "this dramaturgy requires a specific reflection of Indigenous 'being in place and time' in a contemporary world; it is multi vocal and multi temporal."[3] Across the Pacific, Indigenous dramaturgies are explored differently again. Danish Greenlandic philosopher, author, playwright, and dramaturge Ulla Ryum proposes a "spiral dramaturgy," which according to Siri Hansen, is characterized by an emphasis on a cause-effect relationship based on inner associative processes rather than chronological outer actions.[4] Academic research has also shown a recent surge in this field. Based in Toronto, Monique Mojica, Guna-Rappanhock performer, playwright, and dramaturge, has contributed to the field of Indigenous dramaturgy through her seminal works *Princess Pocahontas and the Blue Spots* and *Chocolate Woman Dreams the Milky Way*. Her workshop and performance director, Jill Carter, has written extensively about *Chocolate Woman Dreams the Milky Way* and explains how an organic Indigenous dramaturgical methodology evolves from traditional stories to develop a pictorial score known as a "Guna Laban."[5] Chadwick Allen's "Performing Serpent Mound: A Trans-Indigenous Meditation" also draws upon Mojica's evolving process of creating an Indigenous dramaturgy rooted in land-based embodied research. This process, one that began in 2011 with a team of Indigenous artists, focuses on effigy mounds and earthworks as the first literary structures on this land. Through engaging with the mounds as 'Indigenous literature' Mojica disrupts colonial understanding that scripts are exclusively written texts.[6]

In Aotearoa, Māori are recognized as *tangata whenua* (people of the land), while those who have migrated from the surrounding Polynesian islands in the Pacific are considered *tangata Pasifika* (people from the Pacific). While there is no shared published consensus

3   Rachael Swain, *Listening to Country* (2013), http://www.marrugeku.com.au/listening_to_country_2013/, accessed December 28, 2016.

4   Siri Hansen, as cited in Knut Ove Arntzen, "Sámi and Indigenous Theatre: The Nomadic Perspective and the Notion of a Spiral Dramaturgy," *Trans* 19 (May 2016), http://www.inst.at/trans/19/sami-and- indigenous-theatre/.

5   Jill Carter, "*Chocolate Woman* Visions an Organic Dramaturgy: Blocking-Notation for the Indigenous soul," *Canadian Woman Studies* 26, no. 3/4 (2008): 173.

6   Chadwick Allen, "Performing Serpent Mound: A Trans-Indigenous Meditation," *Theatre Journal* 67, no. 3 (2015): 391–411.

on a Māori or Pasifika dramaturgy, my own conversations with a number of different practitioners, including playwrights, directors, actors, and choreographers, have highlighted a number of shared characteristics. These include observing *tikanga* (protocols), welcome ceremonies, the presence of *kaumātua* (elders), and the non-linear process that involves a community-centric work.[7] These examples highlight that, far from any notion of a generic pan-Indigenous dramaturgical process or even definition, the subtleties and differences between the approaches of different First Nations states (whether in New Zealand, Australia, Canada, or Guatemala, Japan, or Norway) cannot be generalized.

Within an Indigenous performing arts space, dramaturgy also has its own history. For example, Indigenous Australia has a performance history that stretches back 40,000 years. The aesthetics of Indigenous theatre reflect an emphasis on story, song, ritual, ceremony, and dance, as well as a relationship to land and country, oral tradition, mythology, and a notion of time that refuses to be encapsulated in rigid frameworks. The works of Sydney's Bangarra Dance Theatre, for example, depict these performance traditions within a contemporary context. The company has not only resident cultural advisors, but also specific programmes for youth, outreach development, and opportunities to connect to both urban and regional communities. Similarly, the work of Atamira Dance Theatre and Black Grace, both based in Auckland, are also similar in their approach to acknowledging, developing, and expanding a performance history of Aotearoa that existed before colonization. The performance traditions of Australia and Aotearoa are very different, but it is more than simply distinguishing between two Indigenous communities across the ditch. The different nation states in Australia and the different *iwi* (tribes) and *hapu* (subtribes) in Aotearoa also have unique performance histories, languages, customs, gender roles, and presentation styles. The difference, therefore, lies in the fact that, like the conventions and traditions associated with Western performance practice, Indigenous performance-making has an expansive performance vocabulary that is inclusive of its own distinctive dramaturgical structures.

---

7   Dione Joseph, "Towards a New Zealand Dramaturgy: A Maverick Undertaking in 2016, Part I," *The Theatre Times*, January 17, 2017, https://thetheatretimes.com/new-zealand-dramaturgy-maverick-undertaking-2016-part-i/.

Within an Indigenous ontology the act of dramaturgical input is an intervention; it is a process that stretches across a genealogical spectrum inclusive of both time and space, and places story and community at the centre of the work, allowing for a multidirectional dialogue to take place that is upheld through ritual, ceremony, and story. For example, Toronto-based Kaha:wi Dance Theatre's recent production of *Re-Quickening* featured artists from various different Indigenous nations from Turtle Island, Australia, and Aotearoa, and the multiplicity of different Indigenous performance traditions connected and intersected across all three land masses, their natural features, and their Indigenous peoples. There is no broad-brush-stroke category into which Kaha:wi's production can be, or indeed should be, slotted. It is a work that brought together various Indigenous artists to develop a creative trans-Indigenous exploration, but it did so while simultaneously upholding the *mana* (spiritual strength, authority, prestige, integrity, inherent status) of its story-weavers and providing an alternative to both the structure and infrastructure of conventional notions of theatre. It is a form of dramaturgy that goes beyond Lessing's original premise that the practice concerned itself with the "aesthetics of composition, narrative arcs, blocking and audience from a literary historiographical perspective"[8] and invites a far more rhizomatic approach.

Therefore, in academic discourse, cradling space is not scribed as a reflection of paper-based paradigms, but rather as an ontological perspective on embodiment. My offering to the conversation would be that the breadth of ceremony, prayer, ritual, and the connection to the spirit also gift life into the practice, enabling it to extend outwards to serve, heal, shift and empower, and move space. It suggests an understanding of the various layers of performance-making that extends far beyond the binaries of inherited colonial labels and emphasizes the relationship to land and space, its movement, and, in turn, the sculpting of multilayered works.

Again, a suggested relationship between land and performance is not new. According to David Greenwood (formerly Gruenewald), Canada Research Chair in Environmental Education at Lakehead University, if human beings are responsible for the shaping and the making of place, we "must become conscious of ourselves as place

---

8   Lessing, *Hamburgische Dramaturgie.*

makers and participants in the sociopolitical process of place making."[9] Perceiving and knowing that place is always in the flux and
flow of becoming is crucial to ensuring that performance-making
also reflects this state of dynamism. This notion of moving through
space is fundamental to engaging with Indigenous dramaturgy: that is,
realizing that through a variety of verbal and non-verbal forms, performances are one of the most potent expressions of articulation and
that the framing of these performances moves beyond the finite form
of a production on stage. Whether in the form of story, song, drama, or
dance, these forms of performance are both aesthetic and ontological
expressions that affirm the body as a basis for a "mutuality through
which people and land can continue indefinitely through time"[10] and
contribute to a larger discourse that is both community-centric and
committed to the furthering of an embodied narrative. Dramaturgy,
therefore, within an Indigenous context, can also be seen as a performed discourse connecting people with their own and each other's
lived lives directly and immediately while allowing the external expression of the human condition and its interrelations to be produced
within a context highly specific to its own Indigenous ontology.

Canadian dramaturgy experienced its own growth spurt during
the 1970s when developing new works (in both English and French)
was considered critical to the development of the canon. Bruce
Barton's *Developing Nation* is a seminal collection that underscores the
wealth of work on dramaturgy undertaken over the past two decades.
In his introduction he explains that, while "dramaturgy resists the
mantle of stable definition and instead insists on perpetually re-defin-
ing itself in relation to its context ... this wary elusiveness concerning
definitions in no way precludes concrete descriptions and analysis of
its 'working parts.'"[11] Equally, Barton also addresses the conceptual
difference of an "*understanding* of dramaturgy" and the "approach

---

9   David A. Gruenewald, "Foundations of Place: A Multidisciplinary Framework
    for Place-Conscious Education," *American Educational Research Journal* 40, no.
    3 (2003): 627.
10 Annette Hamilton, "Gender, Aesthetics and Performance," in *The Oxford
    Companion to Aboriginal Art and Culture,* eds. Sylvia Kleinert, Margo Neale, and
    Robyne Bancroft (Melbourne: Oxford University Press, 2000), 75.
11 Bruce Barton, "Introduction: Creating Spaces," in *Developing Nation: New Play
    Creation in Englishspeaking Canada,* ed. Bruce Barton (Toronto: Playwrights
    Canada Press, 2008), v.

to its *practice*."[12] He also highlights that when *Canadian Theatre Review* (*CTR*) first published a special issue on new play development in 1986, the authors specifically addressed the "possibilities and—most emphatically—the potential pitfalls in developmental *workshops*."[13] Ten years later, developmental dramaturgy was the focus of the next *CTR* issue and brought a different set of conversations to the fore. Barton points out this includes Sky Gilbert's process-as-product approach, which, when placed next to Bob White's product-as-process practice, suggests that expansion is the only way forward.[14] Fast forward to 2004 and a deepening cultural awareness permeates *CTR*'s third issue with a radical shift to a "move 'beyond the text,'" an argument that suggests that text-based dramaturgy can be enhanced through an "enlarged set of techniques and strategies and an enlivened palette of perspectives."[15] It is within this ongoing and feeling conversation that cradling space finds itself—a dramaturgy of the people and the land shaped by connections to the ancestors, the land, and the experience of the world that is unique to Indigenous people here on Turtle Island.

Saskatchewan, located within the wider context of this rich history, also has its own history of dramaturgy, one that extends to over twenty-five years at the Saskatchewan Playwrights Centre (SPC) and has supported the growth of a number of playwrights in the region. According to Pam Bustin, playwright and long-time member of the SPC, a group of playwrights, most of them members of the Saskatchewan Writers Guild (founded in 1969), came together in 1982 to create a playwright-run organization.[16] According to the website, their mandate is to "provide means for Saskatchewan playwrights to develop plays, and to ensure Saskatchewan voices are heard," and their primary objective is to "foster the development of Saskatchewan plays in a risk-friendly environment."[17] This emphasis

---

12 Barton, "Introduction," v.

13 *Ibid.*, x.

14 *Ibid.*, xi.

15 *Ibid.*

16 Pam Bustin, "Between the Bottles and the Knives: Celebrating Twenty-Five Years with the Saskatchewan Playwrights Centre," in *West Words: Celebrating Western Canadian Theatre and Playwriting*, ed. Moira J. Day (Regina: Canadian Plains Research Centre Press, 2011), 86.

17 Saskatchewan Playwrights Centre, "About," https://saskplaywrights.ca, accessed July 13, 2018.

on developing, but not producing, plays led to a distinctive development strategy, which, as Bustin summarizes, was to "provide an annual series of professional workshops of new Saskatchewan plays including a public event that showcased plays in development."[18] She goes on to highlight that the defining feature of SPC, and one of the contributors to its longevity and success, is the fact that the emphasis is not on production, but development:

> We all want our plays produced, but that's not what SPC does. What we do, and have been doing very well for over twenty-five years, is to develop the stories our members bring to the table—whether or not these stories ever make it to the stage. We are also developing dramaturges, directors, actors, an audience that is excited about new work, and most importantly Saskatchewan playwrights.[19]

Indigenous playwrights in Saskatchewan are distinctive from the wider collective, not simply because of their Indigeneity, but because through an Indigenous understanding and connection to the land, their experience of the same space is markedly different from other Saskatchewan playwrights. Both Kenneth T. Williams and Curtis Peeteetuce have had their work developed by SPC. Three of Williams' plays received dramaturgical support: *Three Little Birds* (2008), *Gordon Winter* (2011), and, most recently, *In Care* (2016). Tantoo Cardinal, playing Annie Bird in the cast of *Three Little Birds*, provided valuable grounding in Indigenous thought and action for the character, while Yvette Nolan was the Indigenous dramaturge on the work *In Care*. Reflecting upon his experiences, as well as the larger dramaturgical landscape in Saskatoon, Williams highlighted that while there is an unwritten and often unspoken commitment to dramaturgy by Indigenous practitioners and for Indigenous practitioners, the actual resources available to support the ongoing development of an Indigenous dramaturgy begin with conversations that investigate the purpose of the work and the world of the play.

"I had trouble with dramaturgy right from the beginning because I didn't have a functional concept of theatre," says Williams. "I was a

---

18 Bustin, "Between," 87.
19 *Ibid.*

short story writer and novelist and I couldn't grasp some of the basic questions of dramaturgy."[20] However, he adds, "I do believe there is an Indigenous dramaturgy because I believe there is a worldview that is unique to First Nations; it evolves from experience and takes shape as the commonalities of the individual experience coalesce." Indigenous dramaturgy, he argues, is one of the leading motivations that continues to propel artists; it goes beyond structures for script and logistics of a production and interrogates the underlying reasons of "why we tell stories about the rez." He explains, the themes of "loss and recovery of language, broken families, the colonial attempts to break the culture by breaking the family continue to occupy our imagination—and these jostle with other stories of ours that showcase our humour, our sense of adventure and free-spiritedness, our myths and our legends." Williams also points out that having an Indigenous dramaturgy supports the context around telling an Indigenous story, especially to an audience that may not be familiar with the history. "Canada intended to wipe out her Indigenous peoples but they didn't do it with guns because they didn't have enough of those—so they created treaties to prove it was surrendered," he says. "These so-called peaceful acquisitions of the land were the bedrock of the starvation policies, the residential (school) policies and the continuation of the children and family services which up to this day are taking the children away from their parents. These are destructive policies and they have casualties on our lives, our lived experience and these seep into the work we make, the stories we create."

Indigenous performance dramaturgy is therefore not about simply providing meaning or undertaking the role of educating a white audience; its functions are more complex than many of the non-Indigenous performance-makers and critics acknowledge. The individual story is powerful and potent. As Māori academic Linda Tuhiwai Smith reiterates, "The point about the stories is not that they simply tell a story, or tell a story simply. . . . [It is] that these new stories contribute to a collective story in which every Indigenous person has

---

20 All quotations of Kenneth T. Williams, unless otherwise specified, are from: Kenneth T. Williams (playwright in residence, Department of Drama Studies, University of Saskatchewan), in discussion with author, September, 2015.

a place."[21] It is this sense of place within a collective cultural space that creates a space where Indigenous artists engage with meaning-making in new and different areas, creating a burgeoning new space where increasing critical discussion can take place. Cradling space as a dramaturgy of 'movement of space' can then also refer to a dialogic space, expressing the intersection of the spiritual, political, and vernacular.[22] Further, as Brazilian performance artist and scholar Eleonora Fabião notes in her remarks on her experiences as a dramaturge, the collective in which she is working is a mobile organism and her work must then take up a mutual agility: "I am in permanent transit. My space moves, or still, my space is movement."[23] This invocation of dramaturgy as a space of movement extends, then, to recognition that the work of dramaturgy is in fact distributed across the various performing agents in the room; it is not necessarily located in the figure of the one who witnesses without doing, an important factor when considering Indigenous dramaturges and their active role in developing the world of the work.

Similarly, Curtis Peeteetuce, playwright and former artistic director of Gordon Tootoosis Nîkânîwin Theatre in Saskatoon, is also a firm believer in the potential of shaping, claiming, and reframing dramaturgy for an Indigenous purpose. The organization's website explains, "we have reinstituted the component of culture in everything we do ... [and] we are excited to open the doors to a new future for the company, one grounded in culture, language and history."[24] This mandate also supports the growing swell of Indigenous-led creative development where the dramaturgical process might conclude

21 Linda T. Smith, *Decolonizing Methodologies: Research and Indigenous Peoples*, (London: Zed Books/Dunedin, New Zealand: University of Otago Press/New York: St. Martin's Press, 1999), 144.

22 Knut Ove Arntzen, "A Metaphorical View on Cultural Dialogues: Struve's Meridian Arc and Reflections on Memories in Eastern and Northern Borderlands," in *The Borders of Europe: Hegemony, Aesthetics and Border Poetics*, eds. Helge Vidar Holm, Sissel Lægreid and Torgeir Skorgen (Aarhus: Aarhus University Press, 2012), 129.

23 Eleonora Fabião, "Dramaturging with Mabou Mines: Six Proposals for *Ecco Porco*," *Women and Performance: A Journal of Feminist Theory* 13, no. 2 (2003): 30.

24 Gordon Tootoosis Nîkânîwin Theatre, "Welcome to Gordon Tootoosis Nîkânîwin Theatre," www.gtnt.ca, accessed July 13, 2018.

in delivering a written text but begins, unequivocally, in an environment that prioritizes land and language.

"Language describes what we do and it is through our Indigenous languages that dramaturgy can offer an opportunity to frame our world view," explains Peeteetuce. "It is essential that our oral traditions are acknowledged and the form of our storytelling is enhanced through the conventions of the theatre."[25] The Eurocentric lens that has currently limited dramaturgy to operating within a particular lexicon has not limited Indigenous practitioners, many of whom continue to adapt, adopt, and develop their own practice in accordance with their own principles of making work. For example, Peeteetuce explains, "theatre convention often speaks of beats as key moments to understand significant change in the narrative arc of a story but when talking to my actors, I ask them to consider these as moments." He says, "Theatre is supposed to be understanding the human condition so we need to understand what's going on this moment and we need to understand that in the context of our experiences, our histories, our language, our ancestors, our world."

Indigenous performance can therefore be seen to function within two concurrent experiences: the moment in which it was created, which is symptomatic of the strengths and weaknesses of those engaged in its manifestation; and the moment in which it is given to the audience, a gesture directed to provoke, not just provide, meaning. Indigenous performance-making has been driven by a number of motivations, but contemporary Indigenous performance, and the growing amount of research that supports its development, highlights the fact that as the narrative changes, Indigenous creators are continuing to create, carve, jostle, and insert themselves into a dialogue that is interested in asking questions, not providing answers. Peeteetuce recalls two words in the Cree language that may offer the beginning of a conversation that places Indigenous practice at the centre of dramaturgy: "*oskâpêwis* are those who help in ceremony and in feasts," he explains. "There is also the Cree term *isihcikêwin* that refers to prayer and ceremony, the stage for the sacred space."

---

25 All quotations by Curtis Peeteetuce, unless otherwise specified, are from: Curtis Peeteetuce (playwright), in discussion with author, September, 2015.

Reflecting back on both their careers as playwrights, actors, and directors, both Peeteetuce and Williams reiterate that dramaturgy has always been intrinsic to the development of Indigenous work. "This is a word that isn't ours," says Peeteetuce, "but at a fundamental level what the word can and could refer to is already what we're doing: shaping plays, strengthening our vision and purpose for the work, and also serving the community." Indigenous performance is more than subscribing to a predetermined narrative. Citing well-known Canadian playwright and dramaturge Colleen Murphy, Williams says, "good tragedy does not have victims. It's people who are acting in their circumstances as positively as they can. They may not always win, but they're pushing, they're acting not reacting." Rather than just working on script or production, Williams tends to believe that, at its core, dramaturgy "draws the truth out from a story, truth that is about characters, not gimmicks or convention." He adds, "We need to explore our past and we need to see those stories. I lived in a residential school until I was eight; however, my parents worked in the school and I was never separated from them like the other children were, and therefore I didn't grow up with the residential school experience like other First Nations children. But it's still a part of our history. In the same way, one of my characters realizes when you're born Indigenous, but born brown in white country, you're also born to be political. Our stories come from struggle, but they only become issue plays when we're not honest about the characters involved. It's about honesty, as much as you can make it, and that's dirty but it's human."

Developing an Indigenous dramaturgy is more than an exercise in widening the existing theatrical lexicon; it is a deliberate and purposeful act to grow, develop, and expand the circle of voices to facilitate a much bigger conversation that takes into full account an Indigenous world view. Cradling space, as this chapter suggests, is one particular facet of developing a vocabulary around Indigenous dramaturgy, and, as both Williams and Peeteetuce advocate, this is an ongoing conversation that can delve deep into finding and refining the language to speak and sing back to the practices that are intrinsic to this place and its space. Expanding the vocabulary around an Indigenous dramaturgy then ensures that an alternative practice can be seen as increasingly conversant within the wider performing arts discourse. Both conceptual and practical, spiritual and robust, at its core the notion of cradling space allows an individual (whether artist or audience) to be welcomed into the rehearsal room/theatre/ performance space with full acknowledgement of his/her/their own unique histories, experience, skills, and knowledge—and not asked to sever any of these from the world of the work. Furthermore, as Indigenous dramaturgy is land based, it is only fitting that it is about acknowledging the ongoing relationship between people and land, and equally the relationship between land, language, and community. The performative histories that are etched into the land and its topography include performance histories that embrace what can be considered the aesthetics of Indigenous performance and include ritual, myth, song, dance, music, mask, oral narrative, mime, and story. Cumulatively, these different features offer a much larger framework that is based on cultural protocol rather than formalized processes.

To conclude, the intention of cradling space as an Indigenous dramaturgical tool is to place itself into an inclusive *kete* (basket) of other approaches and to support, facilitate, and develop further dialogue around the role of dramaturgy within an Indigenous context. Dramaturgy may not be an Indigenous word, but it can be a word that responds to this space and for this place. The future of this conversation has already begun.

REFERENCES

Allen, Chadwick. "Performing Serpent Mound: A Trans-Indigenous Meditation." *Theatre Journal* 67, no. 3 (2015): 391–411.

Arntzen, Knut Ove. "A Metaphorical View on Cultural Dialogues: Struve's Meridian Arc and Reflections on Memories in Eastern and Northern Borderlands." In *The Borders of Europe: Hegemony, Aesthetics and Border Poetics* edited by Helge Vidar Holm, Sissel Lægreid, and Torgeir Skorgen, 127–35. Aarhus: Aarhus University Press, 2012.

———. "Sámi and Indigenous Theatre: The Nomadic Perspective and the Notion of a Spiral Dramaturgy." *Trans* 19 (May 2016). http:// www.inst.at/trans/19/sami-and- indigenous-theatre/.

Barton, Bruce. "Introduction: Creating Spaces." In *Developing Nation: New Play Creation in English-speaking Canada*, edited by Bruce Barton, v–ix. Toronto: Playwrights Canada Press, 2008.

Bustin, Pam. "Between the Bottles and the Knives: Celebrating Twenty-Five Years with the Saskatchewan Playwrights Centre." In *West Words: Celebrating Western Canadian Theatre and Playwriting*, edited by Moira J. Day, 86–92. Regina: Canadian Plains Research Centre Press, 2011.

Carter, Jill. "*Chocolate Woman* visions an Organic Dramaturgy: Blocking-Notation for the Indigenous Soul." *Canadian Woman Studies* 26, no. 3/4 (2008): 169–76.

Fabião, Eleonora. "Dramaturging with Mabou Mines: Six Proposals for *Ecco Porco*." *Women and Performance: A Journal of Feminist Theory* 13, no. 2 (2003): 29–40.

Gordon Tootoosis Nīkānīwin Theatre. "Welcome to Gordon Tootoosis Nīkānīwin Theatre." www.gtnt.ca. Accessed July 13, 2018.

Gruenewald, David A. "Foundations of Place: A Multidisciplinary Framework for Place-Conscious Education." *American Educational Research Journal* 40, no. 3 (2003): 619–54.

Hamilton, Annette. "Gender, Aesthetics and Performance." In *The Oxford Companion to Aboriginal Art and Culture*, edited by Sylvia Kleinert, Margo Neale, and Robyne Bancroft, 68–75. Melbourne: Oxford University Press, 2000.

Joseph, Dione. "Towards a New Zealand Dramaturgy: A Maverick Undertaking in 2016, Part I." *The Theatre Times*, January 17, 2017. https://thetheatretimes.com/new-zealand-dramaturgy-maverick-undertaking-2016-part-i/.

Lessing, Gotthold E. *Hamburgische Dramaturgie*. Hamburg, 1767. University of Duisburg, 2012.

Pavis, Patrice. "Dramaturgeie et postdramaturgeie." In *Alternative Dramaturgies of the New Millennium in Arabo-Islamic Context and Beyond: Selected Papers from the 10th Annual Meeting of the Tangier International Conferences: Performing Tangier 2014*, edited by Khalid Amine and George F. Robertson, 15–21. Tangier: Collaborative Media International, 2015.

Saskatchewan Playwrights Centre. "About." https://saskplaywrights.ca. Accessed July 13, 2018.

Smith, Linda T. *Decolonizing Methodologies: Research and Indigenous Peoples*. London: Zed Books/Dunedin, New Zealand: University of Otago Press/New York: St. Martin's Press, 1999.

Swain, Rachael. *Listening to Country*. 2013. http://www.marrugeku.com.au/listening_to_country_2013/. Accessed December 28, 2016.

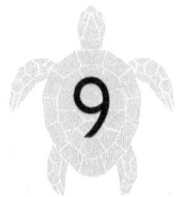

9

STANDING WITH SKY WOMAN: A CONVERSATION ON CULTURAL FLUENCY

Kahente Horn-Miller

t is said that long ago there was a world in the sky inhabited by sky people. One day a pregnant woman drops through a hole created under the roots of a great tree and begins her fall to the world below. As she falls from darkness to light, the animals of the world below talk among themselves, trying to figure out how to help her. A flock of birds rescue and carry her, gently setting her down on the back of the Great Turtle. The water animals have made preparations for her. Bringing mud from the bottom of the ocean, they place it on turtle's back until the earth begins to spread out in all directions. This is the start of life on earth. Turtle's shell becomes Sky Woman's home and the plants that she brought (tobacco and strawberries) are her medicines. The story goes on to contain many more elements, including her twin grandsons and the creation of the natural world and the human race.[1] This story is about human frailty, being in

---

1   The performance *We Are In Her and She Is In Us* is only part of the larger narrative, which was rewritten in its entirety for my doctoral dissertation. For the purposes of the initial performance, the central part of the story, in which Sky Woman falls and lands on Turtle Being's back and gives birth to her daughter, was the focus. I have plans to continue with the development of the rest of the story into a longer performance piece.

relationship, how to endure suffering, and about finding balance. Through it we learn about the importance of family, of our history, and of belonging. We are reminded that we come from somewhere and that the Sky World is very similar to the earth world we know so that we may respect it and nurture it. This is our story.

I have been performing the Sky Woman narrative, *We Are In Her and She Is In Us*, for almost three years. This work describes the transformation of the story from an aspect of my doctoral work to a performance piece and to embodied knowledge where I communicate the history of my people on my body. This is an aspect of my role as a Kanien'kehá:ka (Mohawk) woman: to communicate our culture to our children in a way that prepares and strengthens them for what is to come. This written work is about that performance, about storytelling as ceremony, and about the introspection that takes place when we tell our stories. In this performance I dress in Haudenosaunee regalia with a beaded skirt, leggings, moccasins, crown, and cuffs and tell a portion of the Sky Woman narrative, the Haudenosaunee story of creation.[2] In total, the performance takes about thirty minutes. As I speak, I move around the space in a counter-clockwise fashion, using traditional song and dance, hand gestures, and eye contact to help bring the story to life. During this performance I am she, she is me, we are here together.

....

2   The story begins in the Sky World at the beginning of time and tells of the relationship between the young Sky Woman, her family, and the people of that world. It describes how she was treated because she was special and gifted, and how she learned the ways of her people. It is also about her relationships with others and her marriage. The story is the first place where the clans appear, as well as key ceremonies and songs, and the medicine game of lacrosse; it also describes Sky Woman's descent to the earth world below. It is about the challenges Sky Woman faces that affect her both physically and emotionally, throwing off her sense of balance. As she deals with each of these challenges through critical engagement with herself and those she loves, Sky Woman learns how to think for herself, how to be respectful of others, how to endure suffering—in essence she finds balance. Those challenges prepare her for what is to come as she brings new life to the earth world below. The story teaches us that Sky Woman has a history, a family, and a place where she belongs. We are reminded that we come from somewhere and that the Sky World is very similar to the world as we know it. This is our history.

Dear daughters, this is an explanation of my work on the Sky Woman narrative. This work has taken me on a personal journey that started when you were young, Karonhiokohe and Kokowa, and continued through early motherhood as I began my university studies, looking at Indigenous identity and finding my voice as an academic and writer. It has continued through the births of Iowennakon and Teieswatetah, in my further growth as a mother. The heart of this story was written in that sunny back room at the old house in Kahnawà:ke[3] with Iowennakon as a baby by my side. As I looked into her clear brown eyes I thought out the words I put to paper. I knew the story. I had read it to you from picture books, but I realize now that I didn't fully understand its importance for our people. Through this work and my role as your mother, I have grown. You have all inspired me, informed me, and served to drive my research, writing, and personal growth. You are my ontology; my world view is from the lens of motherhood. This is part of my life's work. You four are my greatest legacy, but this too is part of what I will leave behind for 'the coming faces.'[4] I am hoping that this version of the Sky Woman narrative makes it more accessible for you as we head into difficult times. Mother Earth is suffering. The world you inherit is not a healthy one. I am hopeful that this story and my explanation of it will help deepen a connection to who you are as Kanien'kehá:ka women.

INTRODUCTION

When I began to perform the narrative, the emotional responses from the audience made me reflect on what I was doing. What did this all mean to me as a Kanien'kehá:ka woman? As a mother? As

---

3   Kahnawà:ke is a Kanien'kehá:ka (Mohawk) reserve located south of Montréal, Québec. It has a population of between approximately 7,000 and 9,000 people and a land base of 48 square kilometres.
4   A term used to describe the coming seven generations, the babies yet unborn.

an academic? These questions gave rise to a feeling that I was transforming. I was on a journey of self-discovery and awareness. I began keeping notes on each performance and spent time reflecting on it with friends and family who were there with me. I saw it first as an act of decolonizing the story, of reinvigorating our own storytelling traditions that can be conceptualized as a form of cultural fluency. This involves communicating Haudenosaunee culture in different ways that make it accessible to a new audience of our children and non-Indigenous individuals who want to know more about us and connect with us. I thought about those who had written about the Iroquois, such as the Jesuits, the colonial officials, the anthropologists like William Fenton.[5] What was their goal? To colonize us. Was I taking it out of the hands of those men, who had written down key aspects that were important to them, as men? Or was I building on the work of my ancestors, who had written it out to prevent us from losing it? I had to think logically about what kind of access these male scholars and colonial officials would have had to the women's realm: probably very little. This opened my eyes to why the story seemed so male-centric and patrilineal.[6] As I reflected more on this, I encountered the term *rematriation*. As I put the femaleness back into the story, through inserting Haudenosaunee feminine traditions like burial of the placenta in the family garden, it gained vigour and began to come off the page and back into life. I realized there was more to it than just decolonizing the story.

I encountered the Facebook page *Re-Matriate* (now *ReMatriate*)[7] in the fall of 2015. It is a site started by Indigenous women that projects positive visual images of women. One of the founders, artist Jeneen Freij Njootli, states, "rematriation is a beautiful alternative to the decolonial project.... Whereas decoloniality is an inherent binary, rematriation is something that is generative, is generating. We want to generate and show positive images and depictions of our women

....

5   I use the term Iroquois here to differentiate the non-Indigenous academics and field of study that serve to subjugate our own knowledges from Haudenosaunee knowledge.

6   For an example see Brian Maracle, "First Words," in *Our Story: Aboriginal Voices on Canada's Past*, eds. Tantoo Cardinal et al. (Toronto: Anchor Canada, 2005), 15–31.

7   "ReMatriate." ReMatriate Facebook page (n.d.), retrieved December 31, 2015, from http://www.facebook.com/ReMatriate/.

and of our alliances and identities. And try to dismantle those negative stereotypes and representations of us and gain sovereignty over how our own images are circulating in media."[8] The term, without being clearly defined, resonated with me and with what I was trying to do with the narrative.

This work is a natural extension of me as a Kanien'kehá:ka woman and the larger field of Indigenous womanism.[9] *We Are In Her and She Is In Us* is the culmination of a personal trajectory from academic to performer. As part of a larger transformative experience, I create and perform an Indigenous theory. By examining the process of transformation for the performer and the retelling of the Sky Woman story, this writing provides an example of cultural fluency and the rematriation of our stories where, in particular, we reinvigorate the cultural metaphors in language and the cultural principles of Rotinohnsionni-Haudenosaunee philosophy.[10] Cultural fluency is the understanding and effective use of the hidden cultural currents of communication over time. It's how effective communicators use the language, material culture, subtle nuances in body language, and cultural traditions as they connect with others.

Like others in my community, I had grown up with the Sky Woman story. I had read it to my own children and seen it painted in murals on walls at our local school and youth centre, but I took the teachings of her story for granted. I realized I did not fully understand her until I encountered her again during my doctoral work when the women I interviewed referenced Sky Woman as a living personality, standing with them in their daily lives. I revisited the story, first, in writing to address their inclusion of her as they spoke with me and to understand what Sky Woman meant to the women. After my doctoral work was completed, I continued this journey through the development of the performance piece based on one aspect of the story, from her fall through the hole under the Great Tree to her first steps on

---

8   "The ReMatriate Interview," participants: Ryan McMahon, N'alaga Avis O'Brien, Jenee Freij Njootli, Kelly Edzerza Bapty, *Red Man Laughing* podcast, May 4, 2015, https://www.redmanlaughing.com/listen/rematriate, accessed May 8, 2015.

9   See M. Annette Jaimes-Guerrero, " 'Patriarchal Colonialism' and Indigenism: Implications for Native Feminist Spirituality and Native Womanism," *Hypatia* 18, no. 2 (2003).

10 Richard Hill, email message to author, October 29, 2015.

Turtle Being's back to the birth of her daughter. In doing so, I began to transcend disciplinary boundaries. I moved from researcher to storyteller, to woman, to mother, and finally, to performer. I embody Sky Woman as a form of political agency, as a way to bring her back to life, although she was never gone. Her life and story have been overshadowed by colonization. Her story lost much of its female aspect through the impact of the male, colonial gaze. Her femaleness is viewed through the limited scope of those who wrote her story down. When we look at her life through the female lens, her connection to that life-giving power is understood.[11] That connection is what is missing in these written versions of the story. I connect the listener-audience to her with movements of my body and through the sounds I make. Late in the story, at the point where she births her daughter, I mimic the primal grunt that we women make in the final stages of childbirth as we push our babies out into the world. It is our way of communicating and connecting ourselves to our ancestors through sound. It is our way of saying new life has come! Or I remind them of the physicality of nursing one's baby, of the witnessing of their tiny toes flexing in contentment as they are nourished by our milk. These are the things that one witnesses and experiences as a woman, that the men who wrote our stories down were never able to communicate. So this performance comes out of my role as mother, my relationship with my children and the men and women that I talk to, my confrontations with the page and the limitations of the text.

If we look at the overall idea of storytelling and oral history, it is through multiple tellings that a story is fleshed out, creating a broader, more comprehensive narrative. Each time I tell the story it shifts slightly and I learn something new from it and from the audience response. In turn, I translate that knowledge into the next telling. Such licence does not diminish the integrity of the original narrative. I consistently adhere to the essential elements of the original story. So the story that I tell is perhaps not the exact one my ancestors told, yet it faithfully contains and honours the important elements. The nuances evident in distinct versions of a specific

....

11   For a deeper exploration of breastfeeding as the first treaty and for a deeper understanding of motherhood as ontology, see Leanne Betasamosake Simpson, *Dancing on Our Turtle's Back: Stories of Nishnaabeg Re-Creation, Resurgence and a New Emergence* (Winnipeg: ARP Books, 2011).

history represent a broader understanding of the events and the various ways people have internalized them. The Sky Woman story that I share reflects my experiences being a Iakón:kwe[12] in Kahnawà:ke.

During my doctoral research about how women express their Kanien'kehá:ka identity, I interviewed eight Kanien'kehá:ka women from my home community over a period of six months through 2006 and 2007. Including my own life in the work, I wrote of my own experiences exploring my identity as a Kanien'kehá:ka woman, mother, aunt, sister, and daughter. As they shared their life stories with me they talked about Sky Woman as though she were in the room with us. Sky Woman embodied the same space in which these women lived. This stood out and I thought I should revisit this story myself as a way to understand why this was so. I reviewed versions of the story and what I found did not satisfy me or help me understand what these women were communicating to me about Sky Woman's importance to them. It was important to me, but it didn't play a pivotal role in my life until I began to rewrite it. The existing written versions of the story had partial elements that I kept faithfully. Children's books I had shared with my children contained the segment from when she falls from Sky World to when she lands on the Turtle Being's back. They are meant for children and present key elements in a simple way. Longer versions exist as manuscripts written by colonial officials, anthropologists, and pre-nineteenth-century Haudenosaunee male scholars who were connected to their culture yet also still part of the white colonial project, serving as informants, like Seneca, John Arthur Gibson, and ethnographer and linguist J.N.B. Hewitt.[13] They had limited insights into Haudenosaunee feminine culture.[14] As a result, these writings are more detailed, but they also left me feeling disconnected, and it wasn't until I found Brian Rice's online version on Akwesasne Kanien'kehá:ka historian

---

12 The Kanienke'ha word for Kanien'kehá:ka woman.

13 See John C. Mohawk, *Iroquois Creation Story: John Arthur Gibson and J.N.B. Hewitt's Myth of the Earth Grasper* (Buffalo, NY: Mohawk Publications, 2005). "Myth of the Earth Grasper" was first published in 1928.

14 For further examples of gender neutralization of Indigenous women, with particular focus on the work of Susannah Moodie and her writing, which serves to reinforce this perspective, see Leanne Betasamosake Simpson, *As We Have Always Done: Indigenous Freedom Through Radical Resistance* (Minneapolis: University of Minnesota Press, 2017).

Darren Bonaparte's website, *The Wampum Chronicles*,[15] that something struck a chord. Rice's version was a more modern take on the story that brought in creative writing. It was far different from the anthropological texts I had encountered, and his version was filled with detail and care. Eight years later, as I began to perform the eventual narrative, I also began to reflect on that connection.

The one similarity shared by all the previous written versions of the story is that they are all told from the third-person perspective; I realized that this is key to understanding my own reconnection to the story. When I read through the version Rice posted before he published *The Rotinonshonni. A Traditional Iroquoian History Through the Eyes of Teharonhia:wako and Sawiskera* in 2013,[16] it still felt distant, although the elements remained clear.[17] This was because Rice also writes from the third-person perspective. I wanted to know more.

I sat in the warm sunshine of an early spring day and thought about Sky Woman: what was she thinking, how was she feeling? I was inspired. I wrote out all the key characters and plot of the story I found in Rice's work and listed them in the order they appeared. I then began to write out a narrative of my own. As I wrote the story, I included myself, the lives of the women, key things that they experienced and expressed to me. It felt like a release. I began to immerse myself in Sky Woman's life. She became alive and, for the first time, I felt that I was tapping into what had eluded me: I began to understand and, more importantly, to feel what the women had tried to communicate. I spent the next month writing every day as I tried to understand the connection between Sky Woman and the women in

---

15 Darren Bonaparte, *The Wampum Chronicles*, www.wampumchronicles.com.

16 The original thesis was not purely an examination of the Sky Woman story. The work looked at how Kanien'kehá:ka women from Kahnawà:ke expressed their identity. When I looked for the elements of the Sky Woman story to draw upon for my rewriting, Rice's work seemed to be the most comprehensive examination at the time. Since then the work of others, Kevin Whyte and Amber Adams, for example, has illustrated the multiple ways Haudenosaunee scholars are looking at this story. Their work continues to illustrate its relevance in the twenty-first century.

17 There are multiple versions of the story written by scholars, colonial officials, and community people. Kevin J. White examines this extensively in his doctoral thesis, "Haudenosaunee Worldview Through Iroquoian Cosmologies: The Published Narratives in Historical Context," (PhD diss., University of Buffalo, 2007).

my community. It was my way of grappling with this aspect of my research. That spot in the warm sunshine provided an escape from my busy family life as a mother to three daughters, at that time, and nurtured my creative writing. I knew I was not just writing for the thesis, but also for my children. Understanding this story and presenting it in a way that they and other community members might connect with became a driving factor. As I wrote, I felt fear when Sky Woman felt fear, I felt gratitude and sadness when she did, I felt pain when she did. I felt her frustration and amazement too. I reconnected with the story as it gained more meaning for me.

My interpretation of the Sky Woman story is unique beyond the obvious notion of a simple retelling. To my knowledge, it is the only version of the story written in the first person and the only version that incorporates the influences and impressions of living Kanien'kehá:ka women.[18] This fusion of lived experience, emotions, and thinking produces a narrative that gives insight into Sky Woman's emotional being: the fear and uncertainty she felt as she travelled here, pregnant and alone. These women's stories addressed the fluidity of life, a woman's ability to procreate as she carries a baby inside her. I naturally put them into the story. The women's experiences inform the idea of Sky Woman's experience: her waters protecting life until the birth moment when life on this earth begins and the burial of her baby's placenta in the ground near the home to remind that child of where they come from. The women's own experiences brought me closer to Sky Woman on that sunny porch, allowing me to feel the deep sadness of Sky Woman when her daughter dies in childbirth, giving birth to her twin boys. I made their lived experiences and associated pain and happiness into an integral part of the longer story as a way to infuse Sky Woman's own

....

18 My own narrative and perspective on Kanien'kehá:ka identity is included as part of my larger doctoral thesis and thus included as part of the narrative. For further information see: Kahente Horn-Miller, "Sky Woman's Great Granddaughters: A Narrative Inquiry Into Kanien'kehá:ka (Mohawk) Women's Identity at Kahnawà:ke," (PhD diss., Concordia University, 2009). Also see Kahente Horn-Miller, "Distortion and Healing: Finding Balance and a 'Good Mind' Through the Rearticulation of Sky Woman's Journey," in *Living On The Land: Indigenous Women's Understanding of Place*, eds. Nathalie Kermoal and Isabel Altamirano-Jiménez (Edmonton: Athabasca University Press, 2016), 19–38.

experiences with realness. The death of a child is something that one never gets over, and women I talked with expressed the deep lingering sadness of their experiences. I imagined Sky Woman and her own pain of her daughter's death as these women talked with me. Her pain became real, and in this way, their lives gave voice to Sky Woman and the story became an embodiment of the saying, "we are in her and she is in us," contributing to that never-ending life cycle of writing, performance, and story.

I demonstrate this writing process before each performance with gestures that mimic the fluid movement of water. As it comes in at high tide to crash over the shores and rolls back out, the story itself speaks to that continuous fluidity of birth, life, death, and birth again that my people describe. This telling contributes to its continued life and importance for our people as our master narrative. The wave rolls in in the form of knowledge I gain from my family, my community, and the women of my original study. It rolls out as the Sky Woman story infused with their life stories. This fluidity happens again each time I perform it. The wave comes in through the expectancy of the audience, the gift of their listening ears and open eyes. The movement out is the gift of the telling itself and the cultural knowledge it delivers. The emotion and feedback that come to me afterwards from the listener feeds my repeated interpretation and performance of the narrative. The whole process then becomes a dialogue, a reciprocal and never-ending giving and taking of knowledge. We are then in relationship.

CULTURAL FLUENCY

Each time I prepare for a performance I go through a process of embodying Sky Woman. I begin by thinking about the women I interviewed and how alike we are in our experiences as Kanien'kehá:ka women. I am back on that sunny porch during the writing of the story. It is the memory of Elder Brother Sun warming my hands as I type. Moving on in my memory, I think about the thesis defense and how my voice cracked as I spoke about the women and their gifts to me, most particularly the eldest one, who had since passed on. She is in this story and the very performance itself. I then think about Sky Woman's life and journey here. I feel close to her in these moments.

I too am on a journey. Once I was a child, then I became a mother, a storyteller, an academic, and now a performer.

As I get ready to perform, I am awed as I stand looking at this woman in the mirror. The first time I performed the narrative at the Performing Turtle Island conference, I stared in amazement at my transformation. I remember a calm came over me as I stood looking at myself. My hair was long and fell down my back. I had decided to wear it loose, to remind me of the feeling that Sky Woman must have felt as her hair blew around her as she fell. The elaborate crown sat regally on top of my head. The beaded cuffs were tight on my wrists. I felt armed. I felt protected. I felt othered—in another place. Again it happened as I prepared to perform, standing in the bathroom at Emory University, Georgia: women would come and go quietly, giving me a side glance of appreciation. I wondered about this. Why did they not speak to me? Was I somehow untouchable? It happened once more before another performance at Carleton University. I do not feel alone in these moments. I feel deeply connected to the natural world. I think of my children in these times. I do this because of and for them.

As I leave the changing area, I carry myself differently. I leave with my head held high and a walk befitting a queen. Upon reflection, it seems that is what is expected of me. Perhaps is it the dress? The beaded crown I wear? The Haudenosaunee tattoo designs on my arms? Cree/Métis/Irish artist Meryl McMaster describes her artistic work *In-Between Worlds* where she made elaborate costumes out of natural elements as a form of protection: "There's a protection I feel putting them on," she says. "It's all a character, it's all in my dream. It's who I am. I'm trying to illustrate what goes through my head, or what I think about. But at the same time it's a character, it's something I've imagined. It's real, and it's not."[19] I sit quietly waiting for my cue to begin, also in character. I feel real and surreal at the same time. Those who catch my eye smile slightly. I nod in acknowledgement. I feel like me and yet I imagine it is Sky Woman who has that twinkle in her eye and glances back with a slight smile. I can feel her

---

19 Meryl McMaster, quoted in Peter Simpson, "Meryl McMaster Takes New York; At Just 27, Artist's Elaborate Self-Portraits Score Her a Spot at the Smithsonian," *Ottawa Citizen*, June 13, 2015, F1.

at these times, like she is in me. Smiling and waiting, as I am waiting. Her voice ready to be heard.

I have come to realize that the process of preparation, the telling/performance, and the question and answer period after are ceremonial. This is an aspect of telling our stories or even doing our research as Indigenous peoples. When in ceremony, my people experience deep connectedness to each other and to the natural world. As I perform the narrative and critically engage with the audience responses, I become a ceremonial being. Shawn Wilson, in his work *Research Is Ceremony*, describes ceremony as a continual process of give and take. Wilson writes, "The purpose of any ceremony is to build stronger relationships or bridge the distance between aspects of our cosmos and ourselves. The research that we do as Indigenous people is a ceremony that allows us a raised level of consciousness and insight into our world."[20] The telling of the Sky Woman story also builds stronger relationships and bridges distances. Kanien'kehá:ka midwife Katsi Cook explains in her workshops that the story is our umbilical cord to the Sky World. Sky Woman herself, then, is our connection to that time before, and in telling the story we are activating memory and connection. My body and voice become the vessel through which the viewer/listener travels with me to the other side, much like a baby being carried inside its mother. I carry them with my words; this is embodied knowledge.[21] The listener gains cultural fluency through me.

This story is about new knowledge discovery. Many have never heard the story before, and those who have, have gained a new perspective, a world of insights about the human condition previously unencountered. As for communicative awareness, most specifically, the viewer responds with emotion. This deep emotional and empathetic connection comes as a surprise to many. Kanien'kehá:ka elder Kahntinetha Horn speaks of the Kanienke'ha concept of history, *Tsi ni tia wen'a*, as a telling of things in a way that you can see it.[22] It is about making the story alive in the minds of the audience through

20 Shawn Wilson, *Research Is Ceremony: Indigenous Research Methods* (Winnipeg: Fernwood Publishing, 2009), 11.

21 Heather Ritenburg et al., "Embodying Decolonization: Methodologies and Indigenization," *AlterNative* 10, no. 1 (2014), 68.

22 Kahntinetha Horn, personal communication to author, fall 2014.

the mastery of storytelling. The story and the storytelling become, then, a place, a ceremony where relationships are built between the storyteller and the audience. The performance of this particular story builds the relationship between the audience and not only the Indigenous world, but also the connection between the Indigenous world and the natural world.

Paul Stoller, in *Sensuous Scholarship*, describes this as an attempt to profoundly reawaken the scholar's body by demonstrating how the fusion of the intelligible and the sensible can be applied to scholarly practices and representations. It is about incorporating the sensuous body: its smells, tastes, textures, and sensations. Stoller illustrates that this is paramount in ethnographic descriptions of societies in which the Eurocentric notion of text and of textual interpretations are not important. Perception, Stoller indicates, in non-Western societies devolves not simply from reading, but also from the senses of smell, touch, taste, and hearing. He writes, "in many societies these lower senses, all of which cry out for sensuous description, are central to the metaphoric organization of experience; they also trigger cultural memories."[23] The viewer/listener connects viscerally to the Sky Woman story through the sound of my voice and the movement of my body.

This entire project of retelling the Sky Woman narrative is about communication, about reclaiming and sharing cultural memories. When we speak of cultural fluency we are speaking about communicating across cultures and across time. Cultural fluency is the process through which communication is influenced by attitudes, body language, customs, and other intangible and often ambiguous aspects of communication that are not easy to perceive. It is complicated, multifaceted, and multidisciplinary, and it is generally unconscious.

In another view, Richard Hill Sr. describes cultural fluency as a dialogic process of information sharing that addresses culture loss through colonization. With respect to Haudenosaunee culture, Hill states, cultural fluency is founded in "the ability to understand the cultural foundations, the intent of our culture as expressed through various stories and traditions that we have." Hill adds that cultural

....

23 Paul Stoller, *Sensuous Scholarship* (Philadelphia: University of Pennsylvania Press, 1997), xvi.

fluency requires continued discussion of Haudenosaunee culture and tradition, moving beyond a primary focus on language proficiency. In dialogue we work at rediscovering the thinking of our ancestors and how they determined our way of life. Further, "cultural fluency is always about how we gain this understanding and then put it into action in our lives." He writes, "We are very concerned about linguistic fluency in our communities but at the same time we have to be concerned about how well we understand the culture that the language represents."[24]

My performance is one such conversation. It is akin to the idea of a cultural fluency in that it references the interactions and skills needed to adapt to another culture. Educational psychologist Yukiko Inoue writes that cultural fluency requires "the appropriate application of respect, empathy, flexibility, patience, interest, curiosity, openness, the willingness to suspend judgment, tolerance for ambiguity, and sense of humor."[25] If we look to Inoue's work on the necessary skills for developing cultural fluency when in another country, they have relevance to this discussion. They are described as follows:

- tolerance of ambiguity (the ability to accept lack of clarity and to be able to deal with ambiguous situations constructively);

- behaviour flexibility (the ability to adapt own behaviour to different requirements/situations);

- knowledge discovery (the ability to acquire new knowledge in real-time communication);

- communicative awareness (the ability to use communicative conventions of people from other cultural backgrounds and to modify own forms of expression correspondingly);

24 Hill, email message to author, October 2015.
25 Yukiko Inoue, "Cultural Fluency as a Guide to Effective Intercultural Communication: The Case of Japan and the U.S.," *Journal of Intercultural Communication* 15 (November 2007), www.immi.se/intercultural/nr15/inoue.htm.

- respect for otherness (curiosity and openness, as well as a readiness to suspend disbelief about other cultures and belief about our own cultures);

- empathy (the ability to understand intuitively what other people think and how they feel in given situations).[26]

Like Hill, Inoue's points also describe a dialogue that occurs across cultures. Through a kind of fluency presented through the storytelling, the Sky Woman narrative bridges across time and culture.

IN RELATIONSHIP

The journey of a young woman from Sky World to the Turtle's back is a metaphor for those in-between spaces that people experience throughout life. In her journey, her identity is reflected and refracted by the new world she encounters. As she stands on Turtle Being's back, she becomes Sky Woman and thus the marker for the Haudenosaunee way of living in the world. She is untethered: this is symbolized by her fall from the Sky World to the new world below. Through the telling of the story, we experience a similar unmooring. Through the visual imagery generated by the narrative, of the meeting of water and sky "almost too beautiful to bear,"[27] we are also reminded of this through the sky dome symbolism found in the tattoos on my body and beaded on the traditional clothing I wear for the performance. Through my intonation, movements, and clothing, the narrative performance erases the line of separation between the human and natural world that Western knowledge has demarcated. Through the story and my movements I communicate the inter-connectivity of the social and spiritual worlds that is the Indigenous reality. I portray an alternative world view presenting an ambiguous situation that the viewer must confront. One doesn't really know what is going to happen. As we reflect on the definition

....

26 *Ibid.*
27 All quotations from the script, unless otherwise cited, are taken from the version of the story contained in Horn-Miller, "Sky Woman's Great Granddaughters."

of cultural fluency presented in the work of Inoue as it plays out in this story, we see that tolerance for ambiguity requires the flexibility and adaptability of the listener/audience to accept a woman falling from the sky and animals talking and collaborating.[28] The audience is required to suspend their disbelief and bear witness to a sense of timelessness. Disoriented, their adjustment and curiosity about the narrative is reflected in the questions they ask after the performance.

The Sky Woman performance puts me and the audience in relationship with one another. For the Indigenous and non-Indigenous viewer, it reminds us that we are here together on Turtle Island. You as the viewer/listener are put into relationship with the land by acknowledging the story, listening to it, experiencing the world through Sky Woman's eyes. For the Haudenosaunee or Indigenous viewer, the story itself reminds us that we come from somewhere: Sky World and Turtle Island.[29] These shared relationships, as Wilson describes, "allow for a strengthening of the new relationship."[30] As the storyteller and listeners, we are in relationship.

Wilson and others have indicated that there is no distinction between relationships that are made between people and those that are made with our environment. Both are equally sacred.[31] He emphasizes that we as Indigenous people have a grounded sense of identity, in the literal sense. Drawing on the work of Gregory Cajete, he writes that the ground and environment from which we came is what makes us. Further, "our continuing connection to the land, and fulfilling our role within that ongoing relationship, is centred on our specific environment and the relationships that it holds, rather than on events that may be seen as historically important to others but hold only tenuous connection to our land."[32] The story, because it is of this land, connects us to the land, regardless of whether you are Indigenous or not.

....

28 For a detailed examination of the agency of animals in Indigenous creation narratives, see Vanessa Watts, "Indigenous Place-Thought and Agency amongst Humans and Non Humans (First Woman and Sky Woman Go on a European World Tour!)," *Decolonization: Indigeneity, Education & Society* 2, no. 1 (2013): 20–34.
29 See Horn-Miller, "Distortion and Healing."
30 Wilson, *Research Is Ceremony*, 84.
31 *Ibid.*, 87.
32 *Ibid.*, 88.

Wilson's examination of the term Indigenous is a way to characterize the particular relationship between the audience and the land that this story generates. Wilson, quoting Lewis Cardinal, describes the term as meaning "born of the land" or "springs from the land."[33] It is widely understood that this is the reason why many are comfortable using the term Indigenous instead of Aboriginal. The Kanienke'ha word Onkwehonwe, meaning original people, relates closely to this idea that Wilson describes. As Wilson further clarifies, the word means to be born of this continent, of this environment. Quoting Cardinal again, he writes, "when you create something from an Indigenous perspective, you are creating it from that environment, from that land that it sits in."[34] It is in creating this version of the Sky Woman story and through the performance of it that the relationship between the listener and the environment is strengthened. As I tell the story, in symbolic gesture I extend my hands to the audience, silently gifting them with the responsibility to share in the stewardship of Turtle Island. This is our responsibility as Kanien'kehá:ka women.

CONCEPTUALIZING REMATRIATION

It is these kinds of gestures along with the tone of my voice that evoke powerful responses from the audience. In turn, their responses also make me reflect. At one of my performances a man stripped down to his underwear to show his own traditional Indigenous tattoos. He and others have expressed an identification with Sky Woman and the birth process, and at other presentations men and women cry because they finally felt a reconnection after the death of a loved one. I asked myself, "What was I doing? What did this all mean to me as a Kanien'kehá:ka? As a mother? As an academic? As a woman?" It certainly goes beyond the confines of traditional academic work and speaks to me at a more visceral level. It was more than decolonizing the story. I felt a sense of responsibility to explore this further. This is when I began to examine the rematriation concept, which has relevance to this discussion.

33 Lewis Cardinal quoted in Wilson, *Research Is Ceremony*, 88.
34 Cardinal quoted in Wilson, *Research Is Ceremony*, 88.

The term rematriation has gone through an evolution in its use and meaning. It was first used prior to the 1980s, in the community of Six Nations near Brantford, Ontario, by a group actively seeking to rematriate objects held in museums.[35] Psychologist Gilbert Rose used it in the 1980s with reference to the psychology behind the creative process. The term refers to the relationship of the artist to the mother figure that undergoes a separation in childhood, a traumatic experience. The artist draws on this desire to reconnect and rematriate with the mother as they reconnect through the art.[36] In this sense, Rose's use of the word was a counter-narrative to the term repatriate.

Yet, rematriation is not simply an opposite term used to counter repatriation. Repatriation means to return an object to its country of origin. This use confuses the real meaning of the word 'repatriation' as Indigenous peoples see it. Indigenous writers substitute matri- for patri- to denote a feminized relationship with the earth that is characteristic of the Indigenous world view, a change from 'fatherland' to 'motherland.' The Kanien'kehá:ka word *yethinistenha-ohwentsiate* for Mother Earth reflects how we view our lineal descent and relates to the idea of mother-culture. This is more closely related to the idea communicated by the Facebook page, *ReMatriate*.

Shawnee/Lenape scholar Steven Newcombe used the term rematriation in 1996 with reference to restoring a living culture to its place on Mother Earth. Connecting the term to the Indigenous association with the land, he used it to explain the restoration of a people to a spiritual way of life to regain a sacred relationship with ancestral lands without external interference.[37] As a concept, rematriation acknowledges that our ancestors lived in spiritual relationship with our lands for thousands of years and that we have a sacred duty to maintain that relationship for the benefit of our future generations. Rematriation, then, is an example of cultural fluency. Is it acceptable or fitting to use the term rematriate? In performing the story, am I returning the story to its feminine essence?

35 Paul Williams, email message to author, May 27, 2016.
36 Gilbert Rose, cited in George Hagman, *The Artist's Mind: A Psychoanalytic Perspective on Creativity, Modern Art and Modern Artists* (London: Routledge, 2010), 8.
37 Steven Newcomb, "PERSPECTIVES: Healing, Restoration, and Rematriation," *News & Notes*, Spring/Summer 1995, 3.

Seneca scholar Penelope M. Kelsey used the term in her work *Reading the Wampum* and describes her use of the term as a way to designate the reclamation, re-embodying, and re-enactment (in a new context) of all of our Indigenous knowledges, cultural life ways, epistemologies, philosophies, and so on. She says it is a way to resituate women at the centre in imaginings (and concrete practices) of Indigenous knowledge, nationhood, and community. "I used 'repatriation'," she writes, "to invoke the internalized colonial processes whereby we have normalized heteropatriarchal systems as part of our vision of ourselves and as part of business-as-usual (by which I mean how the mere engagement of the settler colonial state has demanded and continues to demand this kind of patriarchal conformity)." For Kelsey, it is about decolonizing the ways Indigenous women have adapted to patriarchal norms. Further, she advises we use the term: "by using 'rematriation' we can bring women (and children) centrally into the norms of Indigenous nationalism in ways that honour our ways of knowing."[38]

The space and therefore the relationship between humans or between humans and the environment is seen as sacred. This is a key idea within many Indigenous peoples' ways of living. By reducing this space through the sharing of stories like the Sky Woman narrative, we are strengthening the relationship between humans and the natural world. This idea of bringing things together so that they share the same space is what ceremony, and hence storytelling, is about. This is what I am doing as I perform: I am creating an Indigenous space and bringing people into ceremony. Wilson states that research itself is a sacred ceremony within the Indigenous research paradigm, as it is all about building relationships and building this sacred space.[39] Significantly, the women who started *Rematriate* articulate this same idea with reference to the revitalization of Indigenous women's connection to land and feminine identity in opposition to the spaces created between women and the environment by colonization. Rematriation, I've come to understand, is a mental, emotional, physical, political, and spiritual thing—replacing feminist essentialism in a holistic Indigenous way.

....

38 Penelope Myrtle Kelsey, personal communication, February 17, 2016.

39 Wilson, *Research Is Ceremony*, 87.

ACTIVATING KNOWLEDGE ON THE BODY

As I began to embody the term *rematriate* as an aspect of cultural fluency, I also thought about finding a way to give the story more physical permanence in my life, some way for the story to speak for itself. Over the winter of 2016, I tattooed Haudenosaunee patterns onto my lower arms, just below the elbow. The symbols are inspired from beadwork and fine art. They include the sky dome, celestial beings, water, tobacco braid, three sisters, and The Great Tree.[40] The feminine tattooing tradition among the Haudenosaunee has not been documented. Only one reference to it—as a way to relieve tooth pain—is mentioned in any historical sources. In examining the tattooing traditions of other Indigenous peoples worldwide, I and other Haudenosaunee scholars and community people have come to the conclusion that our women did indeed tattoo. There are a small number of people reinvigorating the traditional Haudenosaunee tattooing designs. I believe I remain among the first to tattoo with the intent of marking Sky Woman on my body as way to bring her story off the page and into life. I told my daughters about getting the tattoo. At first my younger daughter didn't want me to get one. When I finished I showed it to her and explained what it meant, and how meaningful it is to me, to us, and she sees it now as a thing of beauty.

The process of being tattooed fits within the entirety of what I am doing to rematriate the Sky Woman story and ultimately the community to which I belong. I am adding tattooing as another medium for cultural fluency. I have put the teachings of Sky Woman on my skin as an activation of embodied knowledge. When I wear the symbols of her story, they speak. When I am out and about, people see the tattoos and ask about them, and I then tell the story. We have a level of agency in this contemporary moment as Indigenous scholars. Through this work, I am fully engaged with my methodology.

40 These symbols reference key elements of the Sky Woman narrative. The sky dome describes the point at which the earth and the sky meet in the horizon, the curvature of the earth. The celestial beings are the precursor to the animals of the earth world who assisted Sky Woman by creating earth on the Turtle Being's back. Tobacco is the Haudenosaunee sacred medicine used to send words upward to the Sky World. The three sisters are the foods corn, beans, and squash, which are a staple of the Haudenosaunee traditional diet. The Great Tree is the tree of life, an important aspect of the Sky World portion of the narrative.

Mine is a contemporary Indigenous methodology. Wilson writes, "If research doesn't change you as a person, then you haven't done it right."[41] In this case, the tattooing is part of an ever-evolving process of personal evolution, adaptation, and development.

CONCLUSION

In a more recent conversation with Abenaki wampum scholar Marge Bruchac about the work we do as Indigenous women scholars, we discussed the importance of women working at the recovery of Haudenosaunee tradition and cultural fluency. With reference to the wampum belts Bruchac described how their manufacture often entailed collaborative projects between men and women. Men made the beads and women crafted the belts, but the symbols within the belts came out of discussion among community members. Yet, through time and colonization, white men's voices overshadowed these objects, much like Sky Woman's story, and the agency of women in the creation and use of the belts was lost. In its written form, the voices of white men still speak on this story. As it is rewritten from a feminine perspective and performed, those voices are removed. Why are Indigenous women crucial to the recovery of these objects, we asked ourselves? Bruchac says that, by the very putting of our hands on these objects, we are "talking over" these stories and objects.[42] This is what rematriation is all about.

Exemplary of this shift in its meaning, we can also look to the Two Row Wampum[43] to grasp the full implications of the rematriation of this story. The Two Row poses a relational conception that provides a

---

41 Wilson, *Research Is Ceremony*, 135.

42 Marge Bruchac, personal communication with author, April 30, 2016.

43 The Two Row Wampum is one of the oldest treaty relationships between the Haudenosaunee and the European immigrants. This relationship is symbolized by two vessels travelling down the river of life together. This relationship is visually symbolized by a woven belt of wampum beads with two purple lines running down the centre. The purple beads are interspersed by three rows of white, which denotes two vessels traveling down the river of life together. One line of purple represents the Indigenous people in their canoe and the other line represents the sailing ship of the newcomers traveling in a relationship of non-interference. This was to be the basis of all further treaty agreements between the Haudenosaunee and other nations.

foundational principle for understanding what rematriation is about in this context. Historians and anthropologists have long interpreted the Two Row as simply characteristic of a balanced relationship between Indigenous people and settlers, one that is based in respect for differences. It is indicative of so much more. Additionally, the Two Row communicates extensive relationships—males—females, humans—animals, animic—inanimate, terrestrial—celestial, living—ancestors—that are found throughout the Sky Woman narrative.[44] We can see this most clearly in the twins of the story. Her story, then, is foundational to understanding this important concept of a balanced existence symbolized in the Two Row Wampum, and by performing it, I am bringing the audience closer to a lived, embodied understanding of this important concept. I am rematriating the responsibility for cultural fluency through the performance, first within my family, then my community, and finally with the world at large.

Rematriation in this instance, then, describes the activation of cultural fluency through the performance of the story, the tattoos on my arms, and serves to expand the binaries created by the colonizers to the point where they disappear. We are no longer us and them, but we. This story goes beyond the anthropologists' understandings, the Warriors on the blockades, and the politicians in the boardrooms.[45] It goes to the heart of what humanity is supposed to be about.

Dear Daughters, I am ending this piece with a continuation of my original letter to you. I want to say that I am saddened that I have not been able to pass on the language to you. That ended when your Tota stopped speaking it to us so that we wouldn't feel out of place. 'I wanted you to belong,' she said. We were out of place. We were the girls with the funny names. Now it's your turn. You are the girls with the funny names. But since I went to school, perceptions have changed. You are the girls with

44 See Horn-Miller, "Distortion and Healing," 19–38.
45 This is with reference to the Oka Crisis of 1990. A seventy-eight-day standoff between the Kanien'kehá:ka (Mohawk) and the Sûreté du Québec and Canadian Army over the town of Oka's attempts to expand a golf course onto a traditional burial ground.

*the funny names among many other children with funny
names. What makes you special is that you are from
here. I have not been able to give you Kanienke'ha but I
have given you a sense of self, pride, and a connection
to your culture. You know you are from Turtle Island.
This is your story. This is my gift to you. Continue to
be proud of who you are and to whom you belong."*

REFERENCES

Adams, Amber. "Teyotsi'tsiahsonhátye: Meaning and Medicine in the Haudenosaunee (Iroquois) Story of Life's Renewal." PhD diss., University of Buffalo, 2013.

Bonaparte, Darren. *The Wampum Chronicles.* www.wampumchronicles.com. Accessed July 29, 2018.

Cajete, Gregory. *Look to the Mountain: An Ecology of Indigenous Education.* Skyland: Kivaki Press, 1994.

Hagman, George. *The Artist's Mind: A Psychoanalytic Perspective on Creativity, Modern Art and Modern Artists.* London: Routledge, 2010.

Horn-Miller, Kahente. "Distortion and Healing: Finding Balance and a 'Good Mind' Through the Rearticulation of Sky Woman's Journey." In *Living on the Land: Indigenous Women's Understanding of Place,* edited by Nathalie Kermoal and Isabel Altamirano-Jiménez, 19–38. Edmonton: Athabasca University Press, 2016.

———. "Sky Woman's Great Granddaughters: A Narrative Inquiry into Kanien'kehá:ka (Mohawk) Women's Identity at Kahnawá:ke." PhD diss., Concordia University, 2009.

Inoue, Yukiko. "Cultural Fluency as a Guide to Effective Intercultural Communication: The Case of Japan and the U.S." *Journal of Intercultural Communication* 15 (November, 2007). www.immi.se/intercultural/nr15/inoue.htm.

Jaimes-Guerrero, M. Annette. "'Patriarchal Colonialism' and Indigenism: Implications for Native Feminist Spirituality and Native Womanism." *Hypatia* 18, no. 2 (2003): 58–69.

Kelsey, Penelope Myrtle. *Reading the Wampum: Essays on Hodinohso Ni' Visual Code and Epistemological Recovery.* New York: Syracuse University Press, 2014.

Maracle, Brian. "First Words." In *Our Story: Aboriginal Voices on Canada's Past*, edited by Tantoo Cardinal et al., 15–31. Toronto: Anchor Canada, 2005.

Mohawk, John C. *Iroquois Creation Story: John Arthur Gibson and J.N.B. Hewitt's Myth of the Earth Grasper*. Buffalo, NY: Mohawk Publications, 2005.

Newcomb, Steven. "PERSPECTIVES: Healing, Restoration, and Rematriation." *News & Notes*. Spring/Summer 1995: 3.

"ReMatriate." ReMatriate Facebook page (n.d.). Retrieved December 31, 2015. http://www.facebook.com/ReMatriate/.

"The ReMatriate Interview." Participants: Ryan McMahon, N'alaga Avis O'Brien, Jenee Freij Njootli, Kelly Edzerza Bapty. *Red Man Laughing* podcast, May 4, 2015. https://www.redmanlaughing.com/listen/rematriate. Accessed May 8, 2015.

Rice, Brian. *The Rotinonshonni: A Traditional Iroquoian History Through the Eyes of the Teharonhia; Wako and Sawiskera*. New York: University of Syracuse Press, 2013.

Ritenburg, Heather, et al. "Embodying Decolonization: Methodologies and Indigenization." *AlterNative* 10, no. 1 (2014): 68–75.

Simpson, Leanne Betasamosake. *As We Have Always Done: Indigenous Freedom Through Radical Resistance*. Minneapolis: University of Minnesota Press, 2017.

———. *Dancing on Our Turtle's Back: Stories of Nishnaabeg Re-Creation, Resurgence and a New Emergence*. Winnipeg: ARP Books, 2011.

Simpson, Peter. "Meryl McMaster Takes New York; At Just 27, Artist's Elaborate Self-Portraits Score Her a Spot at the Smithsonian." *Ottawa Citizen*, June 13, 2015: F1.

Stoller, Paul. *Sensuous Scholarship*. Philadelphia: University of Pennsylvania Press, 1997.

Watts, Vanessa. "Indigenous Place-Thought and Agency amongst Humans and Non Humans (First Woman and Sky Woman Go on a European World Tour!)" *Decolonization: Indigeneity, Education & Society* 2, no. 1 (2013): 20–34.

White, Kevin J. "Haudenosaunee Worldviews Through Iroquoian Cosmologies: The Published Narratives in Historical Context." PhD diss., University of Buffalo, 2007.

Wilson, Shawn. *Research Is Ceremony: Indigenous Research Methods*. Winnipeg: Fernwood Publishing, 2009.

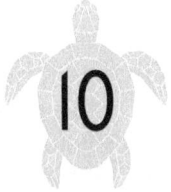

10

RESURGENCE, RECOGNITION, AND REMAINING SETTLED THROUGH *CHANGES* AT UPFRONT '91

Megan Davies

n 1986, the newly formed Tunooniq Theatre[1] from Pond Inlet, Baffin Island, was invited to perform at Expo '86 in Vancouver, British Columbia. Their collective-creation productions, *Changes* and *In Search for a Friend,* were translated from Inuktitut to English for the Vancouver performances, and they were so well received that over the next decade the Inuit theatre company would receive numerous invitations to perform at national and international festivals. At the time Tunooniq Theatre made their southern debut, the Inuit population of the Northwest Territories (NWT) was in the midst of a land claims process, as were the Dene and Métis populations

---

1 Also known as Tununiq Theatre and presently named Tununiq Arsarniit Theatre Group. Here, I will use the spelling used in contemporary 1991 reviews for clarity's sake.

in the NWT. In the next decade, during Tunooniq's southern and international performances, Inuit in the NWT would go through a process of separation, forming their own territorial government, Nunavut, that emerged from the result of a major land claims process. During this decade of performances rife with Inuit and settler-state politics, Tunooniq was invited to perform *Changes* at the Toronto UpFront '91 performance festival in September 1991. UpFront '91 was billed as the first truly Canadian festival which consisted of regionally selected productions that were "outstanding and significant" and were "selected from the alternative side of the theatre tracks."[2] Advertisements and reviews (written by settler-Canadians) of *Changes* categorized it as exotic, but also educational, exotic but close enough for audience members to somehow become insiders of 'traditional' Inuit culture. In this chapter I engage with the interrelated web of strange settler advertisements and reviews, the material culture surrounding UpFront '91 and *Changes*, as they relate to the politics of recognition, reconciliation, and Indigenous resurgence in the Canadian settler-state.

There has been very little scholarship written about Tunooniq Theatre, despite their continuously prolific productions. Scholars such as Sherrill Grace, Jan Selman, and Klara Kolinska who have written about Tunooniq focus on the company's creation process or vaguely describe their subversion of the colonizer's gaze with little to no close reading of the script or audiences' responses. While I agree to an extent with these scholars' arguments about the collective creation process and the script's subversion of the colonizer's gaze, I would like to extend their scholarship here.

I consider that Tunooniq's artistic governance aligns with the vision of the political foundation of Nunavut emerging in the late 1980s and the 1990s, while also drawing on the scholarship of Jarrett Martineau and Leanne Simpson to suggest that *Changes* provided group members and their audiences with resurgence and self-recognition. I then provide a brief overview of popular culture representations of the North to illustrate the context within which Tunooniq was working, and demonstrate, through a close reading of the text, how Tunooniq subverted the colonizer's ethnographic gaze.

....

2   Liam Lacey, "Theatre Festival Set for September," *Globe and Mail*, July 19, 1991: C5.

Next, employing the critical scholarship of Glen Coulthard and Dale Turner, I consider the politics of recognition in the settler-state's relationship to Nunavut and how these politics were also at work at UpFront '91. Finally, I demonstrate how the settler-audience's reactions might be read as a kind of consumptive catharsis influenced by the performances' context, rather than a serious engagement with *Changes'* offer to unsettle settler narratives. Ultimately, I argue that Tunooniq's creation process and the script of *Changes* offered a redemptive form of resurgence and self-recognition for the Inuit performers and audiences that is reflective of the hopeful imaginings of Nunavut's public government. Despite this, the state-imposed politics of recognition and popular culture imaginings of Inuit and the North seeped into UpFront '91 and informed settlers' reception of *Changes*. In the postscript that follows my conclusion I consider what has changed, twenty-five years later, in light of Canada's 150th colonial birthday in July 2017.

STRUCTURES OF GOVERNMENT IN NUNAVUT AND TUNOONIQ

At the time that Tunooniq was performing *Changes* in the late 1980s and 1990s, Inuit in the NWT were negotiating with the government of Canada to separate and resolve land claims. The history of Inuit relations with the federal and territorial governments and the creation of Nunavut is perhaps useful here to situate the company's governing structure and performances.

Peter Kulchyski's *Like the Sound of a Drum* is a study of Aboriginal[3] cultural politics in Nunavut and Denendeh, drawing on decades of ethnographic research. Kulchyski's discussion of NWT history and Nunavut's creation is a useful place here to begin:

> If the period from 1905 to 1921 can be characterized as one
> in which the government was virtually non-existent, and
> 1921 to 1967 as one in which the government was largely
> an administrative apparatus, then the next period, rough-

---

3   For clarity's sake, here and throughout this essay I use the specific language
    that authors and artists have used in their own work (especially since they
    occasionally use those terms in the quotations that I cite).

ly 1967 to 1979, was characterized by the transition from administration to government. Slowly, between 1967 and 1975, the balance between appointed and elected members of the territorial council shifted in favour of elected members. By 1975 the council, Territorial Assembly, consisted entirely of elected members (there were fifteen) led by an appointed commissioner. The council began to look and act less like a coordinating committee of federal civil servants and more like a northern government, albeit highly colonial in nature.[4]

Kulchyski also explains that after 1975, in the 1979 election the majority of the electorate were Aboriginal, but despite this majority, "this did not give them control over the State in northern Canada, a situation that, while the dynamic has evolved markedly, persists."[5] Here Kulchyski suggests that, although there might have been an Aboriginal majority in the NWT government, Canada maintained ultimate sovereignty over Indigenous lands.

More specific to the formation of Nunavut, in the chapter "The Laws of the Land," Kulchyski describes the unique situation of the Inuit in their land claims negotiations. The Inuit were only recognized as "Indian" under the British North America Act in 1939, and as such they could not engage in treaty negotiation with the federal government before this time. As a result, Kulchyski argues, the "eastern Arctic remained uncertain until a Supreme Court of Canada decision in 1973 involving the Nisga'a First Nation in British Columbia, the Calder case, forced the federal government to re-establish a process of negotiating Aboriginal title where it had not been surrendered by treaty."[6] Soon after the landmark Calder case, the Inuit could finally pursue a comprehensive land claim. After 1973, the Inuit began their land claim, which lasted approximately fifteen years. The agreement-in-principle was "finally reached by TFN [Tungavik Federation of Nunavut] with the federal government in 1990," *one year* before Tunooniq performed *Changes* at UpFront '91.

....

4   Peter Kulchyski, *Like the Sound of a Drum: Aboriginal Cultural Politics in Denendeh and Nunavut* (Winnipeg: University of Manitoba Press, 2005), 61.
5   *Ibid.*, 64.
6   *Ibid.*, 80.

In 1999 Nunavut was finally established, which was "the direct result of a comprehensive land claim, known as the Nunavut claim."[7] This claim, however, did not include full Inuit governance; rather it became a popular government that upheld Inuit values solely because of the large Inuit population in Nunavut and remained within Canada's state sovereignty.

In *Made in Nunavut*, Graham White describes the creation process that established Nunavut, focusing on its decentralized government provisions. White notes that "Nunavut came into being as a separate territory, with its own government, as one of the central provisions of the 1993 Nunavut Land Claims Agreement (NLCA), a modern-day treaty signed between the Inuit of Nunavut, represented by the Tungavik Federation of Nunavut and the Government of Canada."[8] As White explains, one of the fundamental tenets of the creation of Nunavut was an emphasis on decentralized government; however, what actually emerged is what White calls a 'deconcentrated' government. White defines a deconcentrated government as a system that contains an increase in positions in locales outside of the capital and the decentralization of some power, but with the majority of power still located in the territory's capital. According to White, the Inuit were not interested in a different government, but a better one "whose very structure and operation were rooted in Inuit culture and values. Decentralization was a critical element in the attempt to realize this goal."[9] During the 1980s and 1990s, the majority of Inuit proposals for a new governance structure were focused on decentralized government, White argues, which were a direct response to the centralized government in Yellowknife. This focus on decentralized government was an Inuit assertion that the government in Yellowknife would not know what was best for individual communities. Instead, the Nunavut decentralized government proposal was based on the assumption that communities, not individual government figureheads, would know what communities needed. According to White, decentralization was an integral focus of proposed governance amongst Inuit in the NWT in the late 1980s

---

7   *Ibid.*, 86, 90.

8   Graham White, *Made in Nunavut: An Experiment in Decentralized Government* (Vancouver: UBC Press, 2015), 3.

9   *Ibid.*, 7.

after the land claims agreement, all the way up to Nunavut's creation in 1999. This decentralized governance can be traced within Tunooniq Theatre's organization structure and their creation process, from the time of their founding in 1986 to the performance in Toronto in 1991, and continues today.

According to Jan Selman and Tunooniq Theatre members, the company "was started as an employment project by artistic director Pakak Innuksuk; his wife, Ellen Hamilton, administers the company."[10] Prior to the company's creation, Innuksuk had begun a drumming group in Igloolik, and later began the Tunooniq Theatre company. The company's productions were created first by working with local elders, who taught them songs, stories, and language, and then they worked collaboratively to create productions from there. As described in the introduction for the script of *Changes* in *Staging the North*,

> Tunooniq is so much a community endeavour that giving credit to individuals presents difficulties. David Qamaniq, (group member) who was most helpful in providing production and other background information, says that all the actors took part in scripting and planning the performances. The Elders taught the actors the traditional dance and some, at any rate, of the *ajajaq*, which are described as traditional folk songs.[11]

Indeed, although the company had two initial founders and has artistic directors and elders providing teachings, Tunooniq Theatre is deconcentrated in the sense that all members equally share the work of script building and performance planning. The collective creation of Tunooniq, then, replicates the popular view of governance in Nunavut at the time and provides a blueprint for the future Nunavut governance structure: decentralization. Much like the aspirations during the creation of Nunavut and beyond, Tunooniq reflects the vision of decentralized governance.

---

10 Jan Selman, "Three Cultures, One Issue," *Canadian Theatre Review* 53 (1987): 12.
11 Tunooniq Theatre, *Changes*, in *Staging the North: Twelve Canadian Plays*, eds. Sherrill Grace et al., 101–13 (Toronto: Playwrights Canada Press, 1999), 104. All quotations from this play and accompanying page references in brackets are taken from this edition.

ACTS OF RESURGENCE IN CREATION
AND PERFORMANCE

Although Indigenous performance cannot be reductively reduced to its ability to provide resurgence and self-recognition, it is one useful lens with which to consider Tunooniq Theatre's production of *Changes*. Both Leanne Simpson's *Dancing On Our Turtle's Back* and Jarrett Martineau's "Creative Combat" address resurgence and self-recognition embedded in Indigenous performance and are helpful guides for thinking through *Changes*.

Near the conclusion of *Dancing on Our Turtle's Back*, Simpson uses Rebecca Belmore's performance piece at *Mapping Resistances*, curated by Wanda Nanibush in Peterborough (2010), to illustrate Indigenous performance's potential to decolonize space. Although Simpson describes the performance in detail, her interests lie in how Belmore's performance transformed colonized space. Below, Simpson articulates this transformation in full detail:

> Belmore drew me into a decolonizing space where my presence and attention became completely focused in a similar fashion to what happens during natural childbirth, or ceremony. I lost sense of time and space. I was transported into a world that Belmore as the artist/storyteller had envisioned—a world where my voice and my meanings mattered. Downtown Peterborough, like any other occupied space in the Americas, is a bastion of colonialism as experienced by Nishnaabeg people. But for twenty minutes in June, that bastion was transformed into an alternative space that provided a fertile bubble for envisioning and realizing Nishnaabeg visions of justice, voice, presence and resurgence.[12]

Simpson's reflection on Belmore's performance theorizes the decolonizing potential of performance. Simpson is attentive to specificity: the potential in Belmore's work functions as a form of Nishnaabeg self-recognition through visions of justice, voice, presence, and resurgence that are specific to Nishnaabeg intellectual thought.[13]

....

12 Leanne Simpson, *Dancing on Our Turtle's Back* (Winnipeg: ARP Books, 2011), 97.
13 Simpson explains that Nishnaabeg intellectual thought is not limited to ▸

In a broader articulation of the political potential for Indigenous performance, Martineau identifies that colonization, despite its invasive structures, is not totalizing. Martineau further claims that "We have always resisted; and our resistance shapes both *how* we imagine and *what* we create. Indigenous creativity provides us with inventive forms of decolonizing praxis: methods of resistance, techniques of resurgence."[14] For Martineau, decolonization strategies cannot be separated from creativity; it is "an art of creative combat, a collective practice of freedom."[15] In this practice of freedom, Indigenous art offers multiple possibilities that can envision, but also mobilize, anti-colonial struggles. Martineau demonstrates this through a variety of performance pieces that are largely collective—in their relationship with audiences and the creation process itself. For Martineau, collective creation is an integral component of Indigenous decolonizing art actions, and he traces this argument through the work of many Indigenous artists, including Christi Belcourt, A Tribe Called Red, Skookum Sound System, Beat Nation (to which Martineau himself belongs), Sonny Assu, and Postcommodity. In both Simpson's and Martineau's works, performance offers imaginings of anti-colonialism, resurgence, and recognition that can come to fruition during the performance and beyond.

The narrative of *Changes* concerns a small Inuit community that endures a range of changes—some associated with colonization, some not—and poses suggestions and questions about ways forward within them. These changes are framed by the beginning scene and the actions of Tapakiak, the spiritual leader of the community. In *Changes*, the performance begins with scene one, entitled "Starting Scene," with the performers filing onto the stage in "traditional caribou skin clothing. Pakak enters last, carrying the drum. They sing the first ajajaq. As the song ends the hunters prepare for hunting" (105). In the script, none of the ajajaq lyrics are listed, so the content of each ajajaq is unknown, although there are examples of ajajaq lyrics from Baffin Island in *Northern Voices* that are suggestive. These

....

◄ the mind, rather it is felt in the body, in the heart, in the spirit, and in engagement with the world around one.

14 Jarrett Martineau, "Creative Combat: Indigenous Art, Resurgence, and Decolonization" (PhD diss., University of Victoria, 2015), 4.

15 *Ibid.*

ajajaq, as previously noted, were taught to the group members by local elders from Pond Inlet, Igloolik, and Hall Beach. In describing the initial intentions behind and Tunooniq's process in "Carrying On the Song," co-founder Pakak Innuksuk states that "Tunooniq Theatre recopied some songs which we learned by listening to the tapes and also we had some elders come to help us to learn some of the songs."[16]

What I find particularly useful about this scene and Innuksuk's statement is what it suggests to me: that Tunooniq's creation process with the actors engaged in performance comprises an act of resurgence and self-recognition. Working with elders and using ajajaq—both the songs and ajajaq as a narrative structure—to (in)form their performance functions as its own combative act. The learning of the songs and using them in performance pose both an anti-colonial imagining that disrupts notions of the 'vanishing Indian' in its interruption of the possibility of a disappearing Inuit culture and, simultaneously, materializes this imagining through the actors learning songs and dances for performance, thus possibly constituting a form of self-recognition that negates colonial imaginings of Inuit peoples in the colonial-occupied space of Toronto.[17] In an interview with Cindy Cowan, actor David Qamaniq suggests this form of self-recognition in stating his initial interests in auditioning for the group: "I wanted to show others—the whole world I guess—how we (the Inuit) used to live; how we used to be independent without the white man's help. I wanted to tell how the Inuit survived . . . I wanted to show this part of Inuit life, even though we don't live the

....

16 Pakak Innuksuk, "Carrying on the Song," *Canadian Theatre Review* 73 (Winter 1992): 22.

17 In Michelle Raheja's book, *Reservation Reelism: Redfacing, Visual Sovereignty, and Representations of Native Americans in Film* (Lincoln: University of Nebraska Press, 2010), in her chapter titled "Visual Sovereignty, Indigenous Revisions of Ethnography, and *Atanarjuat (The Fast Runner)*," she addresses the legacy of salvage anthropology as it relates to Inuit peoples through examining films such as *Nanook of the North*. Raheja also provides a discussion of sovereignty through film, using a term she coins called visual sovereignty (which includes sovereignty that occurs outside of the frame). In her discussion, she describes the material agency that Inuit people exercised while Flaherty was creating *Nanook*, and its use for cultural resurgence today (by preserving Inuit knowledge throughout the film). For more on topics of visual sovereignty, see Raheja's book.

old way, any more."[18] Indeed, the materialized imagining (of independence and survival, as Qamaniq suggests here) through the actors'
performances actually extends to their Inuit audience during their
performances in the NWT and beyond, thus providing a potential
resurgence. Inuit audiences and participants are given the opportunity to learn and envision new futures because the performance
deals explicitly with fluid traditions, changes, and ways of moving
forward. In doing so, *Changes* spreads Inuit knowledge through the
act of creative art making and staging Inuit knowledge (though only
what the collective deems is appropriate to share in performance)
to distribute knowledge and multiple anti-colonial imaginings and
futures. How these moments of resurgence and self-recognition were
perceived by Toronto audiences at UpFront '91 were guided by lingering popular culture expectations and imaginings about the North.

NORTHERN IMAGINARIES AND THE COLONIZER'S ETHNOGRAPHIC GAZE

As Canadian scholar Sherrill Grace has argued, the idea of the North
has captured Canadians' imaginations (including my own) for cen-
turies and forms an integral component of our identity.[19] Grace, a
settler-Canadian literature scholar, has written extensively about
the North's role in the settler-Canadian cultural imaginary. In the introduction to her edited collection of plays, entitled *Staging the North*
(where Tunooniq's scripts are published in full), Grace addresses
the artistic legacy of representations of the North by southern
Canadians. Grace articulates that the problem is not that Canadians

---

18   Cindy Cowan and David Qamaniq, "On Independence and Survival," *Canadi-
     an Theatre Review* 73 (Winter 1992): 18.
19   I think it is important here to note my own relationship to the North. My own
     imaginings have doubtless been shaped by my participation attending, read-
     ing, and performing in plays written by southern settlers about the North, in-
     cluding Wendy Lil's *The Occupation of Heather Rose* and Henry Biessel's *Inuk and
     the Sun*, Judith Thompson's *Sled*, and Geoff Kavanagh's *Ditch*. My imaginings
     have also been shaped by films by both anthropologists and Inuit peoples, at-
     tending multiple Tanya Tagaq performances, anthropologists' recordings of
     Inuit words, and my undergraduate supervisor, who wrote extensively about
     the Franklin Expedition, transcultural whaling shipboard performances, and
     intercultural performances in the North. I have also never been north of 60,
     but not from lack of desire.

produce representations of the North to fuel their identities; it is that they are not seen as representations, rather as truths: "What is sometimes forgotten is that they are *representations* of North and that they do crucial ideological work. As representations, they have great power over our imaginations; we repeat them unconsciously and come to believe them."[20] These representations that Grace describes become problematic when they are projected onto the North and Inuit peoples and seen as truths, while Inuit and other Indigenous peoples populating the North are not permitted to represent themselves to the southern population. Indeed, Grace establishes that "the strongest tradition of northern plays is still one grounded in southern Canada."[21] In "Representations of the Inuit: From Other to Self," Grace fleshes out these representations more clearly, stating that "non-Inuit playwrights have used their representations of the Inuit in many ways,"[22] including for salvage ethnography, as a lens through which to reaffirm a settler self, and as symbols of national identity. Moreover, Grace emphasizes that these representations of the North cannot be "confined to the theatre. Popular representations of the North, and of Canada-As-North that are taken as truths rather than representations, can be traced well back into the 19th century."[23] These representations span a wide range of mediums such as radio dramas, television, films, literature and performance, such as Charles Dickens and Wilkie Collin's *The Frozen Deep* (1856), Robert Flaherty's *Nanook of the North* (1922), radio drama *Renfrew of the Mounted* (1936–1940), television series *North of Sixty* (1992–1998), and Judith Thompson's *Sled* (1997).

These northern representations that Grace identifies as being taken up as truths are most potent in Robert Flaherty's *Nanook of the North* and Farley Mowat's northern fiction. Though both employing different modalities of transmission (allegedly documentary film and literary fiction), Mowat and Flaherty project an ethnographic

---

20 Sherrill Grace, "Degrees of North: An Introduction," in *Staging the North: Twelve Canadian Plays*, eds. Sherrill Grace et al. (Toronto: Playwrights Canada Press, 1999) xi.

21 *Ibid.*, xiii.

22 Sherrill Grace, "Representations of the Inuit: From Other to Self," *Theatre Research in Canada* 21, no.1 (2000): 38–48, https://journals.lib.unb.ca/index.php/tric/article/view/12647/13534, accessed January 24, 2014, 46.

23 Grace, "Degrees of North: An Introduction," xiv.

gaze onto Inuit bodies, cultures, and livelihoods, and achieve troubling affirmations of settler narratives of self. In *Nanook of the North*,
Inuit peoples are relegated to the 'Happy Eskimo' stereotype and
are subject to the colonizer's gaze that designates them as primitive
in comparison to the colonizer's self (read as civilized). Nanook
and his family are shown in this film as barely able to survive, and
cultural vibrancy and other forms of wealth are next to non-exis-
tent. The film assumes a false authoritative truth in its use of documentary film aesthetics, including juxtaposing video scenes and
authoritative narrative text, and quotations from the characters
on screen. In contrast, Mowat's literary fiction produces an alternative way of affirming a settler self in his narratives and audience, but that also projects an inaccurate ethnographic gaze onto
Inuit bodies.[24] Mowat's earlier work, *People of the Deer* (1952), was
allegedly based on his observations of Inuit as a student biologist
at the University of Toronto,[25] providing his writings about Inuit
with a false authorial voice. In his children's novel, *Lost in the Barrens*
(1956), Mowat's protagonist Jamie (a young white teenage boy) finds
his roots and sense of self by surviving in the North and locating
his Viking ancestors, staking a white Anglo-Saxon indigeneity in
the region despite being largely dependant on Awasin, his Cree
best friend, and later on an Inuit boy. In this narrative, Inuit are
described as "Eskimo" and the region they inhabit is described as
unliveable by other Indigenous nations in the novel—hence the
descriptor in the book's title: "barrens." In a literary fiction format,
with an authoritative voice Mowat's narrative affirms a masculine settler self achieved through his conquest of the Arctic and
supplanting of Indigeneity in it, with the help of Awasin and, most

24 For more on the ethnographic gaze and salvage anthropology as it applies
    to the North, see the scholarship of Heather Davis-Fisch in *Loss in Cultural
    Remains in Performance: The Ghosts of the Franklin Expedition* (Basingstoke: Pal-
    grave MacMillan, 2012), as well as Michelle Raheja's *Reservation Reelism* (Lin-
    coln: University of Nebraska Press, 2010). For primary source accounts, see
    Knud Rasmussen, Charles Francis Hall, and Franz Boas. I do not discuss this
    topic in full here, choosing to discuss literary and filmic representations that
    are prominent and easily accessible for the public.

25 Gerald J. Rubio, "Farley Mowat," in *Canadian Encyclopedia*, Historica Canada,
    revised March 4, 2015, http://www.thecanadianencyclopedia.ca/en/article/
    farley-mowat/, accessed December 9, 2016.

significantly for both Awasin and Jamie's survival, an Inuit boy. *Lost in the Barrens* won a Governor General's Award for Juvenile Fiction and a Canada Library Association award at the time of its publication. Just one year before *Changes* was performed at UpFront '91, *Lost in the Barrens* was produced as a made-for-TV film, winning a Daytime Emmy Award in 1991 and two Gemini Awards in 1992.

Gender and masculinity also come into play in these Northern representations; as Kulchyski documents, Inuit women are consistently described in anthropological literature "as servile caricatures."[26] This is most certainly projected onto Nanook's wife, Nyla, in Flaherty's film.[27] Indeed, in Mowat's short story, "Walk Well, My Brother," Konala, an Inuit woman, and Charlie Lavery, a white war veteran who becomes a northern charter pilot, become stranded after their plane goes down somewhere around the Queen Maud Gulf on its way to Yellowknife.[28] Konala and Charlie are stuck together with a language barrier, and Konala struggles to teach and provide for Charlie while sacrificing her own health. Eventually, Konala becomes too sick to continue. Before dying she advises Charlie to "walk well, my brother" in the new pair of boots she made him, but only after teaching him how to live (and thrive) in the Arctic.[29] The gender, racial, and economic politics in Mowat's

---

26 Peter Keith Kulchyski, *Like the Sound of the Drum: Aboriginal Cultural Politics in Denendeh and Nunavut* (Winnipeg: University of Manitoba Press, 2005), 69. I do not discuss gender at length in this essay. This would be a rewarding area for further discussion as it relates to Tunooniq Theatre, especially because of the masculinist British and settlers' relationship to the North. For a more robust discussion of gender as it relates to the North, especially in the nineteenth century, see Lisa Bloom's *Gender on Ice: American Ideologies of Polar Expeditions* (Minneapolis: University of Minnesota Press, 1993), Heather Davis-Fisch's *Loss and Cultural Remains*, or Jen Hill's *White Horizon: The Arctic in the Nineteenth-Century British Imagination* (Albany: State University of New York Press, 2008). Davis-Fisch discusses gender in relation to intercultural relationships and sexual encounters and larger masculinity national narratives, as does Bloom.

27 Tanya Tagaq highlights this in her own version of *Nanook of the North*, first performed at a screening of the film at the 2012 Toronto International Film Festival, in which she provides a sound score that engages critically with the film's ethnographic gaze.

28 This short story was included in a collection titled *The Snow Walker* in 1975, and was later developed into a film in 2003.

29 Farley Mowat, "Walk Well, My Brother," in *The Snow Walker* (Toronto: McClelland and Stewart, 1975), 148.

short story are endless. In all of these examples from Mowat and Flaherty, the Arctic is seen as harsh and barren, but conquerable by a white male protagonist (with the help of the Inuit, as in Mowat's work). Conversely, in some of these representations Inuit people are barely able to survive, as with the depiction of Konala and the family in *Nanook of the North*. In both Flaherty's and Mowat's modes of representation, the Inuit and the North are a culture and a geography to be studied, enjoyed, and consumed by the southern (white) Canadian imaginary. Within these representations and consumptions, Inuit women, as represented by Konala and Nanook's wife, are portrayed as subservient, self-sacrificing, and ultimately consumable.

By the time southern audiences observed *Changes* at UpFront '91, the south had established this century-long legacy of films, plays, literature, and radio dramas that projected an ethnographic gaze onto Inuit people, culture, and livelihoods that seeks to affirm a (masculine) settler self in Canada.

CHANGES TO THE COLONIZER'S GAZE

The legacies of the colonizer's gaze lingered in Toronto audiences, but they were also manipulated by the theatre company for their own ends. Referring to contemporary Inuit drama, Grace argues that "first, the Inuit have taken over this representational activity and, in the process, they are 'returning the gaze,' othering *us*, and, even more importantly, using theatre for their own purposes."[30] In speaking about how Inuit drama is deployed and received, Grace expands on Alan Filewod's description of the colonizer's gaze. Grace applies this concept to plays *about* Inuit peoples, and to how Inuit artists are tactfully returning this gaze, building her argument on analyses of Tunooniq Theatre's productions, *Changes* and *In Search for a Friend*. Expanding on Grace's and Filewod's thought-provoking scholarship here, I want to further analyze this gaze, how it functions, and how it relates to *Changes*.

In the Western tradition, the gaze is a concept that helps to understand how viewers react to what they are watching, based on a specific Freudian psychological process. It is a (dated) Eurocentric concept, but it is a useful tool to consider settler audiences'

30 Grace, "Representations of the Inuit," 44.

spectatorship of Indigenous performance and what I think is Tunooniq's tactful use of it. Building on Freud's work, Laura Mulvey, a feminist film theorist, developed a psychological theory to explain the male gaze in cinema, which is a helpful framework for me to understand how the colonial gaze might function in *Changes*. Mulvey argues that the spectators experience a contradiction during their observer role because of two psychological processes: scopophilia (the pleasure of looking) and recognition (the constitution of the self through identification with the image). Mulvey argues that the recognition process actually produces anxiety for the viewer in some instances. In Mulvey's reading, the female body signifies for the male at once a pleasure of looking at, but also a fear of castration through a process of recognition.[31] Mulvey states that "the tension between instinctual drives and self-preservation continues to be a dramatic polarization in terms of pleasure."[32] If we assume that the dominant theatre-goer for the *Changes* performance at UpFront '91 was a settler, as the performance's reviewers were,[33] then the Inuit performers potentially signified for the colonizer audience at once the pleasure of looking at an object, but also fear, triggered through recognition and racial difference. Moreover, if we consider the dominant popular-culture representation of Inuit peoples, as illustrated by Mowat and Flaherty among others, this ethnographic gaze that constitutes the self through difference is likely already how settler audiences arrived at *Changes*. Mulvey also argues that because of the viewer's objectification and attempt to control the image onscreen, "Man is reluctant to gaze at his exhibitionist like,"[34] meaning that the

....

31 Despite the productive components of Mulvey's argument, her essay has been highly criticized by film theorists and others. Mulvey has also re-examined her thinking since the essay's initial publication. I fully recognize these criticisms, but I still think her argument is extremely useful as it brings together spectatorship, psychoanalysis, and self-recognition in productive ways.

32 Laura Mulvey, "Visual Pleasure and Narrative Cinema," *Screen* 16, no .3 (1975): 6–18, https://academic.oup.com/screen/article-abstract/16/3/6/1603296, accessed March 14, 2014. 10.

33 I was unable to find any reviews or responses to this specific performance by Indigenous people. I have found some writings about Tununiq Arsarniit's performances (not specifically *Changes*) in *Northern News* and other web media from Nunavut.

34 Mulvey, "Visual Pleasure," 12.

viewer does not like to watch something out of their control or see their objectified self on screen (or in this case, on stage).

During *Changes* the power of the colonizer viewer and this ethnographic legacy has the potential to be subverted, I argue, in its staging (or to use Mulvey's term, exhibition) of the *colonizer* through an *Inuit* perspective, out of the colonizer viewer's control. In the production at UpFront '91, Inuit actor David Qamaniq plays the character Bob, the corrupt white trader. Bob is speaking to the audience using the microphone when he says, "The trading is easy and so, I gather, are the women. These savages don't know the true value of a skin and to them a knife or even a mirror is ample reward for their labour" (III), thus putting the Euro-Canadian settler on exhibition. In this scene, Bob trades alcohol for skins and speaks vulgarly about Inuit women in ways that problematically echo representations of the North and Inuit women as up for the taking.[35] In doing so, Bob becomes the savage that he speaks of, while he is also clearly responsible for the changes that will soon face the Inuit community as a result of his irresponsible trading. Qamaniq, productively playing whiteface and in control of the representation of the colonizer enemy, places, by extension, some of the responsibility onto the settler audience.

At the same time, the character of the colonizer (Bob) is not in control of the narrative plot. Rather, it is the Inuit characters and collaborative scriptwriters who control the colonizer's voice and the narrative direction. While Qamaniq's playing whiteface may unsettle settler audience's narratives of self, the script also places the narrated changes (the influence of colonization) in Inuit youth's control, through the voice of their spiritual guide. Directly after the trading interaction, the community becomes sick with alcohol abuse and, as such, cannot hunt as they did at the beginning of the play: "Look at the hunters. Sleeping like babies in the day" (III). However, there are some benefits that come with trade that the youth embrace, and there is a suggestion that the youth can take what is useful and work to discard what is not. Taqiapik/shaman states, "I'm old and I cannot change. But the young, they embrace the changes" (III). The

---

35 Again, this section would be extremely interesting grounds for further research and analysis as it relates to gender because, to some extent, Bob is personifying those gendered non-Inuit representations or perceptions of the North.

narrated changes, then, are to some extent in the young Inuit's control, guided by the voice of their spiritual guide, Taqiapik. This becomes problematic for the southern Ontario Euro-Canadian viewer, who does not have control over his depicted likeness or how the narrative of changes instigated by colonization is *supposed* to go. The colonizer's lack of control is further complicated when we consider the use of language in *Changes*.

In a *Toronto Star* review of *Changes* at UpFront '91, the late Mira Friedlander notes: "They are clad in traditional costumes of sealskin and leather and speak mostly Inuktitut. Only occasionally do the actors use English to narrate the story of their life."[36] Although English was spoken to provide the audience with context for the physical narrative happening in front of them, according to Friedlander much of the dialogue was actually spoken in Inuktitut. As stated in the introduction to the script in *Staging the North*, "the actors' words are not predominant: movement, sound, and visual effects together produce meaning" (103). The narrative is heavily informed by physical action combined with visual and sound elements, rather than relying solely on dialogue to move the story forward. The words that are written in the published ten-page script are likely the only dialogue used in the production, depending, of course, on where they are performing and who their audience is. Expanding on the staging of Indigenous languages in front of settler audiences, Helen Gilbert identifies a majority audience's confrontation with unfamiliar language as a gap or absence, which intensifies "the ambivalent 'fear and desire' responses which codes of difference evoke in a majority audience."[37] These fear and desire responses arguably contribute to the anxiety already produced by the character Bob and Inuit narrative control in *Changes*.

If we speculate that the performers' use of English is specific to key narrative points within the play, it seems most likely to occur when characters speak into the microphone that is written into the published script. Thus, when Bob speaks and characterizes himself

---

36 Mira Friedlander, "Inuit Drama Like Painting that Becomes Alive on Stage," *Toronto Star*, September 22, 1991: C2.

37 Helen Gilbert, "De-scribing Orality: Performance and the Recuperation of Voice," in *De-scribing Empire: Post-colonialism and Textuality*, eds. Chris Tiffin and Alan Lawson (New York: Routledge, 1994), 102.

as corrupt, the southern audience would have understood him because he is speaking into the microphone, as per the script's stage
direction. Directly before and after Bob's speech, however, the
Inuit characters are speaking to each other about Bob, possibly in
Inuktitut, as they do not use the microphone. Before Bob has the
opportunity to speak, Naujak says: "Look . . . Indians are coming"
(110). Directly after Bob's speech at the microphone, Taqiapik states:
"The white man gives and takes. They stay and change our lives"
(111). The stating of Inuit views about Bob is perhaps not actually
accessible for the Toronto audience because these views are spoken
in Inuktitut. When the southern audiences confronted Inuktitut in
that moment, the language gap potentially furthered anxiety that
was already produced by the Inuit man, David Qamaniq, playing the
white trader Bob, and the Inuit narration of northern colonization.

NUNAVUT, *CHANGES,* AND THE
CANADIAN MOSAIC (THEATRE) STATE

The exquisite performance tactics of Tunooniq Theatre provided
opportunities to disrupt settler narratives of self and the colonizer's
ethnographic gaze, and, as mentioned previously, it offered resurgence and self-recognition for performers and Inuit audiences in
Nunavut and beyond. But in addition to the popular cultural legacies
that influenced UpFront '91 audiences, the context of the festival
also exerted its own influences of settler consumption. Dale Turner's
and Glen Coulthard's criticisms of liberal recognition frameworks
in Indigenous and settler-state reconciliation provide a lens with
which to interrogate the creation of Nunavut alongside UpFront
'91's hosting of *Changes.*

In *This is Not a Peace Pipe,* Turner identifies the problems of the
liberal recognition framework for addressing Indigenous rights in
Canada. Turner does so through his examination of the White Paper,
or the "Statement of the Government of Canada on Indian Policy,
1969," Alan Cairns' 'citizens plus' policy, and Will Kymlicka's 'minority rights' view. For Turner, these liberal recognition theories do
not adequately address Indigenous needs for four reasons, three
of which I will recount here: "they do not adequately address the
legacy of colonialism"; they do not "respect the *sui generis* nature
of Indigenous rights as a class of political rights that flow out of

Indigenous nationhood and that are not bestowed by the Canadian state"; and "they do not question the legitimacy of the Canadian state's unilateral claim of sovereignty over Aboriginal lands and peoples."[38] Indeed, Coulthard's scholarship in "Resentment and Indigenous Politics" significantly extends Turner's four-pronged critique, while framing it within anti-colonial scholarship around resentment. Referring to the three forms of reconciliation, Coulthard addresses the most significant in a Canadian context, which "refers to the process by which things are brought 'to agreement, concord, or harmony; the fact of being made consistent or compatible.'"[39] Coulthard likens this third form to Turner's scholarship on the act of making things consistent, which is at the core of "Canada's legal and political understanding of the term: namely, rendering consistent Indigenous assertions of nationhood with the state's unilateral assertion of sovereignty over Native peoples' land and populations."[40] In another essay, entitled "From Wards of the State to Subjects of Recognition?," Coulthard demonstrates explicitly how rendering consistent (a.k.a. recognition) is a continuation of colonialism but with a different face, arguing that this new phase, "is now reproduced through a seemingly more conciliatory set of languages and practices that emphasize *recognition* and *accommodation*."[41] This new phase, Coulthard argues, continues the colonial relationship between Indigenous peoples and the state, which can be visible through a "version of Marx's primitive accumulation thesis,"[42] which addresses the separation and alienation of peoples from their lands and resource extraction. Coulthard's and Turner's suggestion that the third form of reconciliation (making consistent) negates any kind of real reconciliation is strikingly evident in Thomas Berger's

---

38 Dale Turner, *This is Not a Peace Pipe: Towards a Critical Indigenous Philosophy* (Toronto: University of Toronto Press, 2006), 6.

39 Glen Coulthard, "Resentment and Indigenous Politics," in *The Settler Complex*, ed. Patrick Wolfe, 155–172 (Los Angeles: American Indian Research Center Press, 2016), 156.

40 *Ibid.*

41 Glen Coulthard, "From Wards of State to Subjects of Recognition? Marx, Indigenous Peoples, and the Politics of Dispossession in Denendeh," in *Theorizing Native Studies*, eds. Audra Simpson and Andrea Smith, 56–86 (Durham, NC: Duke University Press, 2014), 56.

42 *Ibid.*

2006 final report on the Nunavut claim agreement's implementation. But it is also evident in the organizational structure of UpFront '91.

As we learned earlier through the scholarship of Kulchyski and White, the creation of Nunavut remained under the sovereignty of the settler state. Although Inuit peoples received an enormous land claim and a popular government, the interests of the settler state were upheld. This politics of recognition that negates real reconciliation is apparent in Berger's final report. In this report, Berger suggests a bilingual language program in Nunavut for education (English and Inuktitut), and argues that it is the federal government's responsibility to finance new education policies and programs for future Inuit youth to gain employment in their communities. Near the conclusion of his summation letter, which serves as an introduction to the report, Berger stresses the importance of Inuit culture and the federal government's financial support of education in Nunavut. However, Berger simultaneously assimilates Inuit culture into what Turner and Coulthard have amply diagnosed as a problematic liberal recognition structure. More specifically, Berger does so while entangling this recognition process with Western capitalist drives—what Coulthard might recognize as the continued primitive accumulation phase of colonization:

> Every Canadian must be aware of Inuit achievements in art and sculpture, in film and performance arts, achievements for which the Inuit have won international renown. The Inuit are a bright tile in the Canadian mosaic. Why not Inuit bilingualism? Why not Inuit literature?
>
> I believe Canadians will support this project—the Nunavut Project. They realize that no affirmation of Canada's Arctic sovereignty will be complete unless the people of the Arctic—the Inuit—are partners in the task.
>
> Our ideas of human rights, of strength in diversity, of a northern destiny, merge in the promise of Nunavut. It is a promise that we must keep.[43]

---

43   Thomas R. Berger, "Conciliator's Final Report: The Nunavut Project," in *Nunavut Land Claims Agreement Implementation Contract Negotiations for the Second Planning Period 2003–2013* (Ottawa: Ministry of Aboriginal Affairs and Northern Development Canada, 2006), xii.

In this excerpt, and throughout the final report, Berger suggests that Inuit education has a benefit to Canadians—as a liberalist mosaic nation and as a country whose economy could greatly benefit from Arctic sovereignty that accompanies the creation of, and partnership with, Nunavut. What emerges in Berger's report is an emphasis on Inuit education and cultural resurgence that is accommodated into existing colonial-state structures. Although the focus of Berger's report is clearly pro Inuit language and cultural revival (many might take issue with Berger's use of the term 'revival'), this becomes co-opted by the settler state and tailored to fit within its own capitalist primitive accumulation desires. Likewise, this integration of Inuit cultural content into settler-state interests is evident in the organizational framework of UpFront '91.

Changes was one of ten plays to be featured at UpFront '91 and had five performance slots during the festival. The festival was named after its location—in and around Front Street in Toronto—and it was billed as Canada's first national festival of Canadian theatre. According to Liam Lacey, "unlike the Fringe festivals, which are open to any theatre group, this is by invitation and selected by jury, which means we should be seeing the best from each region."[44] Here, Lacey acknowledges that the selection of performances was based on the festival's own terms—the performances were chosen by a jury implemented by the festival organizers and were selected "from the alternative side of the theatre tracks." But Lacey also notes that the festival was billed as regional as well as national, in that performances were chosen as the best representations from specific geographic locations in Canada rather than solely based on content. Included in this festival were productions from the west to the east coast: *Napalm* by David Craig, *The Noam Chomsky Lectures* by Daniel Brooks and Guerrillemo Verdecchia, *Gaspard* by Le Groupe Multi-Discipline de Montreal, *Tictacteur* by Sonia Cot, *Sincerely, a Friend: The Music of Leonard Cohen* by Bryden MacDonald, *Alkoremmi* by Winnipeg's Primus Theatre, and *Millions Die* by Gina Bastoni of Basta Theatre. In Lacey's description of these to-be-featured productions, he allots the most words to Tunooniq, describing *Changes* as "a collective work about a traditional Inuit family before the

---

44   Liam Lacey, "Theatre Festival Set for September," C5.

onset of civilization."[45] In doing so, UpFront '91 was to showcase the regional Canadian cultural mosaic (albeit a predominantly white mosaic), which included Tunooniq Theatre, and assimilated the only Indigenous theatre company in the festival into the unquestioned Canadian settler state/theatre, which was chosen by a judicial committee on the settler state/theatre's own terms.[46] Here, we can see the politics of recognition that Turner and Coulthard describe directly at work, in the creation of the first national festival of Canadian theatre that placed Tunooniq within the Canadian theatre state and recognized Tunooniq as part of the *Canadian* cultural mosaic. This organization of the festival was accomplished without questioning the settler state/theatre's legitimacy or the terms on which it selected 'the best' of regional performances. In doing so, UpFront '91 participated in what Coulthard and Turner have deemed the politics of recognition without real reconciliation, incorporating Tunooniq's performance into the structure of liberal recognition in Canadian theatre.

CONSUMPTIVE SETTLER AUDIENCES AND NARRATIVES OF SELF

The UpFront '91 audiences, then, would have been given permission to consume *Changes* as part of the settler state's cultural mosaic, further enabling them to project an ethnographic gaze on the performance. Advertisements and reviews for *Changes* and UpFront '91 suggest that this was the case and that the audiences' narratives of self remained intact after the performance, despite Tunooniq's subversive performance tactics. Performance studies and musicology scholar Dylan Robinson's essay in *Theatres of Affect* offers some guidance to think through settler audiences' spectatorship by using the advertisements for and reviews of the production.

In "Feeling Reconciliation, Remaining Settled," Robinson addresses the emotional empathy felt by settler audiences observing

---

45 *Ibid.*
46 I want to point out here that likely the producers had the best of intentions in bringing Tunooniq into UpFront '91. I merely want to point out the larger state-imposed colonial structures that seep into Canada's arts and cultural policies (and their enactment on their ground).

inclusionary performances that assimilate Indigenous content and/ or Indigenous histories, arguing that these performances actually allow settlers to remain settled. More specifically, Robinson situates this argument within two inclusionary performances (intercultural operas) that use Western aesthetic forms that integrate Indigenous content, without actually giving up any of the power to Indigenous peoples or even questioning those asymmetrical power relations. Robinson states: "In both performances, the fundamental tenets of Western musical genres and form remain intact; the inclusion thus reinforces settler structural logic: that the structure of the aesthetic might be enriched by 'other' sights and sounds without unsettling the worldview it supports."[47] Robinson's point here is particularly striking in the performances he describes, performances that seek to produce a kind of reconciliation between Indigenous and settler peoples. In addressing this reconciliation, Robinson points towards performance studies and theatre scholars who write about affective contagion as transformative—so-called 'theatres of change' that potentially enable, through affect and empathy, positive transformations in their audiences. Instead of this hopeful affective contagion, however, Robinson argues that the performances he observed did not effect actual reconciliation. Instead, because these performances "engender embodied felt forms of reconciliation,"[48] audiences remained settled, allowing them to feel reconciled, rather than convincing audiences to unsettle themselves and eventually engage in real reconciliation.

Any descriptive reviews that I could find of *Changes* categorized it as educational, exotic, and authentic (much like the non-Inuit literary and popular-culture representations of the North). Mira Friedlander's review at the time pronounced that it was not theatre, but rather a borderline-real performance of Inuit life. Friedlander described the set as simple; "in some ways it even makes the experience richer."[49] Likewise, Paula Citron, a notoriously sympathetic reviewer for non-Western theatre, was fascinated with having an

....

47 Dylan Robinson, "Feeling Reconciliation, Remaining Settled," in *Theatres of Affect: New Essays on Canadian Theatre*, vol. 4, ed. Erin Hurley, 274–306 (Toronto: Playwrights Canada Press, 2014), 277.

48 *Ibid.*, 278.

49 Friedlander, "Inuit Drama," C2.

"insider's look at a culture," describing *Changes* as one of "the most exotic offerings in Up Front '91,"[50] but also educational in that it supposedly allowed the audience to understand Inuit culture. The reviewers and advertisers' responses to *Changes* characterized the play in contradictory terms—exotic, historical, educational, and traditionally authentic. Despite the script's productive subversion of the gaze, reviewers tended to project an ethnographic gaze onto their writing about *Changes*. What is also striking about these reviews and advertisements is that they contain little to no real challenge of, or reflection on, settler narratives or colonization processes in the North. Reflecting on the last moment of the production, Friedlander states, "and when one actor stands centre-stage at the end and asks, 'The young embrace the changes, but how will we survive them?,' there is no answer. Instead, they all join hands and sing a song of hope, of faith, of despair and defeat."[51] Clearly, most reviewers' descriptions locate colonization in the past tense and/or deem it an inevitable outcome, as Friedlander seems to suggest here in a strange conflation, both of which negate any real responsibility or reflection. Instead of unsettling themselves and their relationship to the script's narrative, the reviewers projected the colonizer's ethnographic gaze onto the performance of *Changes*, the same gaze that the script's performance tactics have the potential to subvert.

My guess is that the geographic distance between Toronto and Nunavut, popular cultural representations, and the politics of recognition of UpFront '91 itself enabled audiences to maintain their narratives of self by projecting an ethnographic gaze onto the performance. The majority of the reviewers, and perhaps the majority of the audience members at UpFront '91, may have felt empathy for the Inuit community on stage, as Friedlander clearly does in the final words of her review. But in reality, as indicated by the reviews, like Robinson's audiences, the audience remained very much settled, perhaps nudged along by the politics of recognition in the festival's framework.

---

50   Paula Citron, "Pond Inlet Troupe Traces Inuit History," *Toronto Star*, September 15, 1991, C3.
51   Friedlander, "Inuit Drama," C2.

CONCLUSION

Despite the colonial structures and performances working around them, Tunooniq's performance of *Changes* at UpFront '91 attempted to subvert the colonizer's ethnographic gaze by staging Bob and the colonization process through an Inuit voice and by speaking primarily Inuktitut to deflect any cross-cultural 'knowing' the settler audience might assume. Furthermore, Tunooniq's artistic governance still reflected the governance of Nunavut in its focus on decentralization and reflection of Inuit values, and their creation and performance process possibly provided a space for resurgence and self-recognition for the Inuit performers and perhaps for Indigenous audience members.

There are many possible interpretations of Tunooniq's prolific performances, and this chapter has sought to untangle only one of them. I hope that, in future, theatre and performance studies scholarship will contain a plethora of writing on Tunooniq's continuing body of work that perhaps expands on or overturns my own thoughts here. I personally would love to read more discussions of ethnographic and gendered representations and how they are subverted in Tunooniq's productions, in addition to topics around food sovereignty and language use for a wide range of audiences.

POSTSCRIPT

Today, Tununiq Arsarniit Theatre Group performs throughout the year in Pond Inlet for local community members, but also now for cruise ships, tourists, and visitors. The profile of Tununiq on the Qaggiavuut Society's (a Nunavut arts organization) website states that the company develops theatre for social issues and public education, using traditional Inuit music, songs, drum dance, and stories. Additionally, the company continues to develop "its plays and performances by consensus, involving elders as actors and writers and always weaving Inuit language and culture in every issue it tackles."[52] Recently, their artistic director, Sheena Akoomalik, has remounted *Changes* in Inuktitut (2016) and the company has developed

---

52 "Tununiq Arsarniit Theatre Group," *Qaggiavuut!*, http://www.qaggiavuut.ca/en/artist/tununiq-arsarniit-theatre-group, accessed December 9, 2016.

an original play titled *Qallupilluk*, which features legends, oral traditions, and the wisdom of elders.

In 2008 Tununiq created a production called *Qaggiq*, which toured the territory for the whole summer and performed well into the fall. Daron Letts from *Northern News Services* published an online article that discusses a performance of *Qaggiq* in Pond Inlet on November 14, 2008, at the Attakaalik Community Hall. This November performance was opened by a high-school drama class's short play, which was created with support from Tununiq's artistic director, Akoomalik, and the high-school drama teacher. In his description of the weekend's upcoming event, based on his conversation with Akoomalik, Letts suggests that the narrative of *Qaggiq* "touches on life in the community during 24-hour sunlight and 24-hour darkness" and seems to have an educational focus, all spoken in Inuktitut. Alongside the play's narrative, Akoomalik explains, "we also talk about how Nunavut became its own territory from NWT in 1999," which, according to Akoomalik, "has changed the map of Canada and the rest of the world." The high-school play that opened Tununiq's performance dealt with stereotyping and racism in the community, among other issues. The drama teacher describes the creation process for the play as "a very collaborative project in that everyone assumes different roles [and] contribute[s] to each other and give[s] each other feedback." In the resulting high-school drama, the character of Bob, the ignorant Qallunaaq from *Changes* reappears, asking the other actors, "Are you a real Eskimo?"[53]

REFERENCES

Berger, Thomas R. "Conciliator's Final Report: The Nunavut Project." In *Nunavut Land Claims Agreement Implementation Contract Negotiations for the Second Planning Period 2003–2013*. Ottawa: Ministry of Aboriginal Affairs and Northern Development Canada, 2006.

Bloom, Lisa. *Gender on Ice: American Ideologies of Polar Expeditions*. Minneapolis: University of Minnesota Press, 1993.

....

53 Daron Letts, "Actor Asks: Are You a Real Eskimo?," *Northern News Services*, November 10, 2008.

Chapman, Geoff. "Festival to Showcase Theatre." *Toronto Star*, July 18, 1991: E1.

Citron, Paula. "Pond Inlet Troupe Traces Inuit History." *Toronto Star*, September 15, 1991: C3.

Coulthard, Glen. "From Wards of the State to Subjects of Recognition? Marx, Indigenous Peoples, and the Politics of Dispossession in Denendeh." In *Theorizing Native Studies*, edited by Audra Simpson and Andrea Smith, 56–86. Durham, NC: Duke University Press, 2014.

———. "Resentment and Indigenous Politics." In *The Settler Complex*, edited by Patrick Wolfe, 155–172. Los Angeles: American Indian Research Centre Press, 2016.

Cowan, Cindy and David Qamaniq. "On Independence and Survival." *Canadian Theatre Review* 73 (Winter 1992): 18–21.

Davis-Fisch, Heather. *Loss in Cultural Remains in Performance: The Ghosts of the Franklin Expedition*. Basingstoke: Palgrave MacMillan, 2012.

Filewod, Alan. "Receiving Aboriginality: Tomson Highway and the Crisis of Cultural Authenticity." *Theatre Journal* 46, no. 3 (1994): 363–73.

Friedlander, Mira. "Inuit Drama Like Painting that Becomes Alive on Stage." *Toronto Star*, September 22, 1991: C2.

Gilbert, Helen. "De-scribing Orality: Performance and the Recuperation of Voice." In *De-scribing Empire: Post-Colonialism and Textuality*, edited by Chris Tiffin and Alan Lawson, 98–111. New York: Routledge, 1994.

Grace, Sherrill. *Canada and the Idea of the North*. Montreal: McGill-Queen's University Press, 2002.

———. "Representations of the Inuit: From Other to Self." *Theatre Research in Canada* 21, no. 1 (2000): 38–48. https://journals.lib.unb.ca/index.php/tric/article/view/12647/13534. Accessed January 24, 2014.

———. "Degrees of North: An Introduction." In *Staging the North: Twelve Canadian Plays*, edited by Sherrill Grace et al., i–xxiv. Toronto: Playwrights Canada Press, 1999.

Hill, Jen. *White Horizon: The Arctic in the Nineteenth-Century British Imagination*. Albany: State University of New York Press, 2008.

Innuksuk, Pakak. "Carrying on the Song." *Canadian Theatre Review* 73 (Winter 1992): 22–3.

Knowles, Ric. "Multicultural Text, Intercultural Performance: The Performance Ecology of Contemporary Toronto." In *Performance and the City*, edited by D.J. Hopkins, Shelley Orr, and Kim Solga, 73–91. London: Palgrave Macmillan, 2009.

———. "Part 1: Theory and Practice." In *Reading the Material Theatre*, 9–104. New York: Cambridge University Press, 2004.

Kolinska, Klara. "Staging *Changes* That Hurt: Contemporary Drama and Theatre of the Inuit in Canada." In *Authenticity and Legitimacy in Minority Theatre: Constructing Identity*, edited by Patrice Brasseur and Madelena Gonzalez, 283–92. Newcastle: Cambridge Scholars, 2010.

Kulchyski, Peter. *Like the Sound of the Drum: Aboriginal Cultural Politics in Denendeh and Nunavut*. Winnipeg: University of Manitoba Press, 2005.

Lacey, Liam. "*Changes* Shows Joys and Dangers of Arctic Life." *Globe and Mail*, September 21, 1991: C4.

———. "Theatre Festival Set for September." *Globe and Mail*, July 19, 1991: C5.

Letts, Daron. "Actor Asks: Are You a Real Eskimo?" *Northern News Services*, November 10, 2008. http://www.nnsl.com/frames/newspapers/2008-11/nov10_08act.html. Accessed 9 December 2016.

Martineau, Jarrett. "Creative Combat: Indigenous Art, Resurgence, and Decolonization." PhD diss., University of Victoria, 2015.

Mowat, Farley. "Walk Well My Brother." In *The Snow Walker*, 132–148. Toronto: McClelland and Stewart, 1975.

Mulvey, Laura. "Visual Pleasure and Narrative Cinema." *Screen* 16, no. 3 (1975): 6–18. https://academic.oup.com/screen/article-abstract/16/3/6/1603296?redirectedFrom=fulltext. Accessed March 14, 2014.

Petrone, Penny, ed. *Northern Voices: Inuit Writing in English*. Toronto: University of Toronto Press, 1998.

Raheja, Michelle. *Reservation Reelism: Redfacing, Visual Sovereignty, and Representations of Native Americans in Film*. Lincoln: University of Nebraska Press, 2011.

Robinson, Dylan. "Feeling Reconciliation, Remaining Settled." In *Theatres of Affect: New Essays on Canadian Theatre*, vol. 4, edited by Erin Hurley, 274–306. Toronto: Playwrights Canada Press, 2014.

Rubio, Gerald J. "Farley Mowat." In *Canadian Encyclopedia.* Historica Canada. Revised March 4, 2015. http://www.thecanadianencyclopedia.ca/en/article/farley-mowat/. Accessed December 9, 2016.

Selman, Jan. "Three Cultures, One Issue." *Canadian Theatre Review* 53 (Winter 1987): 11–19.

Simpson, Leanne. *Dancing on Our Turtle's Back.* Winnipeg: ARP Books, 2011.

Tagaq, Tanya. Musical score. *Nanook of the North.* 2012 Toronto International Film Festival.

"Tununiq Arsarniit Theatre Group." *Qaggiavuut!.* http://www.qaggiavuut.ca/en/artist/tununiq-arsarniit-theatre-group. Accessed December 9, 2016.

"Tunooniq." *Canadian Theatre Review* 73 (Winter 1992): 15–17.

Tunooniq Theatre. *Changes.* In *Staging the North: Twelve Canadian Plays,* edited by Sherrill Grace et al., 101–13. Toronto: Playwrights Canada Press, 1999.

Turner, Dale. *This Is Not a Peace Pipe: Towards a Critical Indigenous Philosophy.* Toronto: University of Toronto Press, 2006.

"UpFront '91 Schedule." *Toronto Star,* September 13, 1991: D6.

White, Graham. *Made in Nunavut: An Experiment in Decentralized Government.* Vancouver: UBC Press, 2015.

CODA:

THE DREAM OF AN
IMPOSSIBLE THEATRE

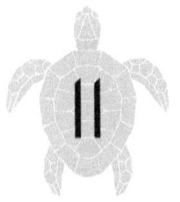

RED PEOPLE, RED MAGIC

Floyd P. Favel

I.
My name is Morning Traveller.
I was born in the Moon when the Chokecherries are Ripe
and I grew up within my language
surrounded by the tales of the old.

I went to school in nearby towns
In winters our bus would be greeted
By the dull explosions against our windows
White snowballs fashioned by hateful hands.

I did not know that
Such a beautiful thing as being an Indian
Could also be such a terrible thing.

I studied theatre
And I have travelled the world,
talked with many wise ones, and many foolish,
counting coup in many enemy lands.

II.
I went to school across the Big Water,
on the edge of the grey North Sea
and amongst the olive groves and vineyards
of the southern country.

And I have returned,
a stranger amongst my tribe.

The road of life is narrow.
It is where the heart is pierced
by the arrows of a hundred
colonial methods and lies.

It is where traitors stand,
Wearing red masks,
knives hidden under blankets.
With a smile, fake handshake
and a forked tongue, they guard
the entrance to the ration house.

Where our People's soul is weighed
in the balance of a government scale.

If I could silence my nostalgia
I would have never returned, but here I am
In the prison of my country,
Nitaskee Oma, Ministik,˙   *This is my land, this Island (Cree)

Turtle Island

III.
When in doubt
Think of your first day in the theatre.

Maybe my first day was
Flying over this country.
Closing my eyes I rested my head on the seat
on my way across the Big Water.

There, amongst the marble colonnades of a foreign city,
I could dream incognito, unremarkable,
and drink espresso at an outdoor café
in a Venetian piazza.

Free from this country
Which has undone so many of my People.

Or maybe it was April 30, 1986.
North Sea coast, Jutland, Denmark.
We awoke, radio solemnly intoned,
Disaster across the Iron Curtain,
Radioactive clouds,
Chernobyl nuclear fallout.

Karin, min elsker, min elskede.*   *My love, my beloved

That was to be my last day with you.
I would never see you again.
At that time I did not know
you would become
a name in a poem, or a story.

I ask forgiveness.

French dramatist Jean Genet
had died the week before,
and the radio played a Schubert lieder
broken by an official voice.

"There has been a disaster in the Ukraine.
Do not go outside, do not drink the milk."
Anxiously we listened to the radio
And the sea waves crashing against the shore

That day I was to leave to seek my master,

who had arrived in the south,
in the Mediterranean lands
where Pan still played his magic pipes

Karin, Karin, Karin,
to say your name breaks my heart.

The night before by candlelight
You read the Rune stones.
Sound of stone on wood,
they echoed the emptiness of our future.

"Make haste! leave this land,
Your fortune awaits!"

 In our last day together
the sun stopped at midday to look.
We were in the garden, you sang.
The church bell in the village
sounded all along the coast.

" . . . I denne evige rejse
Vores sjæle mødes,
i skov, i en regndråbe.
i vinden, i solnedgangen,
og vores hjerter skal smerte,
som vi vil skjule med et bud smil . . . "*

*"In this eternal journey
Our souls shall meet,
in the forest, in the raindrop.
in the wind, in the sunset,
and our hearts shall ache,
which we will hide with a tender smile."

I never saw you again.
I don't know if you are alive.
I could find out, but
I prefer to remember you like this,
in the silence of a September night.

IV.
I walked south,
crossed the border into another language,
a deserted land where radioactive rain fell.
I walked and walked, and by the ocean
I slept the sleep of the vagabond.

I dreamed of an impossible theatre
in this dead and dying land.

In my dream, I awoke
and I was on a grass-covered plateau.
The land was untouched, covered in flowers
and protected by snow-capped mountains.

I saw a man riding from the east.
I walked further and we met at a rock.
He rode a little buckskin horse,
small and intelligent looking.

The rider was old yet vibrant, he smiled
the smile of a man who can laugh at life.
He carried a knife at his waist,
a pen and a small notebook protruded
from a pocket in his military-style jacket.

It was the French dramatist, Jean Genet.

"Have a seat my mon ami'" he called.   * *my friend*

I sat, tired and afraid,
but his presence filled me with calm.
We sat and watched the eagles gliding in the distance.
His horse cropped the grass nearby.

"Moi," like you,   ** *Me*
people walked all over me
and cast me to the shadows of society.
They thought me stupid and worthless,
Like an Indian, a Red Skin.

Moi, I am like you, a poor Indian.   ***Me*
Je suis le peau-rouge   *I am the Red Indian*
de toute la France."""   *of all France.*

He lit and smoked a cigarette.

207

"Mon petit' Red Skin, the theatre came to your shores   *My little
on a rat-infested ship, in the 1500s.
When it landed, your great People
saw the power in this orphan,
this theatre severed from its motherland,
where the practitioners of this strange art were called
whores, witches, and fools.

Your noble sages and sachems
called the theatre their younger brother,
younger brother to their great rituals.
They saw that, on the stage
and in their ceremonies,
these two beings could become brothers
in the act of Performance.

The act of Performance and the act of Ritual
meet at the level of the higher self,
the next dimension closest to this human world
where spiritual beings dwell.

But your spiritual leaders reached out to this younger brother,
'Welcome to this land,
our Sacred Island, Turtle Island,
earth built on the back of a Turtle.
We are the Island's original People.
In the future many of our Nations
will die from massacres and sickness.

We give you permission to stay here
so that many generations from now,
nurtured by this sacred soil,
your healing art will be reborn
from where you have taken root.

One day you will be from here,
that is, if you take sustenance from
that which has already been here.
If you do not you will not become a brother to us.
You will always be a stranger here.
But if you become one with this land,
and become our true brother,
a sacred theatre shall be born, nourished
by the infinite and eternal power of our Island,
and through this art we can shake hands with our ancestors.

We too shall be changed as we embrace you as a brother.
We will take what is good and make it ours.
One day our People will dance, sing, speak
in rhythms and structures derived from our rituals.
The spectators will give us dead flowers.
They will clap their hands together
and we will bow in gratitude
to the seen and the unseen audience.

We will take the power behind our ceremonies
and change the theatre.
We can only do this
if you let yourself be changed by us,
and if you do, then we shall meet you
in the twilight under the evening star,
Soul Brothers, Soul Sisters.

Different but One, their language is
metaphor, simile, abstraction.
Prisms which refract supernatural realities.
Ritual and theatre, though Brothers,
must be different beings.
We cannot mix them up.
Theatre teaches morality on earth;
ritual speaks to the Gods.
Do not mix them
or you will fall into the water.'

Not long ago, a prophet arose
from amongst the Europeans
who have enslaved the world.
His name was Antonin Artaud, a theatre director,
my friend and countryman.

In 1936, he journeyed to your Sacred Island,
to Mexico, and ate a holy sacrament,
Peyote, in the land of the Tarahumara.

He came in Peace.
He did not come to enslave your people,
or steal the land and put you on reservations.
Hand extended, he came, seeking healing,
as that is what your People offered,
and healing is what theatre, the Younger Brother,
must eventually offer.

Without healing, there is no art.

You, my friend, mon ami,
when you go back,
you will see your People, hat in hand
knocking on the white man's doors
wanting to eat at the white man's table
dance on his stages, like a white man.

They will be only white people in red masks,
Red People only on a magic typewriter
Indigenous identity only living on paper.
Your people's spirit will be for sale,
suppressed and silenced
by red masks, bought by a golden coin.

That is not the way, my friend.
You will become lost and foolish
and never find the true way.
The way can only come
from within, and from your own land.

Never forget the fire, the rock,
the trees, the sun, and the wind,
the stars and the moon,
the tipi and the earth lodge, the longhouse—
therein lies the theatre you seek!

Red Skin, Red People of the Earth,
this European civilization must die
within you and be replaced
by the ashes of your civilizations.
From the embers will come a new beginning.

Red Magic, to lift your People's Spirit.

Tout fini!' that is all ... "   *All done!*

"I must continue my journey,
along the road of Stars,
the Wolf Road your People call it,
the path of Stars that goes south
And there the ancestors await me ... "

V.

Slowly he rode and I watched him
until he disappeared over a hill.
Just then, a herd of horses came galloping,
circling me in a cloud of dust
and thundering hooves.
I could not see and became afraid.

When the horses had gone
I looked and nearby stood a young tree,
its leaves trembling in the wind.

And the tree spoke,
"Grandson, our Tribe is bashful and afraid,
but we will stand with you
whenever you raise your hands and your eyes
to our maker, The Great Spirit."

I awoke from my dream.
A little dwarf in a red pointed hat
and a long white beard and pointed shoes
poked me with a curved staff,
and pointed to the west.

VI.

And so, I returned westward
flying high above the clouds,
the last day of one dream,
the first day of another,
challenged, uncertain, and doubtful.

Suspended over my Sacred Island,
one long journey ended as another began
with a vision that roused me from a longer sleep.

I saw my People living in tattered clothes, the elders
in wheelchairs waiting by windows, heads bowed.
Spirits trapped by foreign concepts.
I saw that our Mother, the Land
had become poisoned and ill.

Then a bird flew amongst them and they looked up.
The light entered their eyes
and they saw the birth of a new world.
Lightning flashed and the sound tore the sky in half.
They stood up and gathered on a big plain
around a small timid tree, and they raised their hands.

And they wept and a great crying
rose up across my Sacred Island
as their spirit awoke
and once more they were free.

They were joined by other people
from all races and religions
and together they all stood around the tree,
moving and raising their arms.
Then the bird that had awakened them
came to rest upon the top branches of the tree.

As I looked closer at the bird
I could see that one tear
slowly formed and dropped,
and this became rain
that quenched the earth
of my Sacred Island.

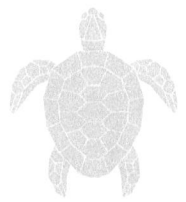

ACKNOWLEDGEMENTS

The editors would like to acknowledge the Social Sciences and Humanities Research Council, SaskCulture, the University of Regina's Faculty of Media, Art, and Performance, the University of Saskatchewan's Department of Drama, and the First Nations University of Canada's Department of Indigenous Languages, Arts, and Cultures for their support of the original vision of Performing Turtle Island. We would also like to thank all the authors for their contributions, as well as the staff at the University of Regina Press for their dedication to this project ever since we began gathering materials in 2015. It has been an exciting journey, and we look forward to ever new adventures on Turtle Island.

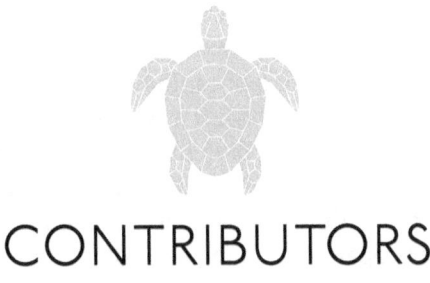

CONTRIBUTORS

MEGAN DAVIES is a white cis-female settler from S'ólh Téméxw, unceded Stó:lõ territory. Megan graduated in 2015 with an MA in theatre and performance studies at York University, Ontario, funded by a SSHRC Canada Graduate Scholarship. Megan is currently flexing her communications, critical thinking, and coordinating skills as a Funds and Community Relationship Specialist at Native Child and Family Services of Toronto. She has written about Indigenous theatre and performance art, and published works on historical reenactments and performative histories across time in the Canadian Theatre Review. Right now, Megan likes to think about the tangled systems of governmental and private funding structures, non-profits, and public policy/politics, and how we are orientated and continue to orient ourselves as individuals within the settler-colonial state of Canada.

SPY DÉNOMMÉ-WELCH, PhD, is an associate professor in the Faculty of Education at Brock University. He is a multidisciplinary scholar and artist of Anishnaabe descent, and writes, composes, and produces work in theatre, opera, and video. His current SSHRC-funded research focuses on Indigenous opera creation, cross-cultural collaboration, and decolonizing performance practices. He wrote, co-composed, and co-produced the Dora-nominated opera Giiwedin, and is now completing his second full-length opera. He is the artistic director of Unsettled Scores.

FLOYD P. FAVEL is a theatre theorist, director, essayist, and Cree cultural leader based in Saskatchewan. He studied theatre in Denmark at the Tukak Teatret, a school for Inuit and Sami people. After which he studied in Italy with Jerzy Grotowski, a Polish theatre director and one of the more influential theatre figures of the twentieth century. Since then he has travelled and worked across the country and the world, developing his own unique theatre process he entitles 'Native Performance Culture', or NpC. Indigenous theatre is an artistic genre with its own methods, techniques, and body of knowledge that is open to all peoples and not defined by 'identity,' and is multicultural in presentation. His researches, investigations, and presentations focus on theatre, Indigenous tradition, healing and health, and cultural rejuvenation. In Favel's view, *'theatre, as a younger brother/sister of Indigenous tradition, must have a healing component and be born on this land.'*

CAROL GREYEYES is an actor, writer, educator and member of the Muskeg Lake Cree Nation in Saskatchewan. She is the former artistic director of the Centre for Indigenous Theatre (CIT) and founding principal of the Indigenous Theatre School in Toronto, Canada. She has worked as a junior story editor for North of 60 and has written for CBC, TVO, Global, APTN, SCN, for radio and series television. Carol has directed and taught in theatres all over Canada and the United States and has acted in film, television, radio, and on the stage. She is currently an assistant professor in the Department of Drama at the University of Saskatchewan and the coordinator of the wîcêhtowin: Aboriginal Theatre Program, in addition to maintaining her professional acting career.

MICHAEL GREYEYES is a graduate of the School of Theatre and Dance at Kent State University and the National Ballet School of Canada. One of Canada's leading Indigenous performers, he has appeared in numerous films and television shows. Also a playwright, choreographer, and director, his works bring both experience and a fresh voice to Canadian Indigenous drama.

KAHENTE HORN-MILLER (KANIEN'KEHÁ:KA), PhD, is an associate professor in the School of Indigenous and Canadian Studies at Carleton University. As an active member of her community, Dr.

Horn-Miller researches and writes on Indigenous methodologies, Indigenous women, identity politics, colonization, Indigenous governance, and consensus-based decision-making for her community and the wider society. Her community-based research involves interpreting and performing Haudenosaunee philosophy. She currently coordinates the development of Indigenous Collaborative Learning Bundles, Carleton's response to the TRC Calls to Action on bringing Indigenous Knowledge into the university classroom.

DIONE JOSEPH is the founder of Black Creatives Aotearoa and co-founder of JK Productions: He Kōrero Ngā Tahi (Telling Our Stories Together). Over the past decade, her commitment to creating, sharing and manifesting opportunities for diverse artists has seen her create work with different communities in Aotearoa and Australia. She has also been active as a stage critic for both theatre and dance and her reviews can be found in the New Zealand Herald, Dance Aotearoa NZ Magazine and Radio NZ. She has an MA in Community and Cultural Development from the Victorian College of the Arts and a BA (Hons) in Theatre Studies from the University of Melbourne. More information can be found on www.dionejoseph.com.

CATHERINE MAGOWAN is principal bassoonist of the Sudbury Symphony Orchestra and Cambridge Symphony Orchestra, and co-founder of the world's first electric-bassoon band, DFM. She was nominated for a Dora Mavor Moore award for the opera Giiwedin, which she co-composed with her collaborator Spy Dénommé-Welch, and their work for voice and orchestra Sojourn premiered at the Luminato Festival as the finale of the dance opera Bearing (Signal Theatre, 2017). Together she and Dénommé-Welch have presented at conferences on topics such as decolonization and intercultural collaboration in music, and run workshops for youth and young adults on music creation and the politics of music.

DANIEL DAVID MOSES is a playwright, poet, essayist, and teacher. He is a Delaware from the Six Nations lands in southern Ontario, Canada. He holds an honours bachelor of arts in general fine arts from York University and a master of fine arts in creative writing from the University of British Columbia. His plays include his first, Coyote City, a nominee for the 1991 Governor General's Literary Award for Drama: *The Indian Medicine Shows*, a winner of the James Buller Memorial Award for Excellence in Aboriginal Theatre; and his best known, *Almighty Voice and His Wife*. He is also the author of *Delicate Bodies* and *Sixteen Jesuses*, poems, and co-editor of Oxford University Press' *An Anthology of Canadian Native Literature in English*, 3rd Edition (2005). His most recent publications are *Pursued by a Bear: Talks, Monologues and Tales* (2005) and *Kyotopolis*, a play in two acts (2008), both from Exile Editions. His honours include the Harbourfront Festival Prize, a Harold Award, a Chalmers Fellowship, and being shortlisted for the 2005 Siminovitch Award. He teaches as a Queen's National Scholar in the Department of Drama at Queen's University, Kingston, Ontario.

YVETTE NOLAN is a playwright, director, and dramaturge. Her plays include *Annie Mae's Movement, Ham and the Ram, The Birds* (a modern adaptation of Aristophanes' comedy), *Alaska*, and *The Unplugging*. From 2003 to 2011, she served as artistic director of Native Earth Performing Arts. *Medicine Shows*, her book about Indigenous theatre in Canada, was published in 2015. She was recently awarded the Mallory Gilbert Leadership Award for leadership in the Canadian theatre community.

ARMAND RUFFO is a creative writer and Queen's National Scholar in Indigenous Literatures and Languages. A member of the Sagamok Ojibway and Chapleau Cree Fox Lake First Nation, Armand is a respected scholar whose work has been instrumental in establishing Indigenous literary studies in Canada. His creative work has been recognized by a wide array of honours and awards: his volume of poetry, *At Geronimo's Grave*, won the Archibald Lampman Award for Poetry in 2001 and selections from it won the Canadian Author's Poetry Prize. His film, *A Windigo Tale*, garnered multiple prizes in 2010, including Best Picture at the 35th Annual American Indian Film Festival in San Francisco and Best Feature Film at the Dreamspeaker Film Festival in Edmonton.

ANNIE SMITH is a theatre artist, educator, and learner. She holds a PhD in participatory performance and pedagogy from the University of British Columbia. Her artistic and research projects include community-engaged theatre, historic re-enactment, and

Indigenous theatre and performance. She teaches Canadian theatre courses for SFU's 55+ Program, with a particular interest in women and Indigenous playwrights. She has published articles and book reviews in alt.theatre magazine, Canadian Theatre Review, SETC Journal, and Theatre Research in Canada.

EDITORS

JESSE RAE ARCHIBALD-BARBER is a professor of English and Indigenous literatures at the First Nations University of Canada. He is originally from Regina and is of Métis, Cree, and Scottish descent. His publications include stories in *The Malahat Review* (2015) and *mite-wâcimowina: Indigenous Science Fiction and Speculative Storytelling* (2016). He is also the editor of the literary anthology, *kisiskâciwan: Indigenous Voices from Where the River Flows Swiftly* (2018), and is a founding producer and co-writer of the *Making Treaty 4* performance (2017). He sees storytelling and performance as a productive way for Indigenous youth to connect to their traditions and for both Indigenous and Canadian communities to work toward decolonization.

MOIRA J. DAY is a professor of drama at the University of Saskatchewan. She is of English, Irish, and Scottish descent and was born in Edmonton, Alberta. A former co-editor of *Theatre Research in Canada / Recherches théâtrales au Canada*, she has published and lectured widely in the field of Canadian theatre, with a particular focus on women and prairie theatre prior to 1960. Editing projects have included a play anthology featuring the work of pioneering Western Canadian playwright Elsie Park Gowan; a collection of plays and an anthology of essays featuring the contemporary theatre in Manitoba, Saskatchewan, and Alberta; and a special issue, with Mary Blackstone, on contemporary Saskatchewan theatre for CTR. As a scholar/teacher she recognizes the importance of personal commitment to the process of decolonization and reconciliation, as part of helping to create a better, fairer world for all our children.

KATHLEEN IRWIN is associate dean in the faculty of Media, Art, and Performance at the University of Regina. She holds a Doctor of Art degree from Aalto University, Helsinki (2006). Trained as a professional scenographer for theatre, notions of space, identity, and representation inform Irwin's creative practice and research. Recent work investigates the intersection of food, activism and performance. She is a former Canadian Education Commissioner for OISTAT; Board Member for Canadian Association for Theatre Research; National Theatre School Alumni; Associated Designers of Canada; and founder of Knowhere Productions and ArtsAction Inc. A few of her contributions include articles or chapters in *Canadian Theatre Research*; *Theatre Research in Canada*; *Performance Design* (Museum Tuscalanum, 2008); *Public Art in Canada: Critical Perspectives* (University of Toronto, 2009); *Sighting, Citing, Siting*, intro and co-editor (University of Regina, 2009); *Scenography Expanded* (Bloomsbury, 2017); *Artistic Approaches to Cultural Mapping: Activating Imaginaries and Means of Knowing* (Routledge, 2018); and *Analysing Gender in Performance* (Palgrave, 2019). As producer of large-scale, cross-cultural, site-specific events, artist residencies, and academic symposiums, including Performing Turtle Island (Regina, 2015), she understands such work to be among a range of creative actions that may play a small part in restoring balance among Indigenous and non-Indigenous peoples in Canada.

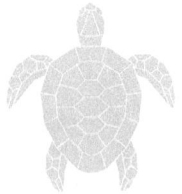

INDEX

www.ingramcontent.com/pod-product-compliance
Lightning Source LLC
Chambersburg PA
CBHW020735180526
45163CB00001B/247